THE THEME OF LONELINESS

THE THEME OF LONELINESS

IN MODERN AMERICAN DRAMA

by
Winifred L. *oesch*
Dusenbury

University of
Florida Press

Gainesville
1960

To all those yea-sayers
who have helped me with this book

A University of Florida Press Book

Copyright 1960 by the Board of Commissioners
of State Institutions of Florida
All rights reserved

Library of Congress Catalogue Card No. 60-10228
Printed by The E. O. Painter Printing Co.
DeLand, Florida

CONTENTS

v

CONTENTS

INTRODUCTION

And God stepped out on space,
And he looked around and said,
"I'm lonely — ...."
—"The Creation," James Weldon Johnson

The feeling of loneliness in mankind is age-old and world-wide, its causes multifarious. Besides the great insoluble problems in men's minds concerning God, nature, death, and the meaning of life itself, specific problems in each society have caused individuals to feel the appalling isolation known as loneliness; and repeatedly, by its embodiment in the communicative medium of literature, men have sought to allay this feeling.

Examples of literary masterpieces concerned with the individual's loneliness are found in all ages. The lonely hero, King Oedipus; the lonely ascetic, Jesus Christ; the lonely revenger, Hamlet; and the lonely psychopath, Hedda Gabler—all are examples of the portrayal of loneliness in individual human beings, each character having his own cause for isolation from the rest of mankind. Study of the place of each in Greek, Hebraic, Elizabethan, and modern literature provides understanding of these respective societies, and indicates that a theme common to all mankind nevertheless takes specific aesthetic forms in particular ages. The recognition that the theme is not of modern origin in literature or in life does not lessen the importance of its appearance with some peculiarly American manifestations in the American drama since 1920. To the modern American dramatist, whose principal mode has been that of realism, all facets of the life around him have supplied material for presentation on the stage.[1] Although there are dramatic qualities to the theme of loneliness which are not limited to a particular time and place, playwrights today have in the main used the theme as a reflection of present-day American life.

1

The concept of loneliness in this book has been arrived at through study of discussions in recent popular and specialized publications, in which the subject is treated frequently and sometimes at length. The suggestion of one writer, however, that "Loneliness is a disease of the soul, and it is strange that it should not appear as such in all encyclopedias and be given as much attention as physical troubles,"[2] has not been acted upon, for a definition of the malady is seldom found in reference books; in those articles and books in which it is mentioned, it is more often described than defined. Of recent discussions of the subject perhaps none has aroused more interest than David Riesman's *The Lonely Crowd*,[3] in which he explains the American loneliness as a recent phenomenon of a highly industrialized, consumer society, in which each man, lacking self-sufficiency, fears that he will be ridiculed if he is different from the crowd, and hence spends his days in quaking and uncertain efforts to conform. A different explanation is given for modern man's acute sense of isolation by Abram Kardiner:[4] "Rugged individualism makes each man maintain defensive hostilities to all around him." These contrasting opinions indicate disagreement between social scientists as to the cause, but not as to the nature or extent, of loneliness.

Among psychologists, one—Karl A. Menninger—[5] attempts to classify individuals of "lonely personality" according to the causes of their isolation; but since he finds—in spite of such causes as geographical isolation, several types of paternal failure, extremes of wealth or poverty, and religious fervor—that the most frequent and serious factor leading to this type of personality is "a real or fancied defect or unfavorable comparison," he perhaps fortifies the position of the sociologists who, with Riesman, claim that America is full of individuals with a sense of their own inferiority and inadequacy. Another, Gregory Zilboorg, who finds the number of lonely men limitless, among the brilliant and among the stupid, says lonely people "feel estranged from the real world, seeking something that they know not and never find."[6] Like other scientists, who have no pat cure for these afflicted, Zilboorg recognizes the serious effects of loneliness on the individual and his society.

Besides sociologists and psychologists, literary men have expressed themselves upon the subject of loneliness. For example, to Thornton Wilder it appears that there is today what he calls "the

American loneliness," which perceptive visitors from Europe observe as typical of many Americans. Transplanted from his homeland, unattached to soil, distrustful of authority, the American, according to Wilder, has been thrown back upon himself. His penchant for joining fraternities and clubs is a result of his being able to feel himself in relation to others only when he is united with them in a project and propelled toward the future. He lives not on the treasure that lies about him but on the promises of the imagination. "Americans can find in environment no confirmation of their identity," says Wilder. They cannot say, as can the Europeans, "I am I because my fellow-citizens know me," and hence they suffer loneliness.[7] Another literary figure, Thomas Wolfe, pretends with romantic fervor to revel in his own isolation: "I have known loneliness as well as any man, and will now write of him as if he were my very brother, which he is."[8] This great subjective novelist concludes that there is a certain joy and sublimity in accepting as comrade the dark-visaged loneliness. Since, however, Thomas Wolfe's epithets for loneliness—"brother" and "comrade"—indicate a hidden hunger for companionship of a different nature, probably lonesomeness, if inspiriting to him, was no more pleasurable than it presumably is to any other man.

Walter Prescott Webb, who has intensively studied the effect of frontier and plains life on the American character, has discovered that the word "loneliness" was used to describe a psychological condition. Quoting a Kansas plainsman, he includes the following description in his book, *The Great Plains.*

> Did you ever hear of "loneliness" as a fatal disease? Once, back in the days when father and I were bringing up long-legged sheep from Mexico, we picked up a man near Las Vegas who had lost his way. He was in a terrible state. It wasn't the result of being lost. He had "loneliness." Born on the plains, you get accustomed to them; but on people not born there the plains sometimes have an appalling effect. . . . "He's got loneliness," we would say of such a man.[9]

Although the loneliness described here is perhaps of peculiar intensity and its cause ascribable to the specific physical environment, it does not differ in kind from that characterized by other writers in different contexts. Summed up in an editorial in *Current Opinion,* in which loneliness is referred to as "the spiritual malady of the age," are the commonly expressed ideas upon the subject. Loneliness, according to the writer,

> springs from a painful sense of separation from those with whom one has a right to feel a sense of intellectual or spiritual kinship, whether they be members of a particular group, or whether we have in mind the whole of humanity or the world or even God! . . . The feeling is one of homelessness of the soul, of being an alien in the sphere wherein one belongs.[10]

Consideration of the specific and general usages of the word has resulted in the concept of loneliness which, as a theme in modern drama, is the subject of this book. The definition of loneliness is taken from an article by Theodore Spencer, "The Isolation of the Shakespearean Hero,"[11] in which the lonely character is described as one whom circumstances have forced into a "suffering self-recognition of separateness." Since the theme of a drama is enacted by characters, it is obviously practical to define loneliness in terms of character. All of the plays discussed, therefore, are concerned with thematically important characters affected by a "suffering self-recognition of separateness."

Loneliness, as used in this book, is not the feeling of bereavement and aloneness which the death of a loved one brings and which time and new interests tend to cure. Neither is the word used in the sense in which nineteenth-century Romantics used it to represent an enjoyable state of melancholia, during which they might contemplate an ever-fleeting object of desire. Nor does it refer to the sort of aloneness of which artists have made use. As Carl Sandburg notes: "There is such a thing as creative solitude—a certain kind of loneliness out of which have risen the works of the creative spirits of the past. They were not afraid of being alone; they had learned how to use their loneliness."[12] Nor does it refer to the self-appointed hermit or to the man who chooses to live alone or to act alone, for such individuals have not been forced by circumstances into a suffering self-recognition of separateness, but on the contrary, they have chosen the way of life which brings them happiness.

The loneliness of the city, the loneliness of the farm, the loneliness of being without a home, the loneliness of lacking friends, the loneliness of success, the loneliness of failure, the loneliness of not understanding oneself, the loneliness of not belonging socially, the loneliness of old age, and the loneliness of youth—all these and loneliness from other causes are discussed for the benefit of the periodical-reading American public, along with suggested panaceas. In general in the discussions there is present the implication that loneliness represents a suffering self-recognition of not belonging to a satisfying object of desire. If those writing on the subject of loneliness can be believed, Americans, in spite of a need for understanding among themselves, seem to feel a distance separating them from each other. Like Willy Loman, they have discovered that they are not well liked. In a world where an optimistic smile and a glad hand are presumably the open sesames to warm companionship, and where the *Rotarian* advises, "Lonely? Get Acquainted!" there must be a feeling of separateness in many American people.

Since drama is an important aesthetic medium for the reflection of life, it is not strange that American playwrights have concerned themselves with the problem of loneliness in a number of important plays in which the feeling of being psychologically isolated from satisfactory human relationships plays an important thematic part in the drama. The theme being the statement of a play's conflict in general terms (as the plot is the statement of the conflict in particular terms), those plays in which loneliness motivates the action or affects or impels the characters are the concern of this book. It is the function of the playwright to represent the life of man, so that by means of his art a deeper truth is revealed than is seen in life itself. Chosen for discussion are those plays concerning loneliness which meet the test of a truthful portrayal of American life, and which, through their aesthetic heightening of the truth, have significance for modern audiences.

If it be argued that the protagonist of any play is a lonesome figure by virtue of the nature of drama, it must be pointed out that the isolation of the hero may or may not be the theme of the play. For example, although Oliver Wendell Holmes in *The Magnificent Yankee* feels desolate at times, and is quite lost after the death of Fanny, the theme of the play is the deep understanding and affection between him and Fanny and the love borne him by all the young law students who served under the childless judge. He stands alone, as a character fearless of Presidents, sure of his own conduct, and at home in the world of men. The loneliness he feels after Fanny's death is normal and serves the dramatic purpose of accenting the theme of the play—the depth of understanding which the two shared through life. Conversely, in *Come Back, Little*

5

Sheba, the lack of understanding between Doc and Lola and the resulting isolation is intricately bound up with the theme—the lonesomeness caused by their failure to realize youth's dreams.

Another example of the contrasting emphasis given to loneliness in the structure of two plays is found in *Dead End* and *Of Mice and Men.* Either play might have been written with emphasis on a sociological theme or on the personal theme of loneliness in men under certain economic conditions, but in *Dead End* Kingsley emphasizes the former, whereas in *Of Mice and Men* Steinbeck makes the plot revolve about the suffering of the wandering ranch hands. The impelling urge of Babyface Martin in *Dead End* to return to see his girl and his mother after six years of criminal life is so strong as to overmaster his reason, which tells him the obvious danger of recapture in his old haunts; likewise, the other characters in this play struggle with personal lonesomeness, but the theme of the play is so patently the debilitating effect of the slums upon human beings that it cannot be considered, as can *Of Mice and Men,* as an example of the American drama which makes human loneliness the motivating idea or theme.

It is with the idea that the theme is of vital importance to the structure of the play and to its meaning that this book is written. Criticizing Shaw's contrary opinion and his claim that the selection of theme is one of the major mysteries of playwriting and a mere matter of chance, John Howard Lawson says, "The theme is the root of the drama. . . . The process by which the artist selects his theme and brings it to life is the basic problem of technique."[13] Lawson's emphasis upon the innate importance of the theme to the play is borne out by a study of the use of the theme of loneliness by American playwrights, for, as is illustrated within the ensuing chapters, the purpose, action, and form of the play are conditioned by the theme.

The plays are grouped in chapters according to what appears to be the playwright's presentation of the basic cause of that feeling of self-recognition of separateness which is loneliness. Each play is discussed within one chapter only, although it should not be assumed that the chapter headings are mutually exclusive. Neither should it be assumed that the classification indicates any particular practice in dramaturgy or in the dramatic effect achieved and least of all in any didactic end. That any modern dramatists have reached deeply enough to present fundamental, rather than superficial, causes for the loneliness which many Americans appear to feel, may be uncertain, but in any case the theme is of recognizable importance to American audiences, whether the playwright has attributed the suffering of a character to personal failure or to homelessness.

The discussion of the theme of loneliness contributes to the understanding of modern American drama as a whole, for doubtless it is a common theme today. A distinguished American critic, Brooks Atkinson, writing on the use of the theme in a number of recent plays, concludes, "In the mystique of today loneliness is a relevant subject."[14] One of America's leading playwrights, Elmer Rice, lists loneliness first among common themes in modern American drama.[15] The fact that the theme of loneliness is frequently interpreted by contemporary dramatists makes significant a detailed consideration of it; for, as Edmond Gagey claims, "American drama of the past thirty years . . . has done far more than reflect passing fads and frivolities; . . . it has portrayed the manners, voiced the creeds, and unveiled the psyche of a brilliant and erratic age."[16] It is hoped that the aims of the book—to establish the causes of loneliness as interpreted by modern playwrights, to delineate the broad scope of the theme, to analyze the dramaturgical effect on the individual plays considered, and to point up the relationship of the theme to American life—may make it profitable to the reader interested in American drama or in American life.

1

PERSONAL FAILURE

Alone!—that worn-out word,
So idly spoken, and so coldly heard;
Yet all that poets sing and grief hath known
Of hopes laid waste, knells in that word ALONE!
—*The New Timon* Part II, Edward Bulwer-Lytton

Personal failure is especially painful in America because personal success is the universally recognized goal of its people. Geoffrey Gorer claims that even to the child "Am I successful?" comes to mean "Am I loved?" For from the beginning the mother's approval is given to her child in proportion to his success. The signs of love demanded in later life are the attention of other people, according to Gorer, and therefore if one is alone, he fears that he is not a success, not worthy of love. "It is these feelings which make loneliness intolerable to well-adjusted Americans,"[1] concludes Gorer in his study of the national character of the American people. Whereas in other countries the gradual deterioration of a family may lead to the dispersion of its possessions, the remnants of the line do not suffer the reprobation of personal failure. They are considered unfortunate but not completely censurable for the misfortune. And if those who cannot trace their family line end up by drinking their days away in the local liquor dispensaries, it is not surprising that, since they come from nothing, they rise to nothing. Not so in the case of the American. No matter where he starts, he is expected to make good on his own, and if he does not, he alone is to blame. As Max Lerner puts it, in America "the indices of belonging are belongings."[2] Lonely is the man, therefore, who fails to make his mark economically and socially in the American world.

Modern American playwrights have presented economic and

social failures in a number of different plays, but in none is the idea better dramatized than in *Come Back, Little Sheba* (1950) by William Inge, *Death of a Salesman* (1949) by Arthur Miller, and *The Iceman Cometh* (1946) by Eugene O'Neill, the last being a study in ensemble of personal failure of many types and the first two being illustrative of the effect of defeat upon one person and those around him. Passed by as an occupational incompetent, disregarded by former friends, and painfully unable to provide for the needs of those dependent upon him, the unhappy victim of his presumably self-inflicted misfortune feels frustrated and isolated. He has "muffed his chance," and finds no sympathizers. Since World War I, novelists and playwrights have been interested in the part which economic and social environments have played in the personal bankruptcy of individuals adversely effected by them. William Inge, Arthur Miller, and Eugene O'Neill in the plays discussed in this chapter, however, see the botching of lives because of a lack of understanding of what makes for success. The resultant loneliness is not that of the social climber whose invitations are not accepted by the best people, nor that of the worker submerged by the capitalistic system, but that of the individual who, starting with the normal chances of attaining his goal in life, fails clumsily through his own inadvertency. Self-recrimination is not his outlet, however, for human nature itself leads him to blame outside forces. His compensation is in dreaming or drinking, or in a combination of both. In either he realizes the grandeur that should be his. In each of the three plays the unfortunate failures drink deep of liquor or daydreams, in order to make a lonely existence bearable.

Come Back, Little Sheba is one of the important American plays in which a woman's loneliness because of her personal failure is presented. It can be said that Regina of *The Little Foxes*, Harriet of *Craig's Wife*, and Electra of *Mourning Becomes Electra* know an isolation which is painful and which is in the larger sense self-inflicted, but all of them successfully attain what, in the last analysis, is their desire. Lola, the sloppy wife in *Come Back, Little Sheba*, however, is vanquished in her battle for home, husband, and baby. Not downright discouragement, but apathy is her response. An adolescent tendency to believe the only happiness in life to be romantic love has remained with her ever since she ardently gave herself to Doc as a young girl, so that instead of

9

making the most of her house, devoting thought to Doc's psychic needs, and becoming acquainted with the seven children next door, she allows her imagination to be stirred by the relationship between Marie and Turk and she derives a vicarious sexual satisfaction from encouraging their love-making. Like thousands of other American women she listens to the soap operas; her dependency upon an outside source for stimulation of the imagination indicates her lack of inner direction, and makes plausible her incompetency in dealing with life's problems.

Although the house is badly in need of cleaning and she herself in need of grooming, she finds the morning unbearably empty after the departure of Doc and Marie, the young roomer. The milkman and mailman offer short respites. Then loneliness overwhelms her. "Come back, little Sheba," is the cry of a woman with a pitiful lack of self-sustainment. Her refusal to admit that her little white dog is not coming back symbolizes her refusal to admit that the romance of her youth is not coming back; but instead of trying to live without either, she forlornly tries to dream them into existence. As substitutes she listens to the radio sob dramas[3] and furtively skirts along the edge of the affair between Marie and Turk, but her loneliness is not the less pitiful because she does not recognize her predicament; and although she once almost admits that perhaps little Sheba is not coming back, as the final curtain falls, she is explaining to Doc, "I had another dream last night," and so it appears that there is no experience which can bring maturity to a woman like Lola. The same motivation on a different social level which justifies the title of "girls" assumed by the plump matrons of Helen Hokinson's drawings,[4] makes Lola a perennial youngster psychologically. Her failure as an adult leaves her isolated from the grown-up world, with little hope that she will ever be able to catch up with her years.

Doc, too, is a failure; but in spite of the fact that he has sought consolation in drink, he takes a much more mature viewpoint than Lola, admits that little Sheba will never come back, and recognizes that his own follies have brought about his ruin. His loneliness is a result of his having fallen in the world from the profession of doctor, to which he aspired, to that of chiropractor, and of having lost contact with the friends whom an intelligent wife and professional success would have encouraged and retained. Apparently he has never complained to Lola that she has failed him,

10

but the deep-seated resentment toward her which he shows when drunk is evidence of a suppressed hatred. Consciously he blames his own ineptitude for his loneliness, but unconsciously he blames Lola. According to Seldes[5] one of the characteristics of the women who, like Lola, derive satisfaction from the soap operas is that each feels that her husband greatly needs her guidance, but that she does not depend upon him. True to this hypothesis, Lola, although she does not get up to fix Doc's breakfast or to clean the house, does insist that he say his prayer for strength each morning. Feeling that she is thus saving him from succumbing to drink, she is actually a cause of his failure. She would accomplish more by looking bright and cooking well. Seldes found that the women who did not listen to the daytime serials were less certain that women know best how to guide the destiny of men. Nor did they look for a magical solution to human problems (like the return of little Sheba) but believed in personal effort and the use of the imagination to cope with unfamiliar situations. The playwright puts into artistic form the deductions of the radio analyst and portrays the effects upon a husband of the type of woman who has no resources within herself. Doc's mistakes in causing Lola's pregnancy before marriage, in failing to take her to a licensed physician, in giving up the study of medicine, were not fatal, and their effects could have been rectified if he had been encouraged by an understanding woman rather than a woman of inner helplessness.

An analysis of the action of *Come Back, Little Sheba* indicates that the move toward the complete isolation of Doc and Lola is led up to and climaxed by events concerning the young college boarder, Marie. Although the lonesomeness of both Doc and Lola is acute from the beginning, it is the opposing attitudes toward Marie and her lover, Turk, which motivate the complete break between the older couple and the shattering downfall of Doc. From the opening scene up to the climax Marie is the focal point of the action. In the final anticlimactic scene, Marie does not appear, for she has departed to be married, and by her very departure has removed the cause of the alienation and made possible a reconciliation, although the audience withholds judgment upon the permanency of the feeling of companionship between Doc and Lola. Obviously their personal limitations make impossible depth of understanding, but through suffering they have broken through

11

the wall of isolation a little and, with Marie out of the way, are more able than before to reach each other.

The action revolving around Marie begins as the curtain opens upon Doc entering the kitchen to get breakfast ready. The jaunty Marie calls "Hi" and gets her orange juice, but refuses his offer, "I'll serve you your breakfast now, Marie, and we can eat it together, the two of us," for she wants to bathe first. No suggestion of inappropriate intimacy is made by the words or action, for Doc's desire to have breakfast alone with the cheerful girl, while not quite like the wish of a father toward a daughter, is nevertheless a normal one, wherein the young girl is idealized as the representation of young womanhood, and not as a symbol of sensual desire. When Lola enters, it is obvious why Doc prefers having breakfast with Marie, for in contrast to Marie's neat appearance and youth, Lola is sloppy and middle-aged. The failure he has made of his life is accented in his mind by the way in which she also has failed, changing from a girl like Marie to the frowsy woman before him. As Lola comments about little Sheba as a puppy and her dreams of the dog, Doc remarks, "Some things should never grow old. That's what it amounts to." Obviously thinking of Lola while he speaks, he takes comfort in the sight of Marie, and on his way out of the house gently fondles the girl's scarf, which is lying on a chair.

Before Doc leaves, however, he and Lola have the first disagreement about Marie's relations with Turk, who even Marie recognizes is "not the marrying kind." Doc insists Marie is too nice a girl to be going out with that kind of man, whereas Lola revels in the fact that she has seen the girl kissing Turk "like he was Rudolph Valentino." Although no open break between them is evident, the difference in their attitudes toward the girl is the first indication of the distance growing between them. To Doc, Marie is an embodiment of that chastity which man idealizes in woman, whereas to Lola, Marie is the recipient of that sexual satisfaction of which woman dreams. It is with an angry show of disbelief that Doc greets Lola's news of Marie's having passionately kissed Turk. When Lola later makes even more explicit her almost psychopathic enjoyment of the love-making of the young couple on the sofa by calling, "Come and look, Daddy," Doc merely scolds his wife for snooping. The intensity of his feeling, however, is made evident by his barely repressed impulse to reach for the bottle of whisky. The incident seems slight, but is extremely significant. Doc's alienation from Lola is almost complete; with Marie in the arms of a lover, Doc is an individual alone on the brink of retreat from reality through alcohol.

Near the beginning of the second act, the incident in which Doc fondles Marie's scarf is repeated as in the first scene. Doc, preparing to leave for the office, again stops to touch this garment which has been around Marie's neck. This morning, however, Doc is less attentive to Lola's chattering, appearing more thoughtful and worried. As he is holding the scarf pensively for a moment, he hears Turk's laughter resound from Marie's bedroom. His body stiffens; almost blind with emotion he stumbles into the table, and, as Lola enters, drops the scarf and rushes out the door. Bitter in the knowledge that Turk has spent the night with Marie, the middle-aged man soon returns for the only friendly thing he knows— the bottle of whisky. Ironically enough, at the same moment Lola is blithely setting the table (for the dinner she is preparing for Marie and her fiancé, Bruce) with the linen and china which Doc's mother had given her as a wedding present. It is the sight of this china, which is still on the table at 5:30 next morning, which enrages the drunken Doc to such an extent that he sweeps it to the floor with the cry, "My mother didn't buy those dishes for whores to eat off of."

This series of incidents in Act II, beginning with Doc's fondling of the scarf and ending with the shattering of the china, is a repetition in a more intense degree of the action of Act I, which begins with the scarf incident, includes the effect of Turk's presence upon Doc, and concludes with Doc's hesitating resistance to taking the bottle of whisky. The actions of Marie, and Lola's obvious enjoyment of the girl's affair with Turk, in both acts motivate Doc's withdrawal from contact with reality. His resistance to reaching oblivion through the bottle in Act I makes more dramatic his fall in Act II through a series of like incidents, which this time build up beyond his strength to withstand.

The rising action continues as Doc tramps past the broken dishes for another drink and returns with a hatchet, with which he threatens Lola. The fact that his threats include Marie reinforces the importance of the incidents concerning the young girl, for even in his semiconscious state, he recognizes that it is Lola's attitude toward the girl's looseness, as well as the immorality itself,

13

which has caused his alienation from both. Had Lola condemned Marie's actions as he did, Doc would have felt closer to his wife, for in their detestation of such behavior, there would have been companionship. But since Lola gets a vicarious sexual pleasure from the relationship of the two young people, Doc is justified in his charge: "You and Marie are both a couple of sluts." With his further charge that Lola is running a whorehouse he almost brings the hatchet down upon her, but collapses before she is injured.

This violent scene ends in utter isolation for Lola. Doc having been taken to the county hospital by two friends, and Marie and Bruce having left to be married, the shaken woman calls her mother, only to be told that her father has not relented about not wishing to see her since her forced marriage to Doc many years ago. She stands by the phone utterly disconsolate as the curtain falls. With no family, no husband, no other human being to turn to, she has reached a state of despairing loneliness. Too crushed even to call for little Sheba, she recognizes her own plight in a deeper sense than at the beginning, when she could dream that Sheba would come back and that Marie's love affairs were her own.

Through the intense suffering of having Doc berate her, and of recognizing her own failure, she advances a step toward understanding and companionship with Doc in the short anticlimactic scene which follows. At least, although she is still telling about her dreams, it is she who is getting the breakfast. It can be said that for the present anyway she is enough aroused by his needs to desire to wait on him and to be concerned about his health. He too has suffered from the loneliness of their estrangement brought about by his vicious treatment of Lola. He begs her, "Honey, don't ever leave me. *Please* don't ever leave me." If true companionship has not brought them together, at least suffering has made them tolerant and needful of a friendly relationship, which they quickly establish.

A study of loneliness, *Come Back, Little Sheba* describes the journey of a couple from loneliness to complete isolation (through a series of incidents involving a boy and girl somewhat representative to them of their own youth) and back to a sense of loneliness, modified by a feeling of belonging to each other because of the suffering each has undergone. Neither is a heroic figure; both are failures according to magazine advertising standards. But in a sense they radiate a kind of optimism at the end because they have

broken through the wall of separation, and are about to eat breakfast together—a solid American breakfast of eggs and bacon, fruit
juice and coffee, toast and marmalade.

The play consists of a series of conversational scenes, in which
the controversy which is to separate the couple builds up slowly;
a scene of extreme violence, in which Doc threatens Lola's life;
and an epilogue-like scene of reconciliation. Because of her lack
of appreciation that Doc's attitude toward Marie's affair is the
opposite of her own, Lola precipitates the action which brings about
Doc's defection from the pledge of Alcoholics Anonymous. His
growing resentment of her results in the scene of violence, which,
after the quiet scenes of which most of the play consists, bursts like
a bomb upon the action of the play. The effect is startling in
that in the previous action no dramatic conflict is obvious, because
the failure of each to understand the other's reactions creates little
opportunity for open controversy; but the anger which grows within Doc builds and is illustrated in the explicit action of his reaching
for the bottle at the end of Act I and of his taking it in Act II. At
the end of the violent climactic scene, oblivion for Doc and utter
desolation for Lola are the results of the hysterical break between
them.

In the last scene, the wheel has come full circle. Except for the
fact that it is Lola instead of Doc who is getting breakfast, "It is
the same Lola, the same life. . . ." The conversation is like that of
scene one, except that with Marie removed, a source of controversy
is gone, and a modicum of companionship is generated by their
thoughtfulness of each other. Their loneliness is less acute than
at the beginning, because they have attained an appreciation,
through the suffering of being separated by antagonism, of the value
of companionship. Inge's study of loneliness builds slowly, bursts
suddenly, and subsides with the suggestion of the impossibility of
a very successful break through the walls of isolation for either
Doc or Lola.

The final scene arouses a keen sense of pity because Doc is as
good-hearted as Lola, but kindliness is not enough to insure success
in a land which requires a certain sturdy drive toward a goal in
life, which neither possesses. Failure together has not meant companionship, however, for neither husband nor wife has the self-
sustaining qualities which might make spiritual success of material
failure. Yet the good will of both is ethically sound and both tend

to be cheerful rather than morose, so that although they might not attract friends, it is almost impossible to believe either could be actively disliked by anyone. But they are both conventional people, and since conventional success has not been theirs, neither has friendship. Their alienation from each other is also inevitable because of their dependency upon a favorable reflection of themselves in each other's eyes, which they do not see.

In another of the most popular American dramas of recent years, *Death of a Salesman,* is to be found exemplification of what David Riesman calls the other-directed individual, who, living in hope of the approval of his peers, is seldom free of a diffuse anxiety lest this approval be withheld.[6] Willy Loman, whose aim in life is to be not just "liked," but "well liked," is too pitifully wrong to be tragic, perhaps, but he represents a failure typical of the times. As Riesman points out, the economy of the country, especially in the past few decades, has given particular emphasis to consuming, for production is able to take care of itself. But to increase consumption, more and better salesmen are needed. In Willy Loman, boxed in his Brooklyn house by towering apartment buildings, trying in vain to grow a few seeds in the darkness of the shadows, is portrayed the lonely traveling salesman, who is not successful because he holds that to be "well liked" is the *aim* of living rather than the *result* of unselfish thoughtfulness of others.

"I was lonely, I was terribly lonely," Willy says to Biff in explaining the woman "buyer" in his hotel room. Wonderingly, on the verge of tears, Willy says to his old neighbor, "Charley, you're the only friend I got. Isn't that a remarkable thing?" To Linda, he says, "On the road—on the road I want to grab you sometimes and just kiss the life outa you. 'Cause I get so lonely—. . . ." No doubt Willy as a salesman is susceptible to a kind of loneliness which to men in other work might not be so keen, for he is "a man way out there in the blue, riding on a smile and a shoeshine." But Willy's isolation and failure come about because, as Biff perceptively says after his death, "He had the wrong dreams. All, all wrong." To see the surface of life was his undoing. Perceiving that the men who made good were well liked (for their money if nothing else) he assumed that to be well liked was to make good and that making good was the end of all living.

On the last day of his life he still did not see beyond that. He

16

recognized his failure in himself and in his sons, but even at the
end of his life he had no vision of the truth. His final words
to the rich brother he imagines stands before him—"Ben! Ben,
where do I . . .? Ben, how do I . . .?"— indicate that he had no
insight of where he had gone wrong. Willy's lonesomeness is of
his own making, but it is of his times as well, for a century ago
there was a chance to own a sunny lot large enough to raise a
garden, and a man was likely to be in creatively productive work.
The play's popularity is testimony to the effectiveness of its characterizations and its dramaturgy, but most of all perhaps to its
dramatization of the plight of many Americans today.

Willy, at one point, in explaining that he did not know his
father and that he would like advice from his older brother, says
to himself, "I still feel—kind of temporary about myself." This is
Willy's way of expressing his loneliness. As Erich Kahler, in his
book explaining the transformation of the individual in the present
age, points out:

> The estrangement between human beings in daily life, the
> lack of immediacy in human contacts and the resulting loneliness
> we frequently witness today, have their roots in man's alienation
> from his own personal human center. Since his "commodity"
> or functional self has taken on such importance, his individually
> human self is left to wane. The perfectly legitimate ques-
> tion, "who are you?" . . . is usually answered with a description
> of one's work; while a feeling of emptiness and falsehood, a
> feeling that one has not at all given an answer to the question
> usually remains.[7]

So Willy, feeling his lack of success as a "functional self" in the
economic world, cannot answer the question of who he is and
consequently has only a sense of temporariness about himself. How
to attain the "individually human self" which would give Willy
a feeling of identity and permanency he does not know.

The play, which might be called "Failure of an American" as
well as *Death of a Salesman*, conveys the idea that, although Willy
might be representative of many, it is nonetheless his own failure—
not that of America—which brings his downfall. If many are in
the same dilemma, the place to look for a solution is not in society,
but in themselves. Willy's affair with a woman on his selling trips
is excusable, at the worst a sordid reminder of the flesh in mankind. Not so, his encouraging Biff to steal the football; not so,

his boasting of the expensive lumber his boys have taken from a nearby lot; not so, his flouting the integrity of the school in proclaiming that the principal would not dare flunk an athlete like Biff; not so, his thanking "Almighty God" that his sons are built like Adonises because they will therefore be well liked.

No wonder Willy feels "kind of temporary" about himself. His sense of honesty is badly distorted, and his recognition of the values of intregrity, truth, and responsibility is very slight. His loneliness results partly from his inability to understand the moral principles, which to a man like his neighbor, Charley, are innate. It is certain, too, that he exaggerates the extent of the hard work which he has devoted to the New England territory. Personality, in his thinking, has always been more important than work. Like Willy, the successful American from the time of the pioneers has had grandiose visions of success,[8] but unlike Willy he has labored to bring them to reality.

The pitiful thing about Willy is his belief that, more than for wealth or fame, he longs for friendship. All his dreams are of friendship and comradeship, and his thoughts of the past include the happy relationship between himself and his boys. His memories of the 84-year-old salesman, who was so successful that he called his buyers to come to his hotel room, revolve not upon the money he made, but upon the friends he had.

> 'Cause what could be more satisfying than to be able to go, at the age of eighty-four, into twenty or thirty different cities, and pick up a phone, and be remembered and loved and helped by so many different people? (Act II)

In those days, recalls Willy, there was comradeship in selling. The actual fact of his not being able to make a living at the end of his life did not hurt Willy half so much as the fact that nobody knew him. His final sacrifice was made so that Linda might have the insurance money, but also in hopes that hundreds of imagined friends would come to his funeral from "Maine, Massachusetts, Vermont and New Hampshire."

Throughout his life Willy had compensated for his failure by dreams of personal popularity, the success of his sons, and recognition by his company. Finally forced to acknowledge that reality has clashed irrevocably with his dreams, Willy at the end makes a fruitless but valiant effort to save himself by feverishly planting

18

carrot, beet, and lettuce seeds in his dark back yard. Even in his distraught state he recognizes that if he can make a little plant grow, he may be saved. With suicide strongly in his mind, getting close to the dirt may make him want to live. If seeds will grow, he still can grow. Although he has sometimes had idealistic dreams of natural scenes of beautiful growing trees and grass in the New England countryside, and of lilac and wisteria and peonies around his own house, he now turns to the soil, not sentimentally, but with a terrible hunger for reality. Imagination has failed him, but in the earth there is still hope—not dreams, but food. It is too late, however. Willy senses that his company does not know him; his buyers do not know him; his sons do not know him; a heart-breaking loneliness tells him it is time to die.

An analysis of the play from the point of view of the function of the theme of loneliness which runs through it must be made with Arthur Miller's statement about the play in mind: "the re-membered thing about 'Salesman' is really the basic situation in which these people find themselves."[9] The situation is of impor-tance in itself, not as a background for the growth of character or for dramatic action. The situation in which a father is separated from his sons, and a mother from both sons and father in trying to mediate between them, is basic to the play. How the family became separated is the story of the play. Told in flashbacks as they come to Willy's mind, the incidents reveal the deleterious effect upon the family relationship of the false ideals which Willy holds and instills in his sons. As the play is constructed, Willy has reached a state of isolation in the first scene, which results in his suicide in the last. In between, the explanation for his plight is revealed in remembered incidents. The situation itself is not dramatic, but the revelation of the causes for it is very dramatic.

Many of these revelatory incidents are plays in miniature with a rising action and climax of their own. For example, the series of incidents which lead up to the climactic scene in which Biff finds his father with a cheap woman in his hotel room are all dramatic. In the opening scene Willy becomes irate when Linda mentions that Biff is finding himself. "Not finding yourself at the age of thirty-four is a disgrace," he shouts. With illogical contradiction in his reasoning with regard to Biff, he continues, "The trouble is he's lazy, goddammit!" and a few speeches later he surprisingly adds, "And such a hard worker. There's one thing about Biff—he's

19

not lazy." Willy's irritation toward Biff for his antagonism carries over into the conversation with Linda in a series of contradictions: "Why do you get American when I like Swiss? . . . Why am I always being contradicted?" Later he says, "Why don't you open a window in here, for God's sake?" She replies, "They're all open, dear." Complaining about the stifling neighborhood in which they live, he says, "there's more people now." To Linda's gentle reply, "I don't think there's more people," he yells, "There's more people! That what's ruining this country."[10] This first scene, in which it is made obvious that an intense feeling has split father and son, lays the groundwork for the following ones concerning Biff and Willy.

The next scene in this series takes place between the mother and sons, who have been wakened by Willy's muttering and have come downstairs to talk to their mother. She berates Biff for his lack of consideration for his father. Biff replies: "He threw me out of the house, remember that." Linda asks, "Why did he do that? I never knew why." Biff's explanation indicates the bitterness of his feeling toward his father. "Because I know he's a fake and he doesn't like anybody around who knows! . . . Just don't lay it all at my feet. It's between me and him. . . ." It is an unusual situation in which a mother does not know why a father has thrown out their son. The question raised is still unsettled as the scene rises to a pitch through a happy interlude of planning for the future, which is abruptly ended as Willy berates Linda for interrupting him in his violent enthusiasm for the boys' plans. Biff rises to his mother's defense: "Don't yell at her, Pop, will ya?" Willy, angered, replies, "What're you, takin' over this house?" Biff is furious. "Stop yelling at her." Willy leaves "beaten down, guilt ridden." The cause of the hatred between them is still unrevealed, but the fact of its existence is made unmistakably evident.

The separation of father and son is revealed in a later scene involving a character outside the family, Bernard, Biff's friend, who has become a nationally known lawyer. Questioning Willy as to why seventeen-year-old Biff seemed to quit trying to be anything after visiting his father in Boston, Bernard explains:

> When he came back—I'll never forget this, . . . it always mystifies me. Because I'd thought so well of Biff, . . . I knew he'd given up his life. What happened in Boston, Willy? (Act II)

Willy furiously replies, "Nothing. What do you mean, . . . What's

20

that got to do with anything?" The feeling aroused in Willy by Bernard's mention of the Boston visit is as intense as that he shows in the scenes with Linda and with his sons. It is apparent that the rift between Biff and Willy is recognized outside the family as well as within, but that its cause is not known either within or without by others than the two involved.

The climactic scene of the series, the scene that reveals the cause of the separation of Biff and Willy, comes unexpectedly in a restaurant washroom, where Willy relives the Boston hotel scene in which Biff finds him with a woman to whom he gives silk stockings. Biff in bitter tears exclaims, "You—you gave her Mama's stockings! . . . You fake! You phony little fake!" and runs out. Willy is kneeling on the washroom floor, pounding with his fists and yelling to Biff to come back, when a waiter enters and Willy realizes where he is. The remembered scene is hardly more sordid than the present one, for Willy's two sons have gone off with two common women, and left the sick man alone in the washroom with no thought for his welfare. Willy's lonesomeness has reached its peak. With dramatic acumen Arthur Miller has imposed the remembered scene, in which father and son are split apart, upon the action of the play, so that one incident reinforces the other, and Willy, although Biff has left with an appeal to Happy to save his father, is deserted by his son in this scene, as in the first.

This melodramatic scene is not the last between Biff and Willy. The reasons for the situation in which the characters find themselves at the beginning are still to be revealed. The series of incidents has reiterated the situation. From various viewpoints it has been made clear that there is an unbridgeable gulf between Willy and his son. Suspense has been created by the obvious emotion of the characters concerning the situation, and by their uncertainty of its cause. "Spite" is the key word of the final scene, which may be called anticlimactic in a dramatic sense but which is absolutely essential to the meaning of the play, for in it comes Willy's explanation for Biff's failure and Biff's counadcharge to Willy. Not the affair of the woman, but the basic controversy of their lives is exposed.[11] "You ruined your life to spite me," is the basis of Willy's argument. "You blew me so full of hot air and false ideals of honesty that I'm a nobody," responds Biff. Willy truly believes his own reiterated charge that Biff ruined his life to get revenge, and in a sense Willy is right—but it is not revenge on Willy for having

21

a woman in his hotel room but revenge for the falsity of the ideals which Willy has espoused throughout his life. Willy shouts,

> Spite, spite, is the word of your undoing! And when you're down and out, remember what did it. When you're rotting somewhere beside the railroad tracks, remember, and don't dare blame it on me! (Act II)

Biff answers,

> I stole myself out of every good job since high school! . . . And I never got anywhere because you blew me so full of hot air I could never stand taking orders from anybody! That's whose fault it is! (Act II)

Feeling still, however, that his dream of the West, of a ranch, of the open air represents happiness, Biff continues, "All I want is out there, waiting for me the minute I say I know who I am! Why can't I say that, Willy?" Thornton Wilder claims that the American cannot say who he is except in terms of his accomplishments.[12] Indeed, how can Biff then say who he is? How can Willy tell him who he is, since Willy cannot tell who he, the father, really is.

Separating Willy and Biff is an irreparable loneliness, which is made all the more poignant by a momentary revelation of the love which could have been between them. Crying in his father's arms at the sordid failure of his life, Biff moves Willy to wonder and amazement that his son loves him; but Biff has already gone upstairs with the words, "I'll go in the morning," before Willy makes his discovery, "That boy—that boy is going to be magnificent!" Willy is immediately dreaming of Biff's success as a high school football star—"There's all kinds of important people in the stands," —just before he drives off to kill himself.

In experiencing a "suffering self-recognition of separateness," Willy exemplifies the individual whose only aim is that kind of success which will gain him social approbation. The playwright, while highlighting the separation of Willy and Biff through a series of emotionally charged incidents, has packed the play with supporting scenes which, in other ways and through other characters, reflect and reiterate the lonesomeness of a character with Willy's lack of understanding. He could have been a good craftsman; he could have belonged by seeing around him his own creations. He could build a porch; he could plaster a ceiling; but a misguided idea of success led him to salesmanship with the mistaken thought that there was "comradeship" in it. Instead there was in it for Willy only biting lonesomeness.

The other characters, through whom the theme is emphasized, appear and disappear as Willy's mind switches back and forth from present to past. The play opens and closes with the music of the flute, thin and poignant, representing the unknown musical father, for whose guidance Willy longs, and whose presence he cannot remember. Uncle Ben, the epitome of false standards of conduct, appears momentarily several times to misguide Willy and to isolate him further from the ideals to which he might have belonged. Charley and Bernard are a contrasting father and son to Willy and Biff. Through ideals of honesty and progress through hard work, Bernard attains the standing of a highly respected lawyer, to whom Charley points with modest pride, and at whom Willy can only shake his head and marvel. The contrast between Bernard and Biff is devastating even to Willy's dream of his son's success. The young boss, Howard, who fires Willy, completes Willy's separation from his work, and isolates him economically, as the others have psychologically. Howard's role is really only the technical fulfillment of the deterioration of Willy as a salesman, and is actually of minor importance.

Happy and Linda, the most important characters next to Willy and Biff, are unattached like them at the beginning and at the end, but in the flashbacks they appear as part of the unified family, reveling in the prospects of future attainments of the hero-sons. It is said of Linda in the stage directions that behind Willy's violence and his need for her she has always sensed in him

a hovering presence which for thirty-five years she has never been able to predict or understand and which she has come to fear with a fear so deep that a moment ago, in the depths of her sleep, . . . she knew this presence had returned. (Act I)

And in the end, in spite of the relief which it might seem she would feel after living so long "from day to day," she is really desolated by his death. Although her ideals were always higher than Willy's—for example, she detested the action of Uncle Ben in tripping up Biff—she never wished to impose them upon her husband. She followed where he led, even encouraging his dreams of success, although she recognized what Willy did not—that the facts did not support the dream. "She had developed an iron mastery of her objections to her husband," according to the playwright, and her encouragement of his idea of himself as an important salesman led only to an essential separation between them. Her reiteration, "Willy, darling, you're the handsomest man in the world," only brings to his mind a woman in a hotel room, as does her mending her stocking recall his gift of stockings to the woman. There is no companionable discussion between them, but only a boosting of Willy's ego by his wife who fears him, yet longs to please him.

Happy, likewise, adds emphasis to the theme of the loneliness of Willy, for Happy is a rubber stamp of Willy. He has not, like Biff, "ruined his life for spite," but he lives in the dream of being a much more important man than he is. Without aim in life or high standards of conduct, he lives on the pleasures of women and drink, and at Willy's funeral his philosophy is still

> He [Willy] had a good dream. It's the only dream you can have—
> to come out number-one man. He fought it out here, and this is
> where I'm gonna win it for him. (Requiem)

Misguided, lonesome—"My own apartment, a car, and plenty of women. And still, goddammit, I'm lonely"—Happy will never be different from his father. In him are seen the results of Willy's teaching personified in a second Willy. Whereas Biff in a sense revolted against his father's materialism, and deliberately became a failure, Happy is not even aware of the faults of his father's ideas and lives by them himself.

Thus Biff is alienated from Happy, who still lives in a dream of the future, and the two boys are alienated from Linda, who berates them for their lack of respect for Willy.

> . . . there's no leeway any more. Either he's your father and you
> pay him that respect, or else you're not to come here. (Act I)

And Linda is alienated from Willy because she knows no way to get along except to give in to him. When Bernard warns that if Biff doesn't buckle down, the football hero will flunk math, Linda says, "He's right, Willy, you've gotta—" whereupon Willy explodes in anger at her, "You want him to be a worm like Bernard? He's got spirit, personality . . ." and Linda, almost in tears, leaves the room. And, of course, the alienation of Willy and Biff plays the central part in the plot. The relationship of Willy and Happy, while not so clearly defined, obviously indicates a lack of friendship,

24

for Willy feels he cannot turn to Happy for help when he loses his job, and says to Charley, who gives him money, "You're the only friend I got."

Thus each member of the family feels an isolation from the others, and thus the play is logically constructed so that the memories which appear upon the stage are those which come to Willy's mind as a result of the impact of his unhappiness. The lonesomeness of the hero is emphasized by this technique, for to him alone come the thoughts which are dramatized in incidents explaining the situation in which he finds himself. All the other characters of the play take part as he wills. The action, however, follows no casual plan in its forward movement. The careful design of the play is illustrated, for one example, by the build-up of suspense in the Willy-Biff series; but the theme of loneliness is emphasized by the fact that in essence the scenes are played by Willy alone with his dreams.

Arthur Miller has skillfully created a drama in which the action and form and purpose all cooperate to the same end. Measured by Francis Fergusson's statement that "in any given tragedy (if it is good) action, form and purpose are one,"[13] *Death of a Salesman* qualifies; for the action, which is made up of the incidents, is appropriate to the form, which reveals the mind of the central character, and both serve the purpose of illustrating the situation (and its causes) in which Willy and many of his fellow Americans find themselves. Study of the meaning of the term "action" as used by critics has led Fergusson to conclude that it can be defined and understood only with reference to a particular play and that, making use of plotting, characterization, and speech, the action points to the object which the dramatist is trying to show. As the action of *Oedipus* might be indicated by the phrase "to find the culprit," so the action of *Death of a Salesman* might be described as an attempt "to discover how to be well liked." The skill of Arthur Miller lies in the fact that he has taken this idea—a concept which is in itself not dramatic, not full of possible plot situations—and composed a drama in which that idea is made the main purpose of the action by the exemplification in plot, character, and speech of the situation of the misguided American salesman.

With artistry the playwright has created a coherence between the action and the form. Disavowing that he makes use of flashbacks, Miller says

25

It is simply that the past keeps flowing into the present, bringing
its scenes and its characters with it—and sometimes we shall see
both past and present simultaneously. (Act I)

The action of the play itself consumes hardly more time than would
be allowed by the neoclassicist, but the range covers many years as
the scenes recalled in Willy's mind emerge. Many times, as, for
example, when Linda's laughter merges with that of the woman in
the hotel room, we see past and present simultaneously. By perhaps no other technique could we be made so aware of the reason
for Willy's failure "to be well liked" as by the flow of scenes from
past to present, whereby we view Willy's mistakes in the light of
the present and whereby we are made aware of the lack of moral
stamina in his character through the years, which has resulted in
his present irrational behavior. The stream-of-consciousness form
of the play is the proper medium for the action. Form and action
cohere to express the playwright's desired purpose.

Arthur Miller has made doubly sure that his purpose will not be
lost by concluding the play with a requiem—a mass for the repose
of a soul—in which the theme of the play is reiterated as various
characters express their opinions of Willy. "He had the wrong
dreams," says Biff. "There's more of him in that front stoop than
in all the sales he ever made." Willy could have "belonged" by
reveling in the creations of his own hands. He couldn't belong by
aspiring to be well liked and chesting his way across New England.
According to Charlie, he couldn't help himself, "A salesman is got
to dream. . . ." America needs salesmen, and they've got to ride on
"a smile and a shoeshine." Nobody can blame Willy, for there is
no "rock bottom" to a salesman's life. Willy had nothing solid
under his feet, and no inner strength sustained him. His failure
represents, says Arthur Miller, "a situation which I have seen repeated throughout my life,"[14] and its application becomes broader
for Americans as the number of salesmen increase in this land of
a consumer society.

Eugene O'Neill, like Inge and Miller, has made a study of failure, but a study in aggregate failure, in which overtones of the
universality of loneliness in mankind tend to predominate over
the portrayal of the individual victims. The characters of *The
Iceman Cometh* are all dreamers. They are also all drinkers. Doc
took to drink and Willy took to dreams, but the failures who in-

habit Harry Hope's bar require both dream and drink to sustain them in their isolation. Even the "iceman" of the title is but a character in the daydreams of Hickey, the gay traveling salesman, who conceals his own sense of failure under a veneer of jocularity and largess in handing out liquor to the habitués of Hope's bar.

A haunted young man, Dan Parritt, attempts to make the dream that he betrayed his mother for money, and not for hate, seem true by constant repetition to Larry, the bartender. Chuck and Cora always dream of their plan to get married and live on a farm, though he as a pimp and she as a prostitute are hopelessly mired in degradation. Jimmy Tomorrow will get a job tomorrow; Harry Hope will leave his bar and see his old friends of twenty years ago around the ward; Rocky pretends he's a bartender instead of a pimp for Pearl and Margie, who insist they may be tarts but not whores. Captain Lewis dreams of going back to England as soon as he gets enough money, and his dreaming companion from the Boer War, Piet Wetjoen, wants to go back to the Veldt; Joe Mott, the Negro, is going to open a new gambling house; Pat McGloin is going back to work as a policeman and Ed Mosher as a circus man.

Hickey decides there is no peace in dreaming. He kills his wife as the only way to rid her of her dream that he will cease his debaucheries with women and liquor. He then forces the occupants of the bar to carry out their dreams. They fail, as he predicts. Now they can live in peace, since they need dream no more. But instead of happiness each one experiences a shattering revelation of himself which destroys even his pleasure in drink. Hickey himself recognizes his mistake, and with great depth of understanding proclaims that he is crazy—a cry they all take up with relief. Hickey is crazy, and drink again brings oblivion. Harry Hope can believe that he came back without visiting around the ward because a car almost hit him. All can take up their dreaming again and enjoy that peace which was shattered by a return to reality. Hope knows that he is irretrievably cut off from all his old political friends, and that life is bearable only amongst those other lonesome souls who listen and who pretend to believe his dream so thoroughly that they fortify his belief. "De automobile, Boss? Sure I seen it! Just missed yuh!" says Rocky, and adds, "On de woid of a honest bartender." I'll believe your dream if you'll believe mine is only fair play, so Harry says, "You're a bartender, all right."

According to George Jean Nathan, O'Neill confided to him that the "dominant intention [of *The Iceman Cometh*] has been a study in the workings of strange friendship."[15] This intention, Nathan believes, is fully realized, but like other critics he senses the theme of the tragedy as "the bogus self-substantiation and the transient, pitiable satisfaction which it bequeaths." The satisfaction which it bequeaths to the tenants of the Hope bar is the ability to get thoroughly drunk, a satisfaction which they lost when Hickey forced them to abandon their illusions, a satisfaction, pitiable perhaps, but one which brings them into a spirit of camaraderie which makes life bearable.

Larry Slade, the only character who continues to live without daydreaming, declares at the end, "Life is too much for me! . . . Be God, I'm the only real convert to death Hickey made here. . . ." While the rest happily shout and sing and drink their liquor, Larry stares out the window, "oblivious to their racket." Undoubtedly O'Neill's thesis is a pessimistic one, for the satisfactions which illusion brings are "pitiable" and "transient," but he insists they nevertheless have the edge over death. We prefer to see Harry Hope singing drunkenly to Larry staring hopelessly out of the window as the curtain falls. It is a pessimistic philosophy if the best possible solution for mankind is to keep on dreaming, but it is not completely nihilistic, because of the "strange friendships" engendered in the process of dream sharing. The alleviation of complete lonesomeness in a world of reality by cooperative exploitation of the dream-world is the only possible, but also a semihappy, solution.

Captain Lewis, who starts to the British Consulate to ask for a job, stops in the park and strolls about, unable to go any nearer reality, when a glance at the neighboring bench shows him his companion, the Boer from Hope's bar, who also can go no farther. When Lewis begins humorously berating him after both have come back to the bar, Wetjoen says, "No offense taken, you tamned Limey. About a job, I felt the same as you, Cecil." With a rejuvenating sense of companionship, he becomes an elated member of the human race. If Willy Loman could have dreamed his dreams in the friendship of another failure instead of in the light of success of his brother, Ben, and his neighbor, Charley, perhaps he would not have cracked mentally. The American lives "not on the treasure that lies about him but on the promises of the imagination."[16] Willy's hopes were incontrovertibly smashed, but Harry's and Jimmy Tomorrow's and Lewis' and Wetjoen's were not, because they would carry them out tomorrow, but not today. Never put to the test, therefore, each one's plans happily characterize him and make his existence, if not bright, at least endurable. There are no converts to death among the gang except Larry.

The difficulty of analyzing *The Iceman Cometh* lies in the fact that the purpose of the play is not clear, or more exactly, that there appear to be two purposes to which O'Neill has tried to make the form and action contribute. To the casual reader or theatergoer the opinion of Richard Watts seems to sum up the play:

> [O'Neill] is merely proclaiming the humanitarian doctrine that mankind, being lost and lonely in a hard and bitter world, is entitled to some sort of illusion to comfort it in exile, . . . and the best intentioned meddler interferes with this right at his own peril.[17]

But the analyst is aware that the "best intentioned meddler" is also lost and lonely and that the play to some extent is constructed to highlight his story. It is almost impossible to have a unified play with two equally important purposes: the effect of the leading character upon the mass of common individuals and the effect of the mass upon the leading character. In all great drama there is reaction between characters, but if in *Oedipus* or *Hamlet* the effect of the protagonists' actions upon the populace or even upon the minor characters had been made as important as their individual growth, the purpose of both dramas would have been lost. Conversely, in *The Lower Depths*, if the effect of the tenants of the cellar upon the reformer, Luka, had been highlighted, the purpose of that play—to show the influence of a Christ-like figure on the most degraded of humanity—would not have been clear.

Eric Bentley, in his analysis of *The Iceman Cometh*, sees what the casual observer does not—that it is perhaps the change in Hickey rather than the action concerning the inhabitants of the bar, in which O'Neill is more interested.

> The main ideas are two: first . . . that people may as well keep their illusions; second, that they should not hate and punish, but love and forgive. . . . In a way the truth-illusion theme is a red herring, and . . . the author's real interest is in the love-hate theme.[18]

What Bentley calls the love-hate theme involves Hickey's hatred of his wife, and the hatred of the wandering boy Parritt for his own mother, as well as the former love and present hatred of Larry for Parritt's mother. These three characters all stand apart from the group of dreamers—Hickey, as the reformer; Parritt, as the conscience-stricken wanderer; and Larry, as the author's commentator on the scene—but they have a relationship to each other.[19]

On meeting Parritt for the first time Hickey insists, in spite of the boy's denials, that he knows him.

> But still I know damned well I recognized something about you. We're members of the same lodge—in some way. . . . I can tell you're having trouble with yourself. . . . (Act I)

Dan Parritt wishes to have nothing to do with Hickey, but he pursues Larry relentlessly. "You know what I want most is to be friends with you, Larry. I haven't a single friend left in the world. . . ." Pursued by the guilt of the knowledge that he has betrayed his mother to the police, Parritt tries to feel himself a part of mankind through Larry, who had once loved his mother and is the logical path to redemption. The relationship of the three is highlighted at the end as Hickey reaches the climax of the long story of why he killed his wife. Parritt, deeply moved, admits that he betrayed his mother because he hated her, and Hickey, subconsciously hearing, bursts forth with curses upon his dead wife. Hickey thus influences Parritt to admit his guilt, but in turn is trapped into admitting his own, although a short time before he had tried to deny the relationship which he first felt between himself and Parritt: "I wish you'd get rid of that bastard, Larry. I can't have him pretending there's something in common between him and me. . . . There was love in my heart, not hate." Larry is influenced by Hickey to urge Parritt to kill himself, and finally to be a convert to death himself, so that the three characters play out a theme of love and hate which contains more dramatic conflict than the illusion theme, and which provides the main interest of the play's climax. Since, however, the anticlimax focuses on the truth-illusion theme, the drama as a whole is organically inchoate and its purpose uncertain.

To trace first the theme in which Hickey is involved, it is necessary to notice that the build-up for his grand entrance is produced by expectant comments by the other characters through most of the first act. Willie Oban says jocularly, "Let us join in prayer that Hickey, the Great Salesman, will soon arrive. . . ." Joe Mott groggily mumbles, "I was dreamin' Hickey come in de door, crackin' one of dem drummer's jokes, wavin' a big bankroll and we was all goin' be drunk for two weeks." Larry explains to the only newcomer to the bar that Hickey is "an old friend of Harry Hope's and all the gang. He comes here twice a year . . . and blows in all his money." By such comments and later excited remarks that some of the gang have seen Hickey, suspense builds up to the point of his entrance, when, with all eyes fixed upon him, Hickey's jovial "Hello, Gang" is greeted with approving cheers from the crowd. "His expression is fixed in a salesman's winning smile of self-confident affability and hearty good fellowship," according to the playwright.

At the time of his entrance, Hickey "belongs." He brings a feeling of fellowship with him, which arouses a like response in the gang and causes Harry Hope to deride the report that Hickey has changed; but, after losing himself momentarily in the greeting, Hickey proceeds to put into effect his plan to make the intimates of the bar face reality, and it is soon obvious to all that he *has* changed. The fact that he decides to sleep awhile without touching his drink indicates his determination to cut himself off from the buoyant companionship of the bar. It is a surprising reversal of the expectation built up through Act I that as the curtain falls, Hickey sleeps fitfully at a table while the others stare resentfully at him.

Their resentment increases to a kind of fury through the first part of Act II—a reaction expected by Hickey. He remains confident, directing the actions of all the characters, forcing them to break out of their dreams, finally making them realize the difference between dreams and action, and then bringing them to desperation. It is when they fail to rally and continue to curse instead of to thank him that Hickey's self-confidence first fails. He pleads with them to react as he expected—to find peace from the abandonment of their day-dreams. "The only reason I can think of is," he charges, "you're putting on this rotten half-dead act just to get back at me! . . . It makes me feel like hell to think you hate me." Angered at their continued lethargy, he realizes that he has reached an insurmountable stage of isolation. According to Larry, "He's lost his confidence that the peace he's sold us is the real McCoy, and it's made him uneasy about his own. . . ." Finally becoming almost frantic as he realizes his separation, he admits his hate for his wife.

In his suffering self-recognition of loneliness he is more to be pitied than are the clay-like human specimens who surround him. Hickey, however, has in him some of the nobility of the tragic hero (unless it is only the hope that he may not die friendless), for looking into Harry Hope's expression of resentful callousness, he takes the step which will save the men from desolation. With "pleading desperation" he claims, "Yes, Harry, I've been out of my mind. . . . You saw I was insane, didn't you?" In a moment the crowd happily takes up the shout, "We knew you were insane. We just acted to humor you," and Hickey goes to his death willingly, spiritually reunited with his friends, as the gang goes back to its dreaming and drinking.[20]

Hickey's progress from camaraderie to a semiexpected isolation, and finally into complete involuntary isolation, with an act of expiation at the end, can be compared in the manner of Theodore Spencer to the progress of Shakespeare's heroes. Spencer sees Macbeth's growth into evil as an implacable progress into isolation, but Hamlet, who is isolated at the beginning of the play, becomes very close to Horatio when he begins to act, and at the end, because of his readiness—the readiness is all—to meet his fate, is not a lonely individual. Othello, like most Shakespearean heroes, is at home in his world when the play opens, but grows more and more isolated through his jealousy; at the end, however, he too belongs again by being ready through passion, as Hamlet is through mind, to meet his fate.[21] Hickey cannot be compared to these heroes because, although he wants to die, he does not recognize in his death a form of surrender to a fate or to justice; his reasoning is:

Do you suppose I give a damn about life now? Why . . . I haven't got a single damned lying hope or pipe dream left! (Act IV)

He becomes what the others are. Without a pipe dream, he, like them, is lost, and nothing can bring him companionship with anyone again. His death is not completely ignoble, however, for he has freed Harry Hope and his friends to dream again by insisting that his whole treatment of them has been mad. With cries as he goes out of "They can't give you the chair! We'll testify you was crazy," the intimates of the bar restore their self-confidence and Hickey thus rises above the mass. His soul has grown to the extent that he has shown compassion for others.

32

The object of the action of *The Iceman Cometh,* according to Fergusson's definition,[22] might be expressed in the phrase, "to find peace." Hickey attempts singlehandedly to help the "whole mis-begotten lot" of them to find each his own peace. He firmly believes at first that he has found his own. The irony is something like that of Oedipus' striving "to find the culprit," when it is he all the time. Hickey has to admit that he has failed to bring the men peace. He does come to the understanding that he has lost his own, however, and goes willingly to his death. Oedipus recognizes with tragic anguish that he is the culprit. As King Oedipus restores his country, Hickey restores happiness to the crowd, and so the little man partakes of the heroism which is Oedipus' in great measure.

Besides the development of Hickey, O'Neill in *The Iceman Cometh* has dramatized the plight of a whole group of men, and whether their theme is a "red herring" or the main interest bears investigating. Americans are interested in the mass of people, the common man; to them his loneliness is as important as that of the hero. It is not so dramatic. The static quality of *The Iceman Cometh* is partly the result of the emphasis upon mankind, rather than upon a man. Some enlightenment concerning this theme is gained by a consideration of Gorki's treatment of a mass of unfortunate souls in *The Lower Depths,* which is frequently compared to *The Iceman Cometh.*

The similarity in characters and in setting is emphasized by the likeness of the plots of the two plays. Gorki's pilgrim performs the function of attempting to arouse from their moral lethargy the miserable specimens of humanity who inhabit the Russian cellar, just as O'Neill's traveling salesman brings a new theory of life to bear on the degenerates of Hope's bar. The intrusion of both is resented. Of Luka after his departure, it is said:

Don't you go and interfere with people as that old fellow did! . . . —the damned old fool—he bewitched the whole gang of us.[23]

Of Hickey, a character remarks,

He was crazy, and he'd got all of us as bughouse as he was. Bejees, it does queer things to you, having to listen day and night to a lunatic's pipe dreams—. . . . (Act IV)

But there is a great difference in the ideas of the two plays, for the philosophy of life proposed by Luka is Christian and optimistic

33

about the future of mankind, whereas that expounded by Hickey is despairing if not nihilistic. Therefore, although the characters in both plays may end in drunken orgy, the theme of the two is different. The preaching of the faith-healer, Luka, may come to nothing, but John Gassner could say of the play:

> Gorki provided a rare dramatic experience by taking as sordid a slice of life as it was possible to find and electrifying it with pity rather than revulsion and with hope rather than despair.[24]

In the case of *The Iceman Cometh,* we see without regret the characters throw off the influence of the misguided Hickey, but we must agree, at least to some extent, with Edwin Engel's comment about O'Neill's attitude toward life as shown in the play. O'Neill feels, he says,

> not only that men are "despicable"—stupid, cowardly, deceitful, treacherous, selfish, greedy—; that truth, justice, faith are untenable; but that love is non-existent.[25]

Those critics who compare the two plays are obviously not thinking of their contrasting ideas of life, nor of the difference in their assumptions about man's isolation from his brothers and from God.

The whole question of the meaning of life and of man's consolation in his relationship with other men is brought forth in both plays by the examination of the nature of truth. To Luka, an imaginative daydream may represent a higher truth than that of the sordid life of reality; to Hickey all daydreams are pernicious in that they prevent a man's making peace with himself. Luka encourages the prostitute to believe that she is an honest woman, the baron that he is of the nobility, the actor that he can be cured of habitual drunkenness; and when accused of lying because to him "life's wonderful," he replies,

> Try to believe me. . . . And, besides, why is truth so important to you? Just think! Truth may spell death to you!

At another time he insists,

> If you have faith, there is [a God]; if you haven't there isn't . . . whatever you believe in, exists. . . .[26]

But to Hickey it is necessary for man to own up to his factual existence and by inference to eliminate belief in that which he cannot see. He admonishes his old friends of the Hope Bar:

I know how damned yellow a man can be when it comes to making himself face the truth. I know . . . you'll grab at any lousy excuse to get out of killing your pipe dreams. And yet, as I've told you over and over, it's exactly those damned tomorrow dreams which keep you from making peace with yourself. (Act III)

Besides the difference between Luka and Hickey as to the need of illusion, there is a great difference in their ideas of the possible relationship of man to man. To Luka man need not be isolated:

Being nice to people never does them any harm. . . . Someone must pity people! Christ pitied everybody—Prison teaches no good . . . but another human can . . . yes, a human being can teach another one kindness—very simply![27]

Luka's whole appeal involves the brotherhood of mankind. Luka is not successful in permanently reforming any of the characters, but for a moment he has brought them a breath of the understanding that man does not stand alone. Hickey's effect is the opposite. Admonishing the occupants of the bar for acting with sullen resentment toward him, he angrily exhorts them.

Why don't you laugh and sing? . . . you suspect I must have hated you. . . . I know I used to hate everyone in the world who wasn't as rotten a bastard as I was! But that was when I was still living in hell—before I faced the truth. . . . (Act IV)

Man stands as enemy to man in Hickey's book. Hatred drives Hickey, as love drives Luka.

The same comment might be made about the faith-healer, Luka, that Thomas Wolfe made about Christ:

The central purpose of Christ's life, therefore, is to destroy the life of loneliness and to establish here on earth the life of love.[28]

The central purpose of the salesman, Hickey, is to demonstrate that man must live alone, and that only his daydreams can bring a modicum of comfort and friendliness—not that they represent the truth, but that the truth means death, as it does for Parritt.

It can be seen that in a unified play like *The Lower Depths* the setting and plot conduce to one purpose—the effect of a Christ-like figure upon degraded mankind. Luka slips into and out of the scene almost unnoticed, bringing a light whose rays shine upon the unfortunates after he leaves. In contrast the emphasis upon Hickey's entrance and exit and his own growth in *The Iceman Cometh* detracts from the effect he has upon the men. The action of Gorki's play can be expressed as the struggle of man "to find the Truth," a noble concept in contrast to that of *The Iceman Cometh,* "to find peace," a selfish aim. Up to a point the theses of the two plays are not very different. Both admit that daydreams are lies. Both admit that weak men need lies. Gorki goes on to say that there should be strong men who don't. That strong men even exist O'Neill doubts and so arises the difference in their attitudes toward man's loneliness. Gorki would defeat it through love as shown by a Luka, full of human sympathy. O'Neill would defeat it by dream and drink, and consider that a triumph over death.

Thus the meaning of the truth-illusion theme, involving the men, tends to contradict the love-hate theme, involving Hickey, Parritt, and Larry. For, in respect to the latter, Edwin Engel is correct in saying that O'Neill prefers "death to life-in-death." But in respect to the former, he prefers life, even though it be lived in an aura of degradation and illusion. Parritt is better off dead than ruing the betrayal of his mother; but the men are better off singing drunkenly than they were hating themselves and each other in a worse-than-death, illusionless state. The theme of man's essential loneliness, however, is common to both strands of the plot. Hickey, like the others, wants to belong. He suffers a self-recognition of apartness, like them, and in the end he concludes that he, like them, needs a pipe dream to survive. Viewed thus, the reactions of Hickey to the mob and upon the mob have a logical interplay, and O'Neill's phrase, "the workings of strange friendship," has a broad application. The traveling salesman thinks that he wants to bring peace to his friends of the bar, but in reality he is seeking peace for himself by companionship with them. He is no different from Willy Loman in feeling the need to be well liked. Joseph Wood Krutch says, "O'Neill's most persistent theme is what has sometimes been called the theme of 'belonging.' "[29] In the end, Hickey by his compassion ascends to a higher plane than is possible for the animal-like beings at the bar, but since his belonging ends in their also belonging in an aura of dream and drink, the themes of Hickey and of the men are united.

Unlike *Come Back, Little Sheba* and *Death of a Salesman,* both portraying the loneliness of personal failure in domestic situations, *The Iceman Cometh* dramatizes the failure of the male habitués of

Hope's barroom. Any relationships which these men have had with women have been unhappy ones, and since only prostitutes appear upon the scene, the play has an aura of abnormality by virtue of its absence of women. *The Iceman Cometh* also contains so many characters of several nationalities, representing so many causes of failure, that the play seems a portrayal of the idea itself of the loneliness engendered by man's inability to face life. All three plays, however, exemplify the lonely plight of the American who has failed to become a success.

2

HOMELESSNESS

... the god constrains the Greek to roam,
A hopeless exile from his native home.
—The *Odyssey* of Homer, Book I, Alexander Pope

In one sense Americans are so used to moving that they are never homeless and may speak of a casual hotel room as home, but in another they are forever homeless, because "home" is not the place where they live, but the place where they lived as a child. The popular song of December, 1954, whose subject is "There's no place like home for the holidays," typifies American ways by explaining: "I met a man from Tennessee, and he was heading for Pennsylvania. . . . From Pennsylvania folks are headin' for Dixie's Southern shores. . . ." The American is not at home where he lives. His "home town" is his parents' home.

Thomas Wolfe, recognizing that to return to one's former home is impossible, entitled a novel *You Can't Go Home Again*.[1] The American can move forward but not back except in memory. What lonesomeness Americans suffer, with a sentimental attachment to a past home but no hope of regaining it in any practical form. Recognizing homelessness as an aspect of modern life likely to be understood by their countrymen, three playwrights have made it an integral part of the theme of loneliness in their artistic medium: Clifford Odets in *Night Music* (1940), John Steinbeck in *Of Mice and Men* (1937), and Eugene O'Neill in *Anna Christie* (1921).

Clifford Odets' *Night Music* is a drama of homelessness[2] very different from his earlier social problem plays. The story is of a boy and girl lost in New York. The boy, who is taking some trained monkeys back to Hollywood for a producer, is arrested when one of the monkeys frightens the girl. He misses his plane and loses his job. The play in which the girl was acting has closed,

38

a failure. Each has as a home merely a tiny, unpaid-for room in a cheap hotel. The actual homelessness of the two main characters is, however, as Odets conceives it, what might be called the Platonic reflection of the *idea* of homelessness. The boy is antagonistic toward the girl from a deep inner feeling of being so lost that contact with another human being is hopeless. Only Steve's guardian angel, the fat detective Rosenberger, saves him and the girl from complete desolation, presumably by providing a place to sleep, but in reality by providing some inner confidence.

> You love this girl? And you mean it? Then fight for love! You want a home?—Do you?—then fight for homes. (III, ii)

George Kernodle says that Odets in this play "sees man's problem as purely a problem of the inner spirit."[3] No menacing industrialists are responsible for the boy's despair. The social scheme may have something to do with his situation, but it is only within himself and through contact with a guiding spirit that he can find happiness. The boy becomes convinced that joining the army is no panacea. The real war of the world is not on the battle front, but on the home front.

Suitcase Steve, as he calls himself, moves through a dozen scenes—from such locations as a New York police station and a stage door to a hotel lobby, a restaurant, and on to Central Park and the World's Fair—among many minor characters who are almost all as impermanent as he. Clurman says that Odets has made homelessness "part of every character, of every scene, almost of every prop. It is not a thesis, it is the 'melody' that permeates the play."[4]

The sense of security which is associated in mankind with home cannot be fortified in Americans by permanent settlement on a family homestead. Rather, the American must learn to carry his home within himself. Odets' attitude is much more hopeful than Wolfe's: "You can go home again—within yourself." Although Thomas Wolfe may be trying to discover that "the way home is the way forward,"[5] Odets is certain that the way forward is the way home.[6] The stolid detective Rosenberger, in bitter pain from advanced cancer, remarks upon learning of someone else with the disease, "These higher-class diseases are universal, like music." Stressing the universality of his theme with such analogous references to the likeness of all mankind, Odets has written a distinctly realistic drama, which with its choppy dialogue and intermittent movement from place to place gives the impression of the search of all men for security and a home and love, in a world in which the people are transient and the environment unfriendly, or at least indifferent.[7] Suitcase Steve and his girl are part of the lonely crowd. It is not until each finds a home in himself that he can communicate with the other and find peace in a hurried world.

Criticism of the play, both when it was first presented by the Group Theatre in 1940 and when it was revived by the Equity Library Theatre in 1951, centered on the unnecessary belligerency of the main character. Whether or not this is the main weakness[8] of the play, about the fact of Steve's belligerency there can be no question. Early in the play he confronts Fay outside the theater with: "Hey, wait a minute, you!" and later, "Look, I'm an eighty octane guy—Ethyl in my veins—and I'm sore as hell!" At another time, after she has tried to help him, he berates her with, "This makes *four* dirty things you done on me." Steve responds to the information that dogs test everything with the nose, babies with the mouth, by announcing, "I test with the fists." With equal acrimony he proclaims to Rosenberger, "I'm an ice-cold feller. . . . I'm a member of the Steve Takis Club. It's a one-man club an' I like it!" When the thoughtful detective sends up some egg sandwiches and coffee to the hungry boy and girl, she gratefully bites into one, but Steve scornfully refuses with the charge, "I say he's a creep!"

Steve, in these instances and many others, evinces a hard exterior, which makes it appear that he is solidly caustic or at least completely self-centered, but both Fay and Rosenberger sense that the belligerency has another cause. At one time, she chides, "You're not that bad, Steve." At another, she says of him: "He's sweet— sweet . . . like a hard-boiled Easter egg." Rosenberger likewise recognizes that Steve's impoliteness is bravado to hide his quaking heart. At the end Steve himself senses that his superior air may be a compensation for his lack of faith in himself. As they are about to part at the airport, Fay speaks of how the monkeys brought them together, and he adds, "An' they showed me what I am. . . . They're not with me. I travel with them! They got the big future. . . . This is petty cash tryin' to be a mint!" When Steve claims he wants to join the army or resign from the human race, Rosenberger says,

> You resign too easy, young man. Army? . . . Your fight is here, not across the water. . . . Who told you not to make a new politi-

cal party? Make it and call it "Party-to-marry-my-girl!" (III, ii)

Finally moved, the hitherto irascible youth, with "a spreading, wonderful smile" picks up his suitcase, extends his arm to Fay, and utters the surprising words, "Thanks. . . . Thanks, Fatso," to Rosenberger, as the three exit together.

It is not at all illogical that a man—homeless and lonely in New York—should react to his situation as Steve does. Perhaps a weakness of the play, however, is that Steve's bitter hostility remains constant through so many scenes—his sudden conversion coming only at the very end. If the play is not an unqualified artistic success from the point of view of the development of the main character, Odets has composed a drama in which the theme of loneliness because of homelessness is harmoniously carried out through a large number of characters. The most important of these is the girl, Fay, who finds a cheap hotel room preferable to the home of her stuffy Philadelphia family. She heartens the boy by her unresentful attitude toward her plight and her calm optimism toward life. As the playwright's mouthpiece in his explanation of his title, she observes,

> Crickets are my favorite animals in all the world. They're never down in the mouth. All night they make their music. . . . Night music. If they can sing, I can sing. . . . We can sing through any night. (II, iv) [9]

It is not what she says, however, but what she is, that finally breaks down the wall between her and Steve, for her conversations with him are short and unimportant. In the Chekhovian tradition, in which each character speaks his mind without reference to the others, she does not expect answers from him. According to Eric Bentley this device of short soliloquies "is perhaps Chekhov's most notorious idea. It has been used more crudely by Odets and Saroyan . . . to express the isolation of people from one another."[10] The technique appropriately reinforces the theme of loneliness by emphasizing the separateness of each character from the others. Rosenberger himself is a lonely individual. After one of his somewhat oratorical speeches he says, "Excuse me. I live alone and sometimes it makes me talk too much." Although he is reconciled to it and not overcome by it, even the raisonneur for the play suffers from his isolation.

Besides Fay and Rosenberger are other characters who appear

for a short scene or two to enhance the melody of loneliness which runs through the play. Homeless Man (Roy Brown), whistling "The Prisoner's Song" on a park bench, is going to join the army in order to get three squares a day and a place to sleep. The second time Roy passes across the scene he is described as "a specter, an image of Steve's war thoughts." He is the same age as Steve, and homeless like Steve, and represents that part of Steve which tends to seek an easy solution to his situation. Fay is worried when Roy appears, for she recognizes in Steve's glance at the young recruit a haunting desire for security at the price of imprisonment in army life.[11] Another character, Mr. Nichols, constantly calls out for nickels for the telephone booth. More nickels obviously won't help him to reach somebody, but he is obsessed with the idea that through a call he can make contact with another human being. An actress, departing from an unsuccessful play, has taken with her the curtains which she always puts up in her dressing room as a psychologically fortifying suggestion of home.

Besides these characters and others who appear momentarily, an important semihumorous theme which reinforces the action of the play, "to find a home," is the suitcase theme. From the first scene to the last, suitcases are important properties. In the opening scene in the police station, a policeman sets Steve's suitcase beside him with an obvious, attention-getting flourish. After some time the boy picks it up with the words, " 'Suitcase Takis' is on the street again," and exits with it several speeches later. In the next scene Steve converses with a chorus girl, who leaves the theater with her suitcase, followed presently by a number of actors and actresses, each carrying a small bag or suitcase, and finally by Fay with her suitcase. As Steve stands talking to her, a thief makes off with his suitcase; he becomes irate at her for not noticing the theft until too late. Rosenberger catches the thief and returns the suitcase. Toward the end of the scene Steve orders Fay to carry his suitcase; bewildered, she starts to pick it up, whereupon he takes it, along with hers, as they exit.

With ironic reversal of the idea that a suitcase signifies homelessness, it is made clear to the sailor who is trying to get a hotel room that he cannot do so without some luggage. He is homeless, but, for him, a suitcase might insure a room for the night so he could be with his girl. When Fay and Steve get adjoining rooms in the hotel, the two suitcases are motivating properties for some movement between rooms, and then, toward the end of the scene, Steve repacks his angrily and later stalks out, forgetting it completely. Fay picks it up and runs after him to the park. After sleeping all night on the park bench, "two lonely pathetic creatures, needing a home," they return to the hotel in the morning with Steve's suitcase, to find her father waiting for them with steely glances at the offending object.

The next episode takes place at the World's Fair, where the young couple have run into Roy Brown again, who must quickly get his suitcase uptown before joining the army. In the last of the suitcase series, Steve packs his bag in his hotel room, preparatory to taking the plane back to Hollywood. An attendant at the airport puts it on the plane, and as Steve, having had last-minute orders to remain, stares at the sky, thinking his suitcase now has wings, Rosenberger, like a faithful dog, trots in with the battered object, thus completing the suitcase theme and also the detective's service to Steve.

On a different level of seriousness the suitcase serves the purpose in *Night Music* that the cherry trees do in *The Cherry Orchard*. A symbol of the transiency of Americans, as the cherry trees are of the old regime of Russians, the idea suggested is ever-present throughout the play because of the tangible object upon the stage. As in Chekhov's play, there are connotations beyond the symbolism, which in *Night Music* extend to include the unsettled condition of the mind and emotions of the characters because of the impermanency of their lives. If Gertrude Stein is a reliable judge of national character, the transiency of Americans has an effect upon their way of thinking and is a cause of their being, unlike the British, unsettled in mind as well as in body.

> Think of the American life as it is lived, they all move so much even when they stay still and they do very often stay still they all move so much. They move so much because in moving they know for certain they can know it any way but in moving they really know it really know as certain that they are not daily living in their daily living. The English just in the other way even when they are travelling are not moving, they do move no one can move who is really living in any moment of their living their daily living.[12]

Odets' play assumes to some extent the lack of "daily living" by Americans because of their always moving in mind as well as in fact. Odets nevertheless rejoices in the American spirit that overcomes the debilitating effects of the social and economic conditions which modern America inflicts upon its people.

A transition play of Odets between those of social protest and *Night Music* is *Paradise Lost,* 1936, in which a man is being dispossessed of the home in which he and his family have lived for seventeen years. But with the furniture on the sidewalk, and the curious crowd trying to peer through the closed windows, Leo Gordon is not shattered by his homelessness. He insists upon giving away some bills, which have been left for him, to two "Homeless Men," who are among the crowd outside. One of the two makes fun of Leo: ". . . millions are homeless and unhappy in America today. . . . You have been took like a bulldog takes a pussy cat!" But Leo replies defiantly:

> There is more to life than this! . . . Men, men are understanding
> the bitter black total of their lives. . . . They become an ocean
> of understanding! *No man fights alone. . . .* For the first time
> in our lives—for the first time our house has a real foundation.
> (Act III)

As in *Night Music* the cry is for courage to face the fact of material homelessness without allowing spiritual homelessness to destroy all hope, either with the help of a guiding spirit or the indomitable faith of a Leo Gordon. *Paradise Lost* is aptly titled, for Leo loses everything which might seem to make his land a heaven, but a sequel would certainly have to be titled "Paradise Regained," because he acquires a faith in the brotherhood of man and declares at the play's end: *"No man fights alone!"*

Four years after *Paradise Lost* Odets made a concentrated effort in *Night Music* to present one cause of the lonesomeness of Americans. The purpose of the play is served by the setting, characters, incidents, and dialogue. The numerous settings afford a visible reminder of the movement of the large array of characters, who engage in their isolated activities in dialogue frequently addressed partially to themselves. The form of the play accents homelessness, for, of the twelve scenes of the play, ten end with the forthright exit of the main characters for other destinations. The scene curtains fall on movement, not static stage pictures. The fifth and last scene of Act I is a contrast to the first four in that Fay and Steve sleep side by side on a park bench, and the fifth and last

44

scene of Act II shows them in a momentary embrace in the hotel room. In all the other scenes they are "on their way" as the curtain falls. Thus homelessness is accented by Odets by every possible dramatic device, and the play is artistically created toward the end of portraying the American's loneliness because of it.

A treatment of loneliness engendered by homelessness of an entirely different nature from Odets' *Night Music* is John Steinbeck's *Of Mice and Men*.[13] In both plays the intense hunger for a home burns in the main characters, as well as in many minor ones; but otherwise—in character, in setting, in structure, in dialogue, in mood, and in form—the two plays vary. Set in the Western ranch country of the Salinas Valley, California, mainly on a river bank, in a bunk house and in a hay barn, *Of Mice and Men* is a realistic depiction of the life of transient ranch hands. The characters are particularized in that they cannot be said to represent man lost in America, as Suitcase Steve might, nor is there any semblance of a guiding spirit to aid them. They are one kind of man lost. The plays are similar, however, in that although both Odets and Steinbeck have shown intense interest in the sociological and economic causes of the unfortunate situations of various kinds of Americans, here they have turned from sociological to personal drama, and Burns Mantle's description of *Of Mice and Men* might apply to both. He praises the play for "its appealing exposure of the tragedy that is found in human loneliness."[14]

The dominant cause of George and Lennie's lonesomeness and of that of all the ranch hands is lack of a home. George and Lennie's dream is: "Someday we're gonna get the jack together and we're gonna have a little house, and a couple of acres and a cow and some pigs and. . . ." The stable buck, Crooks, cynical and doubting, expresses the theme of the play:

I seen hundreds of men come by on the road. . . . Every damn one of 'em is got a little piece of land in his head. And never a God damn one of 'em gets it. Jus' like heaven. Nobody never gets to heaven, and nobody gets no land. . . . I seen guys nearly crazy with loneliness for land. (II, ii)

Steinbeck has made bitterly real the impulsive hunger of the ranch hand for a home of his own. Nothing of the sentiment of the "little grey home in the West" or "land where the tall corn grows" regulates his dreams.[15] He understands the hard work of a farm;

45

he recognizes that farm animals involve a daily responsibility; but his happiness would be in belonging to the land and to the house and to the animals upon the land. Crooks' opinion proves to be correct, however, that for a ranch worker a farm of his own is as unlikely as heaven. Something in his character makes him forever a hired hand, and never a land owner.

In this hopeless longing for a home on the land George and Lennie are like the other ranch hands. In their friendship for each other they are not. Steinbeck makes use of their close relationship to point up the loneliness of the typical ranch hand. Their affection—almost a mother-child relationship—is convincingly illustrated by their great pleasure in conversational byplay. To George's "What I could do if I didn't have the burden of you," Lennie usually replies, "I'll go and hide in a cave." George contritely answers, "No, I didn't mean it. Stay with me." Then Lennie leads into the subject dearest to them both. "I will if you'll tell me about the farm." George now has an audience ecstatically rapt in every well-worn phrase. Emerson, for all his words on friendship, has not expressed the feeling so vividly as has Steinbeck in a few short conversations.

That such a relationship is unusual is evidenced in the doubt of the boss that George's interest in Lennie can be unselfish. He suspects that George is taking Lennie's pay. One of the hands, Slim, also is skeptical: "I hardly never seen two guys travel together. . . . Most hands work a month and then they quit and go on alone." George himself says, "Guys like us that work on ranches is the loneliest guys in the world." "But not us!" continues Lennie, "because . . . I got you to look after me . . . and you got me to look after you." Steinbeck points up the unusual friendship to enhance the tragedy of George's having to shoot Lennie to save him from being lynched, but also to emphasize the aloneness of the typical ranch hand.

So unusual is the obviously genuine feeling between George and Lennie that their dream of a home seems possible of fulfillment to the old bunkhouse keeper, Candy, and finally even to the cynical Crooks, both of whom beg to be allowed to help in buying a small farm. Crooks goes so far as to offer to work for them for nothing if they will take him along. The friendship blows like a breath of love through the lonely world of the ranch hands, who are moved by it to think all things possible, but it inspires the hate of the cowardly boss's son, and proves in the end an ill-fated relationship among workers destined for loneliness. A kind of meanness, which even the dim-witted Lennie senses, pervades the air of the ranch where the two men start work. George's reiterated warnings to Lennie to stay away from Curley and Curley's wife are well founded, but the inevitability of Lennie's becoming entangled with them makes the warnings fruitless. The sustaining dream of a home, which is so vivid as to inspire other lonesome ranch hands with belief, is blasted at the end by the death-dealing shot from the German Luger.

In structure Steinbeck's drama resembles the "well-made play" in its careful plotting and its pointing up of properties and incidents which will play an important part in later scenes. Were it not for the fact that the theme of lonesomeness is made so poignantly real, the play would seem melodramatic. It contains several violent climactic scenes, which, if they had not been motivated by the suffering of the characters, would be only sensational. This is not to say that it deteriorates into mediocrity, however, for, instead of imposing the action upon the characters, the violence resulting from their loneliness is a logical outcome of it, and the technique of the plot does not weaken the encompassing theme.

The obvious framework which contains the play is the use of the riverbank scene at the opening curtain and at the closing, with George's admonishing words in the first scene, "Lennie, if you just happen to get in trouble, I want you to come right here and hide in the brush," fulfilled by his shooting of Lennie in the last. In between there are references to the possibility of trouble and to the place by the river, where the two men first camp for the night. After the boss's son speaks to Lennie with a chip on his shoulder, George reminds Lennie, "Look, if you get in any kind of trouble, you remember what I told you to do." The big, stupid man finally remembers, "Hide in the brush until you come for me." Later Lennie, in response to George's warning to stay away from Curley's wife, senses trouble. "Let's go, George. Let's get out of here. It's mean here." Later when attacked by the sullen Curley, he complains to George, "I didn't want no trouble." Finally when he has killed Curley's wife and realizes that trouble has hit him broadside, he rushes to the riverbank, where in darkening twilight like that of the opening scene, George shoots him while describing the "little place," which had been their dream.

47

Added to the carefully prepared build-up of the likelihood of Lennie's getting into trouble is dramaturgical preparation of the kind of trouble to which Lennie is prone. In the beginning George takes a dead mouse away from Lennie, while Lennie protests that he needs something soft to pet and that he has always tried to be gentle with the mice which his Aunt Clara used to give him, but "I'd pet 'em . . . and then I pinched their heads a little bit and then they was dead." Lennie wishes they could get the "little place" of their own soon, because the soft, furry rabbits would not get killed so easily. To arrive at a ranch where one of the hands is trying to give away a litter of new pups is perhaps what Aristotle would call a possible improbability. It is not long after he has been given a puppy that, as could have been prophesied, Lennie has "petted" it to death. By exposition in the opening scene, George makes clear that Lennie has barely escaped lynching in Weed because of this predilection for fondling soft things.

> You just wanta feel that girl's dress. Just wanta pet it like it was a mouse. . . . You didn't mean for her to yell bloody hell. . . . (I, i)

And shortly after the men first reach the bunkhouse, Curley's wife, whom George rightly calls "jail bait," appears sluttishly perfumed and evokes the comment from the staring Lennie, "Gosh, she's purty."

As if the forecast by incident and exposition of the kind of trouble coming were not enough, Steinbeck has strengthened the play's structure by the pointed use of Carlson's German Luger. Carlson first produces the gun from the bag under his bunk to shoot Candy's old dog. He cleans it obviously before replacing it. Later when George, having found the dead woman, is seen to rush into the empty bunkhouse, the audience is prepared for Carlson's announcement that his gun is missing and recognizes that it is not Lennie, as the men assume, but George, who has taken it. And while George makes Lennie sit and look across the river in the final scene, it is no surprise to see him slowly draw it from his side pocket.

Thus, it is with Ibsen-like precision that Steinbeck lays the stage, but also with Ibsen-like purpose he portrays the tragic loneliness of life on a Western ranch. The isolation which George and Lennie feel pervades every other character. Candy, the old bunkhouse keeper, who has lost his right hand, clings to his blind, stinking dog, until with despairing resignation, he lets the men shoot the miserable animal because of his recognition that they do it with understanding pity for his grief and not with brutality. Curley's wife hangs around the bunkhouse relentlessly, although she is not encouraged by any of the men. To the charge that she is a tart, she pleads innocent and claims that she is only lonesome.

> I got nobody to talk to. I got nobody to be with. . . . I want to see somebody. Just see 'em an' talk to 'em. (II, i)

Crooks, the black stable buck, complains to Lennie:

> You got George. S'pose you din't have nobody. . . . A guy goes nuts if he aint got nobody. . . . I tell you a guy gets too lonely, he gets sick. (II, ii)

Even the boss, after stern questioning of George and Lennie, "relaxes, as though he wanted to talk but felt always the burden of his position." After some jocular remarks, which are turned aside by George, who feels that "He's the boss first an' a nice guy afterwards," the boss "realizes there is no contact to establish; grows rigid with his position again."

So besides the loneliness of the ranch hands because of their homelessness, there is in the play the lonesomeness of debilitated old age, of the Negro because of his color, of the lone woman on the ranch, and of the man in authority. There is a sense of homelessness and temporariness among all these characters and some elemental discussion of the needs of mankind for privacy as well as for companionship. Whereas the hands who live in the bunkhouse long for a room of their own, the black stable buck laments that he must live by himself. George's dream of a farm includes "a room to ourselves," and Candy says to Crooks, as he enters the stable room for the first time, "Must be nice to have a room to yourself this way." But Crooks replies satirically, "All to myself. It's swell. . . . Guys don't come in a colored man's room." There is lonesomeness in being one bunk-inhabitant among many as there is lonesomeness in being segregated. There is lonesomeness in old age and in authority, as there is lonesomeness in being homeless.

Although the suitcase is not the much-used property it is in *Night Music*, Steinbeck, like Odets, has accented the idea of homelessness by its use. Carrying their possessions in blanket rolls, or "bindles," George and Lennie make their first entrance, and in a later scene arrive with them at the ranch bunkhouse, where they stow their few belongings by their bunks. A reminder that all the men are temporarily working at the ranch is Carlson's pulling his bag from under his bunk to take out his gun and the placement of all the hands' possessions from their bags onto the little shelves by their bunks. At the end it is with a "small, cheap suitcase" that Curley's wife arrives in the barn to prepare for her running away from Curley. The suitcases or bindles are used as visual reminders of the homelessness which haunts the characters. They contribute to the theme as well as to the plot.

It is because Steinbeck has made his theme more important than his plot that the play becomes a meaningful aesthetic expression of a phase of American life. The technique of creating suspense by exposition and incident is obvious upon analysis, but its use is justifiable, for the final effect of the tragedy of human loneliness is what remains with the audience. Of far more importance than the plot is the portrayal of the friendship which is blasted; of the isolation of each character; of the mood of meanness which is engendered in the atmosphere of lonesomeness on the ranch; and of the homelessness of the ranch hands. Here loneliness is not only pitiful; it is tragic.

Steinbeck does not share Odets' hopeful attitude that Americans (at least these particular Americans) can have homes by fighting for them. His play may perhaps more properly be called one of homelessness than can *Night Music,* in which a home is seen to be possible within oneself even in unpromising circumstances. In *Of Mice and Men* a home remains forever a dream which only temporarily assuages the lonesomeness of the dreamers.

In *Anna Christie,* a play combining realism and a sense of overhanging fate, Eugene O'Neill presents Anna—homeless at the end as at the beginning, and with her lonesomeness not much mitigated by the promises of her lover and her father that they will return. In mid-drama Anna enjoys a life of almost idyllic happiness in what might seem a ridiculous setting for a happy home—a dirty, chugging coal barge. But to her it is a blissful living place, capable of wiping from her memory past sorrow and degradation. Partly it is the happy, companionable relationship with her old father, the type of companionship she had never known with anyone before, that causes the natural color to come into her cheeks. Partly it is the old man's unconscious love of the sea in any form, which love, although he pretends to curse the old devil sea, he transfers to Anna. But mainly it is because the barge is the home which Anna never knew with her country relatives or in her occupation of nursemaid or as a prostitute. She has finally found on the barge a place which she can claim as hers and which she shares congenially with a loving father.

Lonesomeness, according to her own story, was the cause of her turn to prostitution from service as a nursemaid.

> I was caged in, I tell you—just like in yail—listening to 'em bawling and crying day and night—when I wanted to be out—and I was lonesome—lonesome as hell! (Act III)

To Edwin Engel[16] it is both "novel and improbable" that a woman would substitute prostitution for tending children on the ground "that in the latter position one is 'caged in' and 'lonesome.' " But since O'Neill was free to assign whatever motivation he wished in this expository dialogue, he unquestionably felt lonesomeness to be logical. In the fact that she felt "caged in" O'Neill perhaps indicates that Anna has the family love of the open sea, for she explains also that when jailed for thirty days, although the other girls did not mind it, she became very sick and had to be sent to the hospital. As she returns to health on the open barge, she exclaims, "Gee I wouldn't have missed it for nothing. I never thought living on ships was so different from land." There she is not "caged in" and she is not "lonesome," for she has a father and a home of her own.

There is a certain humor in Anna's ecstatic exclamation about "living on ships," as if it were universally true that all mankind could find a home upon the sea. Anna's failure to recognize the psychological factors which make her situation on the barge a happy one does not nullify their validity, however, nor make less joyous the interlude between the first act, in which she wearily enters the saloon, "a dead stranger in this burg," and the last scene, when, as Chris and Burke prepare to leave her, she says, "And as for me being alone, that runs in the family, and I'll get used to it." Anna is fated to be homeless. Suitcase Steve will find a home if he has faith; George and Lennie's home remains forever a dream; Anna's need of a home is so unconscious that she does not understand the cause of her happiness while she has one; but in the end she somehow recognizes that she is doomed to be without that feeling of security which she has had for a time on the barge. Getting used to "being alone" is not a happy solution for any human being, and for Anna it would seem likely to prove fatal.

It is interesting to note that Anna's homelessness is made explicit by O'Neill, as the same state is by Odets and Steinbeck, by her appearance with a tawdry traveling bag. In the bar scene it is made an obvious property as Anna prepares to depart. In the fourth act, as she is homeless again, her suitcase "stands in the middle of the floor." This visible symbol of her plight startles the half-drunk Chris into realizing that she is planning to leave. Its appearance at the beginning and the end coincides with Anna's unsettled state in the first and last acts and provides conspicuous evidence of her homelessness.

Although the dramatic climax of the action of the play comes at the end of Act III in the hysterical scene in which Anna admits her past life and accuses Mat and her father of being like all the other men she has met, the turning point in the loneliness theme comes in the middle of Act II, as the voice from out of the fog interrupts Anna's happiness. Before she sees who it is or even knows that it is more than a passing fisherman, she mutters "half to herself—resentfully," "Why don't that guy stay where he belongs?" The almost unbearable sense of isolation she knew at the beginning of the play has vanished; now, along with the night air, she joyously breathes in a feeling of belonging as she exclaims:

> I feel . . . like I'd been living a long, long time—out here in the fog. I don't know how to tell you just what I mean. It's like I'd come home after a long visit away some place. . . . And I feel happy for once. (Act II)

Unexplainable as the ecstasy is to her, it is real enough to make her resentful of any interruption at all. Partly because of her inheritance from seafaring folk, and partly because of the "clean" way the sea makes her feel, she has found a spiritual home on the barge. Her own wonder leaves her without words, but according to the playwright she looks "transformed." Her haggard appearance of the first scene has been changed to one in which natural color floods her cheeks and the ring of good health is in her voice. Happy for the first time in her life, she is at home. She belongs.

The transition from her former loneliness—hating the farm,

hating being caged in as a maid, hating her past degradation, and hating men—to her finding a home and peace, is abrupt, for O'Neill has given no indication in the first act that such a transformation could take place. Anna has gone to the barge with the greatest reluctance. Only because of her father's earnest persuasion has she concluded that she will "do anything once." Her sudden union with her surroundings must be accepted as a somewhat incomprehensible wonder to the audience as well as to Anna herself and to Chris. And the rest of the play, which in reality contains most of the action, thus becomes anticlimactic.

After falling in love with Mat, Anna cannot have happiness without him, but since she is forced into admitting her past life, she cannot have happiness with him. The peaceful home with her father can never be recaptured after his trouble with Mat. The entrance of Burke signals the end of Anna's belonging. Her struggle to regain some sense of companionship throughout the rest of Acts II, III, and IV overbalances the action, which continues with melodramatic scenes that sustain excitement, but do not contribute to the theme. Had the play begun with Act II, showing Anna in a state of harmony with her surroundings, it would be perhaps a more consistent portrayal of her steadily losing struggle to regain her original peace in the world. O'Neill accents the misery which Anna has suffered inland by his portrayal of her scene in the bar, but he might have contributed more to the theme of her "belonging" on the sea if he had begun *in medias res*. The climactic scenes in which Mat and Chris battle for her, in which she proclaims her past iniquities, in which it is revealed that both men have signed on the same ship, thus leaving her alone again, would have even greater intensity if Anna had not appeared as a prostitute in Act I. Her appearance in Act I makes the conclusion of the play a return to the beginning as far as her lonesomeness is concerned. Better dramaturgy might have made the last scene the climax of an uninterrupted progress into isolation.

The idea that Fate, represented by the sea, rules the life of the Christophersons would have been more forcefully dramatized if Anna had first appeared at peace on the sea. It is only indirectly that the sea can be blamed for her condition as she first appears. For generations the fateful sea has been ruling and, according to Chris, ruining the lives of the family, but Anna appears to take joy in hearing about them, and to conclude that the sea is infinitely preferable to the farm. "Was the men in our family always sailors—as far back as you know about them?" she asks enthusiastically. From her whole account of life inland, it appears that the inhibitions of the land had proved fatal for her, who instinctively longed for the open air of the ocean, and Chris's attempt to attribute her grief and loneliness at the end to the "old davil sea" lacks the conviction it might have had, had she never appeared as an inland girl except in retrospect.

The stories of Anna and Chris might seem more dramatically unified as well if they had both begun on the sea. As the play is written, Anna's loneliness at the end is attributed by Chris to the ways of the fateful sea, from which she, as a Christopherson, is bound to suffer. Her plight, *she* attributes to the ways of the land. Only as she is Chris's daughter and he suffers because of her plight is the sea the causative agent of her isolation. It is merely the irony of fate that out of the very sea she loves there arises the object which destroys her sense of being at home in the world. Her half-conscious effort "to find a home" is thwarted by the very home itself. Her story, as the play is written, seems quite separate from Chris's and loses some of the tragic implications which it would have if it were not confused with his.[17]

Chris is not homeless. The sea has made others around him suffer, but he is at home there. Pretending to despise and fear the water, he claims that his work as captain of a coal barge "ain't sea job," but obviously it is the pull of the sea which keeps him happily chugging up and down the shore. His explanations for deserting Anna are nothing more than excuses, with the "old davil sea" taking the brunt of the blame for his own lack of responsibility in regard to his mother, to his wife, and finally to his daughter. He is no doubt sincere in not wanting his daughter to marry a seaman, because he is aware of the misery of the women connected with sailors, but not because he dislikes the sea himself.

Therefore, although it is necessary to take into account the superstitious feeling of Chris toward the sea as in part the motivation for his treatment of Anna, it is important not to confuse Anna's lonesomeness with the theme of Chris and the sea. The play is not the coordinated study of human lonesomeness which either *Night Music* or *Of Mice and Men* is because of the mixture of themes, but O'Neill has tried, as he has in his other plays, to indicate that the protagonist's attempt to belong to something outside himself, some-

thing greater than himself, is the prime object of tragic drama.[18]
He has also made a semisuccessful attempt to portray the mythical
effect of the sea upon folk devoted to her and to indicate that although life on the sea brings a devastating loneliness, it is not
possible for some people to find a home anywhere else.

It is inevitable, therefore, that Chris should go to sea again. It
is also inevitable that the audience should view skeptically Anna's
plans at the close of the play: "to get a little house somewhere"
and to make "a regular place for you two to come back to."
Questionable, too, seems Mat Burke's promise: "You'll not be lonesome long. I'll see to that with the help of God. 'Tis himself
[Chris] here will be having a grandchild to ride on his foot, I'm
telling you." More in keeping with O'Neill's themes of loneliness
and fate are the foreboding words of Chris: "It's queer, yes,—you
and me shipping on same boat dat vay . . . it's dat funny vay old
davil sea do her vorst tricks." Burke agrees that Chris is probably
right for once, and, as the old man watches the fog with sombre
preoccupation, Anna and Burke stare at him. The curtain falls
to the accompaniment of the "mournful wail of steamers' whistles."
O'Neill feared that he had not sufficiently pointed up the tenuous-
ness of the happy ending. "The happy ending," he claimed, "is
merely the comma at the end of a gaudy introductory clause, with
the body of the sentence still unwritten."[19] The introduction is
not such as to make a happy conclusion probable or surcease from
loneliness likely for Anna Christie.

It can be seen from the consideration of three plays that home,
if conditions are right, can be anywhere to an American—a bench
in Central Park, a little farm with a cabin on it, a coal barge along
the coast. O'Neill has recognized "home" in various settings in his
plays. Although Rob, the dreamer in *Beyond the Horizon,* finds
life on the farm a cause of bitter despair, Andy Mayo, who always
planned to be a farmer, happily adjusts himself to a life on the sea.
Ridiculous as it may seem, the reviewer who decided that the bar
of *The Iceman Cometh* was a home was not incorrect.

> They're all there, this profane unregenerate lot, dreaming out
> their lives in Harry Hope's haven for the half dead, a place that's
> home, even though it smells of rotgut.[20]

In *Desire Under the Elms* a New England farm is the home where
the Cabots belong to the soil, almost as do their animals.

The psychological tranquility which makes a place home can be shattered by many causes. Of course, the number of displaced persons bodily removed in groups by fiat or war is perhaps smaller in America than in any other large nation. But the practice of the members of each generation of removing from their home towns and entering other work than that of their fathers has made Americans unsettled, and the failure of old industries as new ones arise has effected among the American people a transiency which has made them feel bereft of home, and lonely.

Odets and Steinbeck and O'Neill have all found dramatic values in the presentation of a human loneliness caused by utter homelessness. None has made socioeconomic conditions the villain. In each play the emphasis is upon the suffering individuals whose adjustment of self and place is disrupted and whose efforts to overcome loneliness make up the action. The aesthetic effectiveness of the situation of the characters is intrinsic; for although Suitcase Steve and George and Lennie and Anna Christie[21] all carry their few belongings in one small bag or bundle, many an American who has travelled with more baggage knows their loneliness and responds emotionally to their plight.

3

AN UNHAPPY FAMILY

God setteth the solitary in families.

Psalms 68:6

"Happy families are all alike; every unhappy family is unhappy in its own way," says Tolstoy in the first line of *Anna Karenina*. If there is one place where the individual should find comfort and understanding, it is within the family. When, therefore, social or hereditary or personal causes bring about a rift in the family's cohesiveness, the bitterest kind of loneliness may result for some of its members. Happy families are all alike in sharing the feeling of belonging to a mutually satisfying, socially recognized unit of human beings. The outrages against family unity which the dictatorships of the twentieth century have practiced (encouraging brother to testify against brother) have emphasized the sacredness of family loyalty to Americans and have made them, in spite of the fact that no solution has been found to stop the rising divorce rate, view the breakdown of the family with foreboding.

In view of modern social conditions as well as in view of the fact that family relationships have frequently been the subject of dramatic treatment, it is not strange that American playwrights have explained one cause of loneliness as an unfortunate situation in a family. According to Eric Bentley,

Drama has so often and over so long a period been a defense of family piety. In Greek tragedy it is the desecration of this piety that horrifies us. In the comedy of Moliére it is the desecration of this piety that we find ridiculous.[1]

Like Antigone, who stands alone against the state for her dead brother's honor, and Agamemnon, whose family is doomed by the actions of its forebears, many characters of Greek drama are involved in that social unit called "family." Hamlet and Lear, too, are caught up in the tragedy of family difficulties. American drama- tists, like their predecessors, have not failed to find dramatic possi- bilities in the theme of loneliness of those characters suffering from lack of normal family relationships. Three of these are Carson McCullers in *The Member of the Wedding* (1950), Eugene O'Neill in *Mourning Becomes Electra* (1931), and Sidney Howard in *The Silver Cord* (1926).

The most recent of these plays, *The Member of the Wedding,* is the study of the isolation of a young girl whose mother is dead, whose father is too busy to talk to her, and whose chief source of comfort is Berenice, a middle-aged Negro housekeeper, who, no matter how understanding she is of the girl, cannot be a substitute for a cohesive family. Like all children Frankie is interested in her family, and like Willy in *Death of a Salesman* she tries to get others to tell her about the dead parent she cannot remember. She says,

> Jarvis talked about Granny. He remembers her very good. But when I try to remember Granny, it is like her face is changing— like a face seen under water. Jarvis remembers Mother too, and I don't remember her at all. (Act I)

At another time she says, "I know six dead people in all. I'm not counting my mother." She does not pretend to know her mother, even as dead. About her father she is as candid. For her emotional needs he is almost as nonexistent as her mother. She explains,

> Papa was bent over working on a watch when I went by the store. I asked him could I buy the wedding clothes and he said charge them at MacDougals. But he wouldn't listen to any of my plans. Just sat there with his nose to the grindstone and answered with—kind of grunts. He never listens to what I say. [*There is a pause.*] Sometimes I wonder if Papa loves me or not. (Act II)

Frankie is justified in wondering about her father's love, which at best is not an understanding love, for after he has dragged Frankie from the wedding car near the end of the play he says, "Well, it looks like the show is over and the monkey's dead," as she "stares at him resentfully." He has refused to notice her wedding clothes, of which she was so proud, and has hurt her feelings by remarking that he thought they were a "show costume," and then has em- barrassed her by bodily pulling her from the car. It is not strange that Frankie feels lost and without family, especially at times when

Berenice is not there and her little cousin has gone home. Near the end of the first act as she looks unhappily at the empty house, she calls across the yard to seven-year-old John Henry. "Come over and spend the night with me," and when he refuses, "I only asked you because you looked so ugly and lonesome." She does not understand that it is her own feeling of lonesomeness which has made her call, just as she does not understand that it is the lack of a family which makes her want to join her brother's wedding.

Besides not having a family to give her a feeling of belonging, Frankie does not belong to the club of neighborhood girls to which she aspires. Berenice, expressing the theory of clubs in America, gives her good advice:

> Frankie, the whole idea of a club is that there are members, who are included and non-members who are not included. Now what you ought to do is to round you up a club of your own. And you could be the president yourself. (Act I)

Frankie denies all desire to be associated with "those little young left-over people." Nevertheless she is extremely hurt by not being chosen "the new member" of the club of girls, and later with her mind still occupied by the subject, she remarks, "I bet Janice and Jarvis are members of a lot of clubs. In fact, the army is kind of like a club." Suffering from her feeling of not belonging to either family or club, Frankie associates all kinds of "belonging" with the couple who have so fired her imagination that she can think of nothing else. It is no wonder that she wants to belong to them herself.

Carson McCullers has presented the character of this lonely young girl in a play which creates a mood and illustrates a situation, not in conventional dramatic form, but in a way dictated by the theme of loneliness. According to the playwright, *The Member of the Wedding*

> is an *inward* play and the conflicts are inward conflicts. The antagonist is not personified, but is a human condition of life, the sense of moral isolation. In this respect "The Member of the Wedding" has an affinity with classical plays—which we are not used to in the modern theatre where the protagonist and antagonist are present in palpable conflict on the stage.[2]

By her statement Mrs. McCullers indicates her intention of pre-

59

senting a universal problem by dramatizing the theme of moral isolation in an American scene in a way which she considers atypical of the usual methods of dramaturgy today. She also indicates that, although the protagonist is an adolescent, the theme is applicable to human beings of all ages. As the critic of the New York *World Telegram* wrote: "The terrible unwanted isolation of this child may be only a brief experience of sensitive youngsters, but it has flavors of truth for everyone, no matter how old."[3] Mrs. McCullers dramatized her own novel of the same name because of her dissatisfaction with the version which a professional dramatist had produced, but it is not through amateurishness that the dramatic structure is not traditional, but because of the playwright's belief that her theme is better interpreted by a flowing, conversational style than by a tightly-climactic, dramatic structure.

The mood of the play through the first two acts, which consume much the greater part of the playing time, is created perhaps mainly by three dramatic devices: the action seems unplanned and casual; the conversation is frequently desultory and irrelevant; the characters are not always understood by each other and sometimes cannot express their own feelings. All three devices tend to indicate a kind of isolation between people which could not be portrayed in an integrated drama in which characters react to each other in a steady march to a climax. Even in the third act the exciting events take place off stage and are not of importance for themselves, but are, as the author says of the whole play, to illustrate "the weight of time, the hazard of human existence, bolts of chance."

That the action seems unplanned and casual is perhaps the main factor in creating a mood of unornamented reality in which the isolation of the characters seems logical. For example, Frankie at one time during the long scenes in the kitchen takes off John Henry's glasses and makes him try to identify the coal scuttle, a large sea shell, and finally an ant on the floor to prove that he does not need glasses. At another time she breaks into conversation to wonder where her cat has gone, pours cream into a saucer, and calls the police to notify them of the cat's disappearance. Again she makes much of trying to take a splinter from her foot with a large butcher knife. For lack of anything else to do John Henry at one time rummages through Berenice's pocketbook. There is other stage business of the same sort with such properties as a bottle of perfume, playing cards, and Berenice's glass eye. The action is such as might easily take place in any dilapidated backyard and kitchen on a warm summer's day. These seemingly extraneous incidents create a mood of quiet living dictated only by chance and the changing emotions of the characters.

That the conversation is frequently desultory and irrelevant follows logically from the lack of relationship of the incidents to each other. John Henry asks, "You serious when you gave me the doll a while ago?" but receives no answer from Frankie, who is pondering the possibilities of getting away from her home town. Later he asks again, but this time Frankie is inwardly contemplating her brother and his fiancée. Frankie at one point jumps from worried cogitation about her own increasing height to the question of whether "those freaks" ever get married or go to a wedding. Berenice's puzzlement is finally resolved, and Frankie, Berenice, and John Henry all enter into a short discussion of the freaks at the fair last October. The conversation about the missing cat and the telephone call to the police appear to have very little relevancy to the action of the play. A short game of three-handed bridge ends abruptly when it is discovered that John Henry has cut up the face cards, making the bridge hands unplayable.

> Berenice: Now Candy, how come you took our playing cards and cut out the pictures?
> John Henry: Because I wanted them. They're cute.
> Frankie: See? He's nothing but a child. It's hopeless. (Act I)

It is with an appreciation of the aesthetic effect she is creating that the playwright makes use of these and other apparently meaningless topics of conversation. She appears not to work toward the play's climax but rather to drift toward it, swept back and forth at times by the nature of human beings trying to communicate with each other.

The difficulty in communicating with others and even in expressing one's own thoughts is evident in *The Member of the Wedding*, as it is in life, and exemplifies the loneliness consequent upon fruitless attempts. For example, during the bridge game, Frankie's mind is on her brother and the bride:

> Frankie: My heart feels them going away—going farther and farther away—while I am stuck here by myself.
> Berenice: You ain't here by yourself. By the way, where's your Pa?

Frankie: He went to the store. I think about them but I remember them more as a feeling than as a picture.
Berenice: A feeling?
Frankie: They were the two prettiest people I ever saw. Yet it was like I couldn't see all of them I wanted to see. . . . And then they were gone. (Act I)

It is obvious that even the understanding Berenice is not able to follow Frankie's feeling any more than she can at another time:

Frankie: J.A.—Janice and Jarvis. Isn't that the strangest thing?
Berenice: What?
Frankie: If only my name was Jane. Jane or Jasmine.
Berenice: I don't follow your frame of mind. (Act I)

And again Frankie has her sympathetic old friend baffled:

Frankie: Listen, Berenice. Doesn't it strike you as strange that I am I and you are you? Like when you are walking down a street and you meet somebody. . . . Yet when you look at each other, the eyes make a connection. . . . You go into different parts of town, and maybe you never see each other again. Not in your whole life. Do you see what I mean?
Berenice: Not exactly.
Frankie: That's not what I meant to say anyway. (Act II)

Frankie tries again, but still does not succeed in putting into words what she feels she wants to say; and hard as Berenice tries to explain things to Frankie, neither can she make herself understood to the young girl. Frankie complains, after Berenice has gone to great lengths to explain a lesson from her own life, "I don't see how it is a warning applied to me." So Berenice tries to be more explicit, but still fails to convince Frankie that her comparisons are valid, or even to make the girl see very clearly what her meaning is. Carson McCuller's play is not subject to the criticism which John Wharton makes of modern American stylized stage dialogue.

The characters in current plays are extraordinarily well-educated . . . they do not ever say "It don't" or "These kind of things." . . . Moreover, they are unbelievably polite. . . . On stage people politely wait for each speaker to conclude his point before speaking in turn. . . . They are also outstandingly articulate . . . seldom correct or repeat themselves. . . . stage characters have an ability to stick to the point and avoid wandering off on tangents to a degree unequalled in real life.[4]

By disregarding these unnatural dictates of stylized dialogue, the playwright has created an atmosphere in which the theme of loneliness is poignant, for the isolation of the characters seems inevitable rather than contrived.

In the failure of these artless characters to communicate there is nothing of the disillusionment experienced by the characters in T. S. Eliot's sophisticated verse play, *The Cocktail Party*. Edward's exclamation, "One is always alone," is echoed later by Reilly's insistence that one path of life is "No lonelier than the other," and is climaxed by Celia's complaint: "It no longer seems worth while to *speak* to anyone!"

> No . . . it isn't that I *want* to be alone,
> But that everyone's alone—or so it seems to me.
> They make noises, and think they are talking to each other;
> They make faces, and think they understand each other.
> And I'm sure that they don't. (Act II)

Here the isolation is a source of agony or at the very least of blighted expectation. But Carson McCullers' characters do not expect to communicate well. They do not, therefore, suffer the frustration of Eliot's. Of course they do not have the urbane reasoning prowess of Eliot's characters by which to express their reactions. But this inferiority granted, their anxiety is not so extreme because their anticipation is not so great. In the process of verbal intercourse, they succeed or fail as chance will have it.

In contrast to this background of unplanned interchanges, the action which finally leads to Frankie's belonging pulses forward with sustained and steady growth. The first act consists of Frankie's gradual formulation of what she sees as a practical plan to eliminate the loneliness of which she has been made acutely aware by the visit of her "brother and the bride," as she enjoys alliteratively phrasing it. From such expressions as "I just can't understand how it happened," and "I bet they have a good time every minute of the day," Frankie moves onward from wonderment to the wish that they had taken her with them, and then to the complaint, "They came and went away, and left me with this feeling." Although Berenice taunts her with having "a crush on the wedding," Frankie has a growing belief that the solution to her dilemma is to accompany the wedding couple. Indeed, the sight of them has made her aware of a kind of belonging that she had never recognized

63

before. There is some logic in her announcement: "Until yesterday, nothing ever happened to me," because within a few hours she has come to a self-recognition of her apartness which is wholly new. As the culmination of the first phase of her development, Frankie stands outside the dark and empty house and concludes with inevitability,

> Not to belong to a "we" makes you too lonesome. . . . I know that the bride and my brother are the "we" of me. So I'm going with them, and joining with the wedding. (Act I)

Through an act of apparently haphazard conversations and incidents Frankie has grown strong in her resolve to conquer loneliness.

Throughout the second act Frankie comes to recognize that "joining with the wedding" is not a complete fulfillment of what she understands as the urge to belong. Her father's lack of interest and Berenice's stolid resistance to persuasion on the matter dampen her joy (although not her intention of going) ; but these reactions of adults to her plans as well as her own emotional pitch lead her to extend her expectation of what "joining with the wedding" will include, until gradually she evolves an almost idealistic conception of belonging. By the end of the act Frankie has decided that she really wants to belong to the whole world—no mean concept, even for a philosopher. On her shopping trip she stops to tell everybody she passes "about the wedding and my plans"—not from selfish, gloating motives, but with the hope of sharing some of her buoyant expectancy and with the sincere belief that others would partake of her joy. After the wedding she imagines that she and Jarvis and Janice

> will just walk up to people and know them right away. We will be walking down a dark road and see a lighted house and knock on the door and strangers will rush to meet us and say: Come in! Come in! . . . We will have thousands and thousands of friends. . . . We will be members of the whole world. (Act II)

It is obvious that she has come a long way from the end of Act I, when the painful realization of her own loneliness suggested the idea of accompanying the two who were so obviously a part of each other. She has come to broaden her viewpoint to include the whole of humanity. Without any of the inhibitions and prejudices which society imposes on the adult, she would like to make a realization of the brotherhood of man in her own experience. In this idea she steps over the bounds of childhood, for, although few people have thought of going off with the bride and groom, many have considered what form of brotherhood might bring surcease from loneliness.

The part which Berenice plays in Frankie's growth through the first two acts is very important. As an analogous representation of a lonely character, the part has significance, but as an influence on Frankie the part is indispensable. In actuality, although Berenice is almost the last of her family and is left sitting alone as the final curtain falls, she has within her a sustaining faith which gives her a feeling of belonging. Her loneliness, therefore, is not internal, and for this reason she can help Frankie develop an emotional maturity. With assuredness she tries gently to explain the nature of love by illustrations from her own life, and thus to warn Frankie that "joining with the wedding" will result in trouble. So vividly does she describe her love for Ludie that Frankie says, "It seems to me I feel sadder about Ludie than any other dead person." Berenice is not so successful in convincing Frankie not to repeat her own mistake of trying to find love in other men, who were only "little pieces of Ludie." Falling in love with weddings, Berenice claims, could become a dangerous "mania," but Frankie refuses to change her mind. As Frankie appears a happy girl at the end of the play, however, it is evident that Berenice's kindly reasoning has had its effect in helping the girl break through her wall of isolation. Berenice's ability to view life with unselfish understanding has brought Frankie through a crisis. Berenice's own sense of belonging is illustrated as she sits alone in the empty kitchen, thinking of her dead brother and of little John Henry's death and the breakup of the household; for it is with placidity that she responds to Frankie's offer to come to see her often: "No, you won't, baby. You'll have other things to do. Your road is already strange to me." Without Berenice, Frankie might have remained a lonely child. With her help Frankie has gone onward and outward with a new understanding of belonging.

After two long conversational acts follows a short third act full of exciting and tragic events. Frankie is dragged from the wedding car and runs off with her father's pistol to shoot herself; Berenice's brother Honey hangs himself in prison; and John Henry dies after suffering severely with spinal meningitis. The balmy southern atmosphere changes, and wind, thunder, and lightning cause the doors to slam and the lights to go out. So much external action is in contrast to the internal action of Frankie's growth during the first two acts; but it is not melodramatic because most of it takes place off stage and because it is not contrived for excitement, but is used to illustrate the relativity of time and the isolation of human beings. It is all purposeful for Frankie. She returns home at four o'clock in the morning, admitting to Berenice that her plans have been "child plans," just as Honey dashes through the kitchen, obviously on his way to disaster for slashing a white man but proclaiming a new found freedom: "No more 'boy this—boy that'—no bowing, no scraping." With her growing confidence Frankie catches his mood of triumph in defeat. Honey's breathless outpouring, "All my days have been leading up to this minute," seems to Frankie to reflect her own experience. As he now belongs to himself, she, reborn on a new level of competence, sees herself up to now as a child, but with her child's days leading to the moment of her freedom from loneliness in an adult reliance upon herself.

It is Honey's quick passage through the kitchen which prompts Frankie's remark, "Now for the first time I realize that the world is certainly—a sudden place." Combined with the events of the wedding and her young cousin's illness, Honey's flight climaxes the feeling within her of the rapid changes of existence, but most sudden and of most importance is the change within herself. Berenice, well as she understands the girl, fails to grasp the real extent of her growth in so few hours, and lost in her own grief, replies, "Sometimes sudden, but when you are waiting like this it seems so slow." Carson McCullers has artistically characterized the world from two viewpoints in terms of time and thereby emphasized her theme of individual isolation.

The slow-moving first and second acts and the climactic third all conduce to illustrate the theme of loneliness in people as a whole and especially in an adolescent girl. The first-night reviewers, not realizing the purposefulness of Mrs. McCullers' dramatic method, wrote like Brooks Atkinson:

> . . . the play has no beginning, middle or end and never acquires dramatic momentum. Although Miss McCullers has taken the material out of the novel she has not quite got it into the form of a play.[5]

Confronted with its obvious emotional appeal to the audience, they attributed its success to the actors' excellent performance of the three major roles. Since the play has proved successful on the amateur stage as well, the critic today must be forced to admit that, unorthodox as the dramatic structure may be, it is eminently suited for the portrayal of the growth of a girl from extreme loneliness to a mature self-reliance. In the epilogue-like last scene, Frankie classifies the tragic events of the week of the wedding along with the fact that "in that same week . . . I met Mary." It might seem humorous to consider a new friend of as great moment as the griefs of the week; but to Frankie, meeting Mary was of even greater importance. After years of loneliness, she finally "belongs."

In her desperate struggle to avoid loneliness Mrs. Phelps in Sidney Howard's *The Silver Cord* brings havoc to two lives and leaves her mark upon two others. In this play the theme of loneliness is viewed in the effect of the lonely individual upon others rather than in the effect of loneliness upon herself. The greatest weakness of the play, aside from the fact that it is perhaps too baldly propagandistic, is that the playwright does not clarify the extent to which Mrs. Phelps' actions are conscious; hence, although it is very clear that she threatens or brings disaster to others, it is not clear whether she recognizes lonesomeness as a force which drives her or whether she only pretends to. Just as the emphasis in Christian theology is upon the suffering of Jesus because of Judas' kiss, rather than upon the motivation and suffering of Judas, so the emphasis in Sidney Howard's play is upon the suffering of her sons and their wives rather than upon the possible real suffering of Mrs. Phelps. She is not the sympathetic lonely character found in many plays concerning loneliness, and her desperate fear of being left alone is only partially explained. In contrast to Arthur Miller's stated purpose of explaining the "situation" in which Willy finds himself, Sidney Howard is interested in explaining the situation in which Mrs. Phelps places others. This makes Mrs. Phelps a villainous character and exposes her as an invidious influence upon her family. It does not make her character subject to subtle analysis, but it makes the play a great success as an exposure of "Momism," which, according to Philip Wylie, is extensively prevalent in America today.[6]

If the loneliness which Mrs. Phelps feels is not completely explained, the isolation into which she thrusts the other characters, against which they struggle with varying degrees of success, is effectively dramatized. Although more emphasis must therefore be put on the four young people, the tragedy of Mrs. Phelps must first be considered whether her cry of "Oh, Robin! I'm so lonely! So lonely!" is an artificial and plotted attempt to hold her son or the unconscious outpourings of a woman afraid of being alone. According to Mrs. Phelps' interpretation, the failure of her husband to understand her has made her turn to her sons, in a relationship which, although she does not admit it, is so intense as to be unnatural.

> I knew at the end of a week how miserable and empty my marriage was . . . he never dreamed of bringing the least atom of happiness into my life. Or of romance . . . I didn't live without romance. I found it . . . in motherhood. (Act III)

On another occasion she charges David with having hurt her more than she had ever been hurt by anyone else before, "even by your father." The warped relationship between husband and wife is presumably, therefore, the basic cause of the warped relationship of the sons to the mother.

Christina, the scientist and author's mouthpiece, admits the likelihood of the explanation, but refutes the plea that it provides any justification for Mrs. Phelps' mania. Generalizing from the single case, Christina exposes her protesting mother-in-law as an example of a pitiful type of lonely individual in America today.

> You belong to a type that's very common in this country, Mrs. Phelps—a type of self-centered, self-pitying, son-devouring tigress . . . there are normal mothers who are people, too, and don't have to be afraid of loneliness after they've outlived their motherhood; . . . But you're *not* one of the normal ones, Mrs. Phelps! (Act III)

Christina charges that it is their inner emptiness which causes such mothers to refuse to allow the silver cord to be severed. Those who are "people, too," have resources within themselves which make them recognize their children as adults and their function as parents concluded; those who are animal-like devour their children because of their paralyzing fear that life has nothing else to offer them. The loneliness which overwhelms them comes not because of their children's departure but because of their own lack of psychic strength. The Momism in America today, with its destructive creation of "adult children," is the result of the failure of mothers to build within themselves a sustaining power to live creatively after their children's normal need of them has ended.

Mrs. Phelps' self-styled loneliness receives both sympathetic and unsympathetic consideration—the former from her sons and the latter from Christina and Hester. It is her cry, "I'm so lonely! So lonely!" which makes Robert agree to break off his engagement to Hester. With a triumph which she is "unable to repress," Mrs. Phelps greets his acquiescence with the words, "And I won't have to be lonely now! I won't have to be lonely!" In the later scene between Robert and Hester the discussion of Mrs. Phelps' loneliness reveals to Hester the character of the older woman and to the audience the fact that Robert will unhesitatingly tell a lie to his fiancée in his mother's defense. After Hester finds that Robert has previously talked with his mother about breaking off the engagement the scene reaches a climax.

> Robert: . . . You may be as hard as you like on me, but you mustn't be hard on poor splendid lonely Mother.
> Hester [savage—under her breath]: So she's lonely, too! [The meaning here is that she is lonely as well as splendid.]
> Robert: You *will* twist my meaning!
> Hester: You *said* "lonely."
> Robert: Perhaps I did. But Mother didn't. You know she never talks about herself. (II, i)

Even Robert recognizes, although he has been greatly moved by her appeal, that for his mother to claim her own loneliness as a reason for breaking the engagement puts the older woman in a conspicuously reprehensible position. It is obvious, in the scene in which Hester, having regained some composure, charges Mrs. Phelps with breaking the engagement, that Robert's mother recognizes the fact as well.

> Hester: Can you tell me what he meant when he said that the happiness of *three* people was at stake?
> Mrs. Phelps: He must have been thinking of your happiness as well as his own and mine.
> Hester: What about your loneliness?
> Mrs. Phelps: This *is* contemptible of you! (II, i)

Sidney Howard in these instances has used the theme of loneliness to technical advantage, being able to highlight several scenes by the emotional impact of the word. One suspects that it is as a device to hold Robert that Mrs. Phelps first makes the plea of her own loneliness rather than with any deep, suffering recognition of her need. There is irony in the fact that she probably does not recognize her own inner emptiness and loneliness even while she claims it. The playwright makes eminently clear at the end that Mrs. Phelps is genuinely lonely even though she keeps one son clinging to her. With a morbid selfishness which obviously means sorrow for her and complete ruination for him, she repeats, "mother love suffereth long and is kind; . . . hopeth all things; endureth all things. . . ." There is no true belonging for her ever. To the end of her life her fanatical absorption in her son means isolation from any sustaining faith in herself. From a dramaturgical viewpoint, however, she triumphs and is not lonely, because she keeps one son "engulfed forever." She believes that she has played her cards right to insure herself an adoring and devoted child to the end of her days. To the perspicacious, Howard has presented a picture of the real loneliness of "Moms," but on the literal level, his play illustrates the vicious damage which their pretense to loneliness inflicts upon others.

Most seriously afflicted is the younger son, Robert, whom Mrs. Phelps calls Robin. Apparently happy in his engagement to Hester at the beginning, it is clear by the end of the first act that Mrs. Phelps wields a power over him which will isolate him from his fiancée, as well as from a normal life. "It's a wonderful gift you've given us. . . . A wonderful ideal of womanhood. . . . Your own marvelous self, Mother!" he exclaims to her, as he sits with his head in her lap before the fire and then "My blessed, blessed mother!" as they conclude the conversation with his agreement to break with Hester. He carries out the agreement, but is somewhat appalled at Hester's hysterics and later shattered into a period of self-revelation for a short time by Hester's near-death in the skating pond. He turns on his mother with "sudden, cold fury" as he expresses regret about his treatment of Hester.

> Mrs. Phelps: Robin! You're not holding *me* responsible.
> Robert: Who put the idea in my head? Who persuaded me? Who made me promise?
> Mrs. Phelps: Are you implying that *I* came between you?
> Robert: Well, if you didn't, who did? (Act III)

This short scene is the only one in which Robert belongs to him-

70

self or to anyone except his mother. The restraining wall which she has built around him is too high for him to climb. After this short revolt, "suddenly and involuntarily, the boy reverts and is a child again," with the pitiful cry, "What are we going to do, Mother?" His isolation from healthy existence, as illustrated by the action concerning Hester, is obviously complete and permanent. The pity which the playwright evokes for Robert is increased by the fact that he dimly senses that he is caught, but has not the strength to break the cord which binds him. Sullenly he mutters, "We're just like Macbeth and Lady Macbeth, aren't we? . . . We've got into a mess we can't ever get out of. We'll have to get in deeper and deeper until *we* go mad." His suffering self-recognition of apartness, as in many other plays dealing with loneliness, is the emotion-rousing factor which the playwright uses to exemplify the theme. Robert is portrayed as already so ruined by his mother that his final fall into the slough of Momism at the end is not tragic, but it is pitiful.

The story of David, the older son, runs parallel to that of Robert, with alternating climaxes through the play, the main difference being that David, with the help of a clever wife, is able to sever the cord and to belong irrevocably to his wife and expected child. It is by no means certain, however, until the very end of the play, that his escape will be possible. Symbolic of Mrs. Phelps' attitude toward her older son is David's bedroom in which she has left all his belongings (including his baby pillow) untouched since he went to college. With symbolic significance, also, she has insisted on putting him in a bedroom which adjoins hers and placing his wife at the far end of the hall. Her plotted attempt permanently to separate them begins with this maneuver. David resents his mother's intrusion into his room, and as she insists that "the bond between mother and son is the strongest bond on earth," he anxiously wishes that Christina would enter. It is not long, however, before his mother's cleverness, and old habits, are too much for him. With his, "You are a great woman, Mother!" comes the change which portends his break with Christina. Deeply in love with his wife, he is torn by separation from her. Recognizing instinctively that his mother's love for him means his destruction, he still succumbs.

Mrs. Phelps: Then I've still got my big boy, after all?
David: You bet you've got him!

71

Mrs. Phelps [*in triumph*]: O, Dave! Dave! Dave!
David: Now, Mummy! (II, ii)

The similarity of this scene to the one between Mrs. Phelps and
Robert reinforces the theme of loneliness by repetition, and makes
Mrs. Phelps almost a caricature of a "Mom" in her desire to keep
her sons not only from all women, but from any work which she
could not oversee, for by this time she has persuaded David not
to go to New York, but to stay and design houses for her in Phelps
Manor.

David remains isolated throughout the rest of the play. Christina charges him with having in him what she thought was No
Man's Land—a place she could not reach—but now she knows:

It isn't No Man's Land at all. It's your mother's land. Arid,
sterile, and your mother's! You won't let me get in there. Worse
than that, you won't let life get in there! (II, ii)

Only at the very end of the play does David abandon this land
where life can't come. With the slam of the door as Christina
leaves with Hester, he "comes suddenly to life." With a frantic
cry, he runs out after her, exclaiming, "She said we were trapped.
We *are* trapped. I'm trapped." He must push his mother from him
to get away, so persistent is her attempt to hold him. The suspense
which lasts until the end as to whether David, like Robert, will
dwell in eternal loneliness with his mother makes the play one of
the most dramatically exciting studies of a form of human isolation
which the American theater has produced.

Besides alienating her sons from everyone except herself, Mrs.
Phelps is unbelievably successful at separating them from each
other. The rivalry she builds up between them aids her in holding
them. To Robert she says, ". . . you are *my* son. David takes
after his father." To David she says that Robert is like his father.
"You're *my* son, you know." It takes only a suggestion from his
mother that she prefers David as a son to make Robert distracted.

Robert: . . . I'm damned if I'm going to let you turn Mother
against me!
David: Do *what?*
Robert: You heard me! . . . I know from experience what to
expect when you and Mother get together . . . if you try any
of that old stuff tonight, I'll lose the only prop I've got left. . . .
You don't realize that I'm desperate. (II, ii)

Any real companionship between the boys would break the tie by which she has them caught, since for her nefarious purpose, absolute isolation is necessary, as she discovers when she tries to break David from Christina.

Of the two girls, Hester, much the younger, goes through the devastating experience of being blatantly jilted. Calling to Christina to send "these awful people" out of her sight, she envisions getting away from the house as the only thing which can save her from contamination. Recognizing, as Christina does when she speaks of meeting life "healthily," that the relationships in the Phelps family are sadly distorted, she is almost drowned in her attempt to escape. Until the end it appears that Hester will never recover psychologically from the blow of being separated from the man whom she loved, but as she leaves the house, she announces with a smile that she is going "to marry an orphan." She is obviously restored to health by an inner sense of relief at her escape from the Phelps household. Her story is one of passage from a state of belonging to her fiancé, to a bitter isolation from him through an outside agent, to a final belonging to herself.

Christina's greater age and experience help her take her trial less hysterically, but she too passes through a period during which she suffers from the fear of being alone. Upon her realization of the kind of woman that Mrs. Phelps really is, she says,

> I've been through the most awful experience of my life tonight. And I've been through it alone. I'm still going through it alone. It's pretty awful to have to face such things alone. (II, ii)

And later in an agony of fear she explains to her bewildered husband her feeling of being lost.

> Hester's escaped, but I'm caught! I can't go back and be the old Christina again. She's done for. And Christina, your wife, doesn't even exist! . . . I'm going to have a baby by a man who belongs to another woman! (II, ii)

That each son does indeed look upon his mother as his mate is indicated by their playing "king and queen" together or referring to themselves as "Macbeth and Lady Macbeth." Christina is not inaccurate in her charge that her husband belongs to his mother instead of to her. Self-assured though Christina is, she lives through a period of suffering and loneliness, not knowing whether she can hold David against his mother's wiles, but knowing surely that she cannot have David unless she can break completely the cord which binds him. She leaves with Hester unhesitatingly, therefore, to face the future alone if need be. She does arouse her almost lost husband to rejoin her, but even if she had failed, she could have sustained herself by the knowledge that she had the courage to make the decision necessary and to refuse to live compromisingly with a woman of Mrs. Phelps' character.

The moral of the play is laid on with a heavy hand at the end through a long scene in which Christina, as a trained biologist, decries the viciousness of women like Mrs. Phelps, insisting that they are not fit to be mothers at all. So striking are her metaphors that it is sometimes overlooked that she does show pity for the whole situation as an ill-begotten attempt to avoid loneliness through prolonging the early family relationships into maturity. Christina cries,

> You're all of you perfectly miserable! . . . you're not really bad people, you know. You're just wrong, all wrong, terribly, pitifully, all of you, and you're trapped. (Act III)

At the time she speaks they are all three—Robert, David, and Mrs. Phelps—"trapped" in isolated misery, the boys embracing the false and debilitating idea of motherhood which has been instilled in them, and Mrs. Phelps irrevocably devoted to keeping their physical presence as well as their emotional powers at her beck and call. The whole play is a well-dramatized diatribe against Momism, showing its isolating effects upon those involved and those less closely related to it, thus making it out to be a social as well as an individual evil in America today.

It is hard to conceive of a family more isolated from society and from each other than the Mannons in Eugene O'Neill's *Mourning Becomes Electra*. One of the chorus of the townspeople in the beginning explains, "They've been top dog around here for near on two hundred years and don't let folks fergit it." It is with trepidation that the townsfolk come close enough to the house to look it over, even though the daughter of the family, Vinny, has given them permission. A thick wall of fear and jealousy separates the Mannons from all the neighbors. Within the family the hatred for some members by others and the incestuous love of two couples make each of the four live in lonely misery. Christine, the mother, hates Ezra, the father; the daughter, Lavinia, hates her mother; the son, Orin, hates his father. There is an intense love between mother and son and between father and daughter, which isolates each couple from the other. Lavinia is also in love with her mother's lover, Captain Adam Brant, which gives her two reasons for wishing him dead—that she cannot have him, and that he has disgraced her father. Ezra loves his wife and *she* loves Captain Brant, so that neither Lavinia nor Orin is the undivided recipient of a parent's love which they desire.

Writing on psychiatry in literature, Frederic Wertham says: "The theme of family hates and jealousies is the oldest of plots. Freud would say it is the only one." Adding heavy-handed Freudianism to an ancient dramatic plot, that of Aeschylus' the *Oresteia* trilogy, O'Neill has Americanized the universal emotions of loneliness and sex in an aura of the Puritan conviction of man's guilt.

With its vengeful God and its unnatural repression of sensual delights, Puritanism[8] furnishes an ideal motivation for more emphasis than the Greeks gave to loneliness and sublimated sexual instincts. Throughout the three parts of the play there are references to the damaging effects of Puritanism, some made consciously by the characters, some made with unconscious, ironical lack of understanding. But all are made with inferences of the failure of love and the isolation of individuals in an atmosphere of dogmatism. Christine, who has "a fine, voluptuous figure," and who "moves with a flowing animal grace," mocks bitterly at Puritanism in speaking to Lavinia.

What are you moongazing at? Puritan maidens shouldn't peer too inquisitively into Spring! Isn't beauty an abomination and love a vile thing? (Part One, Act III)

Since her wedding night Christine has suffered a hatred of Ezra for taking her in lust instead of in love. But neither could he be her lover nor let himself be loved, for his belief that "love is a vile thing" is too strong to overcome his normal affectionate feelings. It is her hatred of Ezra and his recognition of it—he says that there has always been "a wall hiding us from each other!"—which motivates the play's action. Feeling isolated from his wife, Ezra has turned to his daughter, Lavinia, for love, and has so entrenched himself in her affections that she says, "I'm not marrying anyone. I've got my duty to Father." Christine has turned to Orin, who was born when his father was away fighting in Mexico.

75

These intense attachments have made any normal family relationships impossible, for they have engendered hate between the mother and daughter and between the father and son.

After Ezra comes back from the Civil War with its horrors still in his mind, he has some inkling of what Christine has long known—that the Calvinistic background of the Mannons has made duty, not love, their ruling passion. He says that all the deaths around him finally made him think of life.

> Before that life had only made me think of death! . . . That's always been the Mannons' way of thinking. They went to the white meeting-house on Sabbaths and meditated on death. Life was a dying. Being born was starting to die. . . . How in hell people ever got such notions. (Part One, Act III)

For the first time in his life Ezra tries to express his love to Christine, but says, "Something queer in me keeps me mum about the things I'd most like to say." With desperate pleading he protests,

> I want to find what that wall is marriage put between us! You've got to help me smash it down! . . . I'm sick of death! I want life! Maybe you could love me now. (Part One, Act III)

Of course Ezra's self-revelation comes too late. Generations attending the white meeting-house have influenced his life too thoroughly for him to be able to remake it. A wall has shut his life from all human beings. As a soldier he has been dubbed Old-stick-in-the-mud, because of his devotion to duty, but he has not been loved. And as he admits, all his affection for Vinnie has been compensation for his failure with Christine: "A daughter's not a wife."

Orin's lack of regard for his father is partly due to jealousy of the attention of the father to his sister, but he too recognizes something of the fatal influence of Puritanism upon Ezra and consequently upon himself. He addresses his father's corpse with mockery.

> Death becomes the Mannons! You were always like a statue of an eminent dead man—. . . looking over the head of life without a sign of recognition. . . . You never cared to know me in life—but I really think we might be friends now you are dead! (Part Two, Act III)

In the light of Ezra's own words about life and death, Orin's somewhat facetious remarks about the naturalness of finding his father dead are appropriate. He recognizes that death will look familiar upon himself as well. Toward the end of the play, after he has tried to find life with Lavinia on the South Sea Islands, where the natives live in a natural state, he admits:

> But they turned out to be Vinnie's islands, not mine. They only made me sick—and the naked women disgusted me. I guess I'm too much of a Mannon, after all, to turn into a pagan. (Part Three, I, ii)

Pursued by a guilty conscience, Orin finds death his only recourse and commits suicide. His isolation from the living has become complete. Only in death can he hope to belong.

Lavinia suffers a more remarkable change than does her father. His experiences during the war, which made him long for love, not death, are as nothing compared to her experiences on the Islands.

> I loved those Islands. They finished setting me free. There was something there mysterious and beautiful—a good spirit—of love— coming out of the land and sea. It made me forget death . . . the natives dancing . . . without knowledge of sin! (Part Three, I, ii)

From a thin, black-dressed, unattractive girl she has become a voluptuous creature like her mother, who even affects her mother's colors in dress and who, according to Orin, has stolen her mother's soul. With almost embarrassing passion she appeals to Peter to marry her. Her reaction against her Puritanical upbringing makes her want to break free for eternity. But finally, she too is beaten by the past.

> Peter! You trust me with your happiness! But that means trusting the Mannon dead—and they're not to be trusted with love! I know them too well! (Part Three, Act IV)

Puritanism wins the day. No belonging to anyone is possible under its reign. It even isolates those indirectly affected. Peter, the most kindhearted and gentle of men, becomes alienated from his mother, his sister, and his town through his relationship to Lavinia.

> Peter: I hate this damned town now and everyone in it!
> Lavinia: I never heard you talk that way before, Peter—bitter!
> Peter: Some things would make anyone bitter!
> Lavinia: You've quarreled with your mother and Hazel—on account of me. (Part Three, Act IV)

The loneliness which Lavinia must suffer the rest of her days is the logical outcome for a family which has been governed by Puritanical tenets. As Lavinia enters the empty house, never again to leave it, she says with a kind of gloating, "I know they will see to it I live for a long time! It takes the Mannons to punish themselves for being born!" Neither from Puritanism nor from her own loneliness could she escape more than momentarily; then she accepts the retribution of the family background for the rest of her life.

Besides the isolation of human beings in an atmosphere in which beauty and love are considered sinful, the theme of loneliness is stressed in *Mourning Becomes Electra* by the use of recurring symbols in many contexts. One of the most important of these is "the island." Suggesting separation from adjoining land and isolation by virtue of the surrounding water, the word is usually used in the play to convey also the idea of escape from a confining environment and from hereditary influences. It also symbolizes paganism in contrast to Puritanism. There, love is not a sin and the God is Pan, not Jehovah. Ironically enough, although the island itself is isolated, it represents a hope of belonging to the world of nature in the minds of those who dream of it. The beauty of the world, which is negated for the Mannons in New England, might become real if they could escape to the island. With despair each one discovers that the island is unattainable and that his loneliness is the more bitter for having dreamed of it. It is, indeed, as in nature, a spot set apart by an insurmountable barrier.

Early in the play Captain Brant first describes the islands in the South Seas where he was once shipwrecked. The islanders "live in as near the Garden of Paradise before sin was discovered as you'll find on this earth." Although Lavinia resents his being in the house and openly charges him with being her mother's lover, she cannot help being fascinated by his description.

> The clouds like down on the mountain tops, the sun drowsing in your blood, and always the surf on the barrier reef singing a croon in your ears like a lullaby! The Blessed Isles, I'd call them. (Part One, Act I)

At the end of the third part of the play it is Lavinia's inadvertently calling her fiancé "Adam" which makes her realize that she has always loved Captain Brant, but his Blessed Isles, which enraptured her first in imagination and later in actuality, are not for the Mannons. She ends trapped in her "tomb" of a house, from which neither Peter nor anyone else can save her.

It is strange that Ezra visualizes escape to an island, for he has never seen such a one as Captain Brant describes and could not appreciate its beauty if he were there. He pleads with Christine:

> I've a notion if we'd leave the children and go off on a voyage together—to the other side of the world—find some island where we could be alone for a while. You'll find I have changed, Christine. (Part I, Act III)

Ezra looks on a faraway island as the place which might break down the "wall" he feels between them. He recognizes that he needs distance—half the world between him and his environment; but she realizes that he cannot escape from himself and that the wall can never be broken through. She cries,

> I loved you when I married you! I wanted to give myself! But you made me so I couldn't give! You filled me with disgust! (Part I, Act III)

Ezra's island has no meaning for Christine, but Orin's has. Since Brant has replaced Orin in her affections, she listens with some dismay to Orin's dream, but an "agonizing tenderness" overwhelms her with pity. Orin tells her that he read and reread *Typee* during the war until the South Sea Islands came to represent "everything that wasn't war."

> There was no one there but you and me. And yet I never saw you, that's the funny part. I only felt you all around me. The breaking of the waves was your voice. The sky was the same color as your eyes. The warm sand was like your skin. The whole island was you. (Part Two, Act II)

Orin visualizes his mother as "the most beautiful island in the world" and one which, being removed from all else, he alone possesses. It is no wonder that, when Christine has admitted killing Ezra in order to have her lover, Orin screams with "savage irony":

> To think I hoped home would be an escape from death! I should never have come back to life—from my island of peace! But that's lost now! You're my lost island, aren't you, Mother? (Part Two, Act III)

79

Christine is lost to Orin as she is lost to herself. His peace is also lost, for as the crowning blow, Orin overhears his mother making love to Adam in the ship's cabin.

> You have me, Adam! You have me! And we will be happy—once we're safe on your Blessed Islands! (*Then suddenly, with a little shudder*) It's strange. Orin was telling me of an island. (Part Two, Act IV)

Orin's island from *Typee* is very similar to Brant's South Sea Isle. Both represent sensual delight. Both represent an escape from the Mannon background, from which even Brant suffers. Both represent an escape from the baseness of man by return to Mother Earth. Brant, as well as Orin, sees a mother image in Christine, for her bronze hair reminds him of his mother's. Both men visualize in the islands a sense of complete belonging. The peace of the womb and the sensual delights of man in a natural state combine to make an image of utter fulfillment.

As Christine wrings her hands and moans over her lover's death, Orin, desperately trying to justify himself for killing Brant, feels he has reason:

> I heard you planning to go with him to the island I had told you about—our island—that was you and I! (Part Two, Act V)

As she continues moaning, he pleads distractedly, "We'll leave Vinnie here and go away on a long voyage—to the South Seas—." But Christine can find peace only in her own death.

After the return of Orin and Lavinia from the Islands a year later, Lavinia has become her mother in looks, in dress, in her sensual desire. The Islands have so remade her that she excitedly assures Peter:

> We'll make an island for ourselves on land, and we'll have children and love them and teach them to love life so that they can never be possessed by hate and death! (Part Three, I, ii)

Unfortunately Lavinia uses the island image here as an escape from "folks and their evil talk"—as a place of isolation, not belonging; as a necessary evil, not a happy solution. She is torn between wishing Orin would marry Hazel so she might be free of him, and fear that he will confess their crimes if he marries. She needs an island to escape from Orin as well as from "folks," especially since Orin clings to her, claiming that Hazel is "another lost island"!

At the end, as Orin goes to clean his rusty pistol, he speaks in a hypnotic state. "Yes! It's the way to peace—to find her again—my lost island—Death is an Island of Peace, too—Mother will be waiting for me there." In Orin's last utterance the island image has come full circle—from that of sensual enjoyment to that of death, from the peace of the womb to the peace of the tomb. The search of the Mannons to escape from the precepts of New England Puritanism has failed, and the island which they hoped would bring them happiness has proved barren.

Another symbol of the loneliness of the Mannons is the "mask-like look" which they all wear. The stage directions as each enters reiterate this characteristic. Christine appears to be wearing "a wonderfully life-like pale mask, in which only the deep-set eyes . . . are alive." Lavinia gives the same "strange, life-like mask impression." Of Ezra Mannon, O'Neill says, "One is immediately struck by the mask-like look of his face in repose." Even Ezra's portrait in the study has the same "semblance of a life-like mask," which his corpse also retains. Orin has the "same life-like mask quality" as his father and Adam Brant. As Christine is about to commit suicide her "face has become a tragic death mask," and after Orin's death, on Lavinia "The Mannon mask-semblance of her face appears intensified now." Even upon the mansion, "The temple portico is like an incongruous white mask fixed on the house to hide its somber gray ugliness." The chorus of townspeople who peer at Christine at the play's opening explain:

> Minnie: Ayeh. There's somethin' queer lookin' about her face.
> Ames: Secret lookin'—'s if it was a mask she'd put on. That's the Mannon look. They all has it. They grow it on their wives. Seth's growed it on too, didn't you notice—from bein' with 'em all his life. (Part One, Act I)

The refusal or inability of the Mannons to communicate with others has led to their assuming a false face behind which to hide their emotions. Their own feeling of inner isolation has probably been the cause of its assumption. But the mask, once accepted, has also had the effect of making their isolation, not only from outsiders but also from each other, immitigable. The use of the temple portico as a mask upon the Greek-revival mansion of the family indicates a kind of symbolism in the theater which O'Neill well understands. In his article, "Eugene O'Neill as Poet of the Theatre," Alan Downer[9] points out that the playwright in most of his plays enhances the significance of his themes by such symbolism as the appearance of the mansion, which, although realistic, is suggestive also. Its "Puritan gray" walls remind Christine of a tomb, and when Ezra comes home from the war with a new view of life he says, "I can't get used to home yet. It's so lonely." Ezra is of course referring to the feeling which the family as well as the house gives him. O'Neill has made the family and the setting so much a part of each other that the house seems to assume the mask of the Mannon family and the family assumes the coldness of the gray stone, each thus increasing the loneliness of the other. Orin has a realization of this transference of loneliness as he returns.

> Home at last! . . . But the house looks strange. Or is it something in me? . . . Did the house always look so ghostly and dead? (Part Two, Act I)

O'Neill wrote for the stage; his setting enhances his theme. On the symbolic level the cold mansion of Puritanism makes human love impossible except through escape to a pagan South Seas island, half a world away.

The purpose, action, and form of *Mourning Becomes Electra* all conduce to the effect of a unified drama. The purpose of the play—to show the disastrous effect of man's attempt to repress his sensuous nature—is well served by the action, which consists of one incident after another portraying the alienation of Ezra from Christine, of Orin from his father, of Lavinia from her mother, and then of Lavinia from her father, of Christine from her lover, of Orin from his mother, and finally of Orin from Lavinia and of Lavinia from Peter. The form controls the action with climactic separations through death at the conclusion of each of the three Parts. At the end of "Homecoming" Lavinia cries to her dead father, "Don't leave me alone. Come back to me!" At the end of "The Hunted," Orin grieves frantically for his mother. "I've got to find her! I've got to make her forgive me. . . . But she's dead—She's gone." At the end of "The Haunted" Orin kills himself and Lavinia enters the house to live "alone with the dead." Each death brings retributive action which results in another death, until Lavinia is left alone to suffer for them all.

Along with this picture of the separation of the Mannons from each other, however, is a kind of mystical expression of the oneness of mankind. Orin says of his war experiences,

> Before I'd gotten back I had to kill another in the same way. It was like murdering the same man twice. I had a queer feeling that war meant murdering the same man over and over, and that in the end I would discover the man was myself. Their faces keep coming back in dreams—and they change to Father's face—or to mine. (Part Two, Act III)

Each man who is killed takes with him some part of the man who kills until the killer himself is dead. Orin's dream becomes reality as he looks at the body of the murdered Adam Brant.

> Do you remember me telling you how the faces of the men I killed came back and changed to Father's face and finally became my own? (*He smiles grimly*) He looks like me, too! Maybe I've committed suicide! (Part Two, Act IV)

Orin has killed himself in killing his mother's lover, for he is driven crazy by her hatred and to suicide by her death. O'Neill's constant emphasis upon the likeness of Ezra and Brant and Orin suggests the likeness among members of the great human family; and Lavinia's transformation into her mother emphasizes, not that one generation follows the next, but that one becomes the next. O'Neill has, therefore, made it the more tragic that either man or Mannon makes his own loneliness in life, when he could so easily belong by loving instead of hating.

When O'Neill wrote *Desire Under the Elms* five years earlier he portrayed a New England family in which an Oedipus complex and other Freudian drives also play an important part in the motivation of the characters. The family background of the Cabots, who are debased, illiterate farmers, hardened by the struggle of making a living from the rocky soil, however, is a far remove from that of the Mannons. The greatest difference between the two plays, nevertheless, is in the themes: that of belonging in the earlier play contrasts with the failure to belong in the later. In spite of the tragedy of their lives the characters of *Desire Under the Elms* are left with a kind of exultant grief because of their courage and love. As Abbie is being taken to prison for smothering the baby which her stepson has fathered, Eben comes to her:

> I'll say we planned it t'gether. . . . I got t'pay fur my part o' the sin! An' I'd suffer wuss leavin' ye, . . . 'r bein' alive when yew was dead. I want t' share with ye Abbie—prison 'r death 'r hell

'r anythin'. . . . If I'm sharin' with ye, I won't feel lonesome, leastways. (Part Three, Scene IV)

The lonesomeness of the Mannons is not theirs, for as they go with the Sheriff's men, Eben points to the rising sun, "Sun's a-rizin'. Purty, hain't it?" and the pair stand together looking up "raptly in attitudes strangely aloof and devout." Sordid as their love has seemed, it has brought them into a spirit of belonging to man and to nature. Edwin Engel says of *Desire Under the Elms*: "All of the principal characters in the play 'belong,' for their unity with what Macgowan called 'the dumb, mysterious processes of nature' is clearly established. . . . Flowing and uniting with all natural objects, they display a process of merging that would have delighted Whitman."[10] The hard, cruel old man, Ephraim Cabot, feels uneasy in the cold house, but happy down at the barn, where it is warm and restful. "I kin talk t' the cows. They know the farm an' me. They'll give me peace." The idea of the Mannons of getting close to nature on a South Seas island is only a dream, but the Cabots really belong to the earth. Their passion is unrestrained by the Puritanical forebodings which make loneliness inevitable and mourning becoming to the Mannons.

O'Neill's great posthumously-produced play, *Long Day's Journey into Night*, by its heroic self-revelation of the playwright, illustrates that O'Neill was able to portray loneliness in so many aspects perhaps because his own family was so devastated by it. Much as they seem to want to belong to each other, the father is separated from the sons by his parsimony, the sons and their father from the mother by her addiction to dope, and saddest of all, the sons from each other because of Jamie's admitted hatred of his brother. When O'Neill wrote his happy family comedy, *Ah, Wilderness*, he said: "To me the America which was (and is) the real America found its unique expression in such middle-class families as the Millers among whom so many of my own generation passed from adolescence into manhood."[11] But in the play written of his own "dead" he remembers only bitter isolation among "the four haunted Tyrones," and in most of his other plays he saw common grief for the family of man.

The pity aroused in *Long Day's Journey into Night* is the greater because the revelation of the causes of Tyrone's niggardliness, of the mother's dope addiction, of the sons' feelings toward the family and each other would seem to bring about an understanding among the four, but instead, although it enlightens the audience, it leads to increased loneliness for all the characters. Edmund speaks for O'Neill when he says, "I will always be a stranger who never feels at home, . . . who can never belong. . . ." Arthur Miller in an essay, "The Family in Modern Drama," says:

> Now I should like to make the bold statement that all plays we call great, let alone those we call serious, are ultimately involved with some aspect of a single problem. It is this: How may a man make of the outside world a home? How and in what ways must he struggle, what must he strive to change and overcome within himself and outside himself if he is to find the safety, the surroundings of love, the ease of soul, the sense of identity and home, which, evidently, all men have connected in their memories with the idea of family?[12]

If Miller is right, O'Neill's drama may well qualify as great by virtue of its explicit delineation of the tragedy of those who have not even "memories" of a happy family to return to; life under such circumstances is indeed a long day's journey into night.

Of the three plays, *The Member of the Wedding*, *The Silver Cord*, and *Mourning Becomes Electra*, the last is much the most all-encompassing study of loneliness. The adolescent, unattached Frankie portrays the suffering of a girl in a particular stage before a happy maturity. Mrs. Phelps represents a type of vicious lonesome character in American society; but the Mannons exemplify "lonely family," unfriendly to neighbors, mutually split asunder, doomed to cold isolation without and within. Although Carson McCullers and Sidney Howard have written moving plays on the theme of loneliness resulting from the lack of harmonious family relationships, O'Neill has created a trilogy which does high honor to American drama; and the charge that he required the aid of Aeschylus is refuted by the release of *Long Day's Journey into Night*, which is a play of comparable worth on the theme, and all his own.

4

THE FAILURE OF A LOVE AFFAIR

If two lives join, there is oft a scar,
   They are one and one, with a shadowy third;
One near one is too far.
                              —"By the Fireside," Robert Browning

In the typical Hollywood movie the love affair is never a failure. Boy meets girl, and after a series of misunderstandings, they marry and live happily ever after, for in the movies love and marriage are inextricably combined. But in the serious American drama of the last thirty years love is not always found in marriage, nor is the extramarital love affair an acceptable or happy adventure. In each of the three plays in this chapter the lonely one returns to his legal mate, reconciled to the fact that more happiness is to be found in following the dictates of society than those of personal rapture. But a galling sense of loneliness and frustration is involved in the return, because the defection from marital fidelity has been motivated in the first place by a feeling of isolation from the partner in marriage. The lover, also, returns to the loneliness which he had known before the affair. The joy of belonging completely to another is no longer his, and in the eyes of society his beloved has never been his, so he can compensate only in memories for his loss.

Loneliness, according to Max Lerner, is the cause which so wholeheartedly propels Americans into their love affairs:

The surrender of the American to love has about it for the moment an appearance of completeness not frequently found in other cultures. . . . There are suggestions in [Henry] James that this may be because the American brings to whatever he touches a fresh and generous energy that contrasts with the somewhat jaded feeling of the European. It is more likely, however, that

86

the impulsion comes not from surplus energy but from the loneliness of the American and his impulse to escape from it into a secure harbor where he can find the absolute of love with his loved one.[1]

In the stage medium, as in the American movie, the lovers involved are raised to an ineffable state of ecstasy. The more bitter, therefore, is failure when it comes. Three modern plays in which loneliness is the cause of, and also the result of, a love affair are: Eugene O'Neill's *Strange Interlude* (1928), Philip Barry's *Tomorrow and Tomorrow* (1931), and Clifford Odets' *Rocket to the Moon* (1938). In a lengthy nine-act play O'Neill personifies the relationship of father, lover, husband, and son to a woman whose life revolves among them. The conflict within her because of her love for one man and marital duty to another, however, furnishes the main interest of the play. Philip Barry in *Tomorrow and Tomorrow* has romanticized and modernized a Biblical passage in which a presumably barren woman conceives a son. Elisha becomes, in the modern version, a noted doctor and lover of the attractive wife of a prosaic businessman. To the unsuccessful, middle-aged dentist of Clifford Odets' play, an affair with his pretty, incompetent office girl is like a rocket to the moon. In each of the three plays a deep sense of loneliness is engendered by the impossibility of a happy conclusion to the love affair which has created an aura of complete belonging while it endured.

In *Tomorrow and Tomorrow* Philip Barry has dramatized the story of II Kings 4: 8-27, in which it is related that Elisha, the man of God, goes with his servant, Gehazi, to Shunem, "where was a great woman." She provides him lodging and he tells her, "At this season, when the time cometh around, thou shalt embrace a son." She doubts him, but as Elisha had prophesied, a son is born. One day, when the boy is old enough to go with his father and the reapers, he becomes ill and seems dead, until the mother brings Elisha, who breathes life back into the child. Of this briefly told story, Barry has made a play, in which the love affair is beautifully dramatized, and the facts are biologically and psychologically modernized.

As the play opens, Eve Redman is awaiting the return of her husband from his class reunion, but it is soon evident that his entrance does not remove the emptiness from her life. Although their greeting is affectionate, Eve indicates in various ways that she feels a terrifying need of something more than his presence; and when he drops off to sleep in his chair during her ecstatic recital of her desire for a child, she feels completely desolate. She appeals to him to help her satisfy her longing for a baby.

> If loving children made you have them, I'd have a houseful. . . . I shouldn't mind any kind of pain at all. I'd welcome it. I'd know then that I was living—making—and not slowly dying, a little more each day like this. . . . Heaven shine on me, rain on me. . . . Don't keep me empty this way any longer. (I, i)

"Help me to life, Gail," she pleads as she reaches out her hand to him. He does not take it, for he has dropped asleep after a long day's driving. Her own hand drops lifelessly into her lap. Her loneliness is like the darkness of the stage after she has urged him to bed and has turned out the lights.

During the conversation, Eve has explained that she has invited a lecturer, Dr. Nicholas Hay, to stay with them while he gives a four-week course at Redman College, named after Gail's grandfather. The reasons she gives for inviting him, like the rest of the conversation, indicate her lack of satisfaction in the marriage.

> . . . the hotel is so bad. Besides, I thought it would be pleasant to have—you know—someone to do for. He'll probably have whiskers, and be very cranky.—And then again, he may be rather sweet. I hope he's like Father was—I hope he's so old and absent-minded he can't do one thing for himself. . . . You see, I have no one to look out for anymore. (I, i)

To Eve, Gail seems completely self-sufficient. Obviously he has no understanding of her loneliness, for he is very casual with his remark that there is nothing wrong with her. "You just get lonely, that's all," he explains dispassionately. He is quite unsympathetic as well to her wish that she attend classes when the college becomes coeducational. She begins, "Oh, Gail—I must do something! Somehow or other I've got to find *some* way to—" but breaks off, realizing the hopelessness of trying to make him understand her suffering.

When the handsome, young, unattached Dr. Nicholas Hay appears, feeling ". . . oh, if I weren't so stale. The whole world's stale," it is no wonder that an immediate and irresistible attraction pulls him toward Eve. Dr. Hay has given up a general practice because all he really cares for in the world is "human emotion and the whys and wherefores." Disillusioned about the benefits to mankind of the practice of medicine, he is going abroad with his secretary, Gillespie, to make "findings" which he hopes will change the future of the human race. He is lonely and resentful of his need to earn money for the trip, and he pleads with Gillespie to get him a hotel room where he can be alone because, he says, "I've lost the gift of talking to people, if I ever had it. I can still lecture, but I can't talk." Obviously his need of Eve is as great as hers for him. Their passionate affair becomes the theatrical representation of what Lerner calls the "absolute of love."

Hay explains to his secretary the effect which Eve Redman has had upon him.

> . . . when I came here three weeks ago I was in pieces. I wondered when they'd come to sweep me up. . . . But just to have been in the same house with her, to have heard that quiet voice, . . . To have walked with her over that lovely lawn, through those lovely meadows— (I, iii)

His effect on Eve is similar. Her feeling of emptiness, of being an "artist without an art," as Hay expresses it, fades while he listens understandingly to her recital of an experience of complete belonging when she was fifteen.

> . . . there was one very bright night, and I went walking by myself. All at once I came upon the bank of laurel. It was—I can't tell you. I've never known beauty like it, before or since.—I think it was the first time I ever felt myself alive. But when I could I ran from it. I haven't been back there since. (I, iii)

Eve is afraid she may have changed, or the laurel may be different. She fears that if she went back, she might lose even the memory of this rapturous moment. Hay thinks she is afraid that the beauty of it will seem too real again and her own life too desolate.

The last evening of his stay, Gail being away still on a business trip, Hay reproaches Eve for her three-day absence. "You had to run again from what was real," he charges, and then insists, "Is the laurel in bloom, Eve?" In a moving love scene Nicholas Hay and Eve Redman become two human beings involved in a mystical experience. Of the midnight supper she has prepared, he says, "I'm not hungry for this." Besides the laurel as a symbol of belonging, the playwright makes use of two candles. "Let them stand for us," says Eve, "You— . . . and me." Hay thinks they are not melting away. "They are a special kind I have. They last forever," she assures him. A love so strong as theirs will never burn out. His threat to extinguish the candles if she is afraid to go with him to see the laurel gives her courage. She opens the French windows to the moonlight. "Come," she says, holding her hand out to him, "I should like you to see the laurel. I think there is nothing will ever change it." As she leads him out through the windows and across the porch, the stage becomes dark, except for the two burning candles.

At the end of the first scene the complete darkness of the stage symbolizes Eve's estrangement from her husband. At the end of the love scene the two burning candles symbolize her ecstatic belonging to her lover. Thus, love shines in a dark world. Thus, love becomes a relationship to all nature, the moonlight, the River Willing, the laurel in bloom. Thus, love means an eternal and mystical unity with life. The laurel, which gave the girl her first intimation of the feeling of being alive, has been replaced by the lover, whose kiss gives the mature woman "the same sense that the laurel gave." Transported beyond the fear that she cannot face the beauty of the blooms, she abandons her inhibition and enters completely into a state of belonging.

In the morning the two candle-lamps are still burning slowly. Gillespie is carrying suitcases out to the waiting car. Gail Redman, who has arrived home in the early morning hours, announces that Mrs. Redman will not be down. Hay, who has taken a walk to the river, comes laden with laurel. He asks Gail to give the flowers to Eve. "I wish I might lay it at her feet," he says, as he keeps a twig for himself. At the end of the scene, Eve is left alone arranging the laurel in vases, but Gail on his way to work turns back: "Eve—You look so pretty, standing there with all those flowers." He has not left her alone as he had in the first scene. By her courageous acceptance of the love which Hay brought her, she has become less separated from her husband, and when, two months later, she tells him there is no need to send the letter applying for the adoption of a child, they enter into a more understanding relationship than they have had before.

The child is named Christian, according to Nicholas Hay's suggestion. Eve and Gail are happy in their mutual love for him, but when, at the age of seven, he takes a serious fall from a horse and almost dies, they disagree about the cause of the coma into which he has fallen. Eve has obviously learned from the love affair with

Nicholas what she has tried to teach her son. "I want him to be himself—to the furthest reaches of himself—but himself, first, last and always. That isn't easy for a son of mine to learn." When Gail complains that the boy has not learned to read, she insists that he has been occupied with "real things." "He has a sense of the strangeness of the world, of himself in it." She explains that she thinks Gail has forced the boy to ride horses against his will and that Christian is like her "until not so very many years ago"—anxious to please, but afraid to be himself. She has bent all her efforts toward helping Christian to a sense of belonging.

As the boy sneaks out of his bedroom, his head swathed in bandages, to try the jump again, Eve is listening entranced to the voice of Dr. Nicholas Hay, who is giving a radio lecture to which Gail has tuned. Although she has not seen nor heard from him in almost eight years, she is spellbound by his voice.

> Emotion is the only real thing in our lives; it is the person, it is the soul. . . . the highest point a human being can reach is that at which he knows he has earned the right to depend upon emotion to prompt action. (III, i)

"Nicholas," she breathes as he tells of the power of the smell of certain flowers, the rush of the river to recall emotions which are never lost. She hardly sees Gail as he now stands before her with the limp, feverish child in his arms; but as she looks up, she moves without hesitation to call the station in Chicago from which Nicholas Hay is broadcasting. *"He* will know what to do," she murmurs. It had been part of the pact between them that if she ever needed him, Nicholas would come to her, but if she called him, she must be willing to go with him.

The love between them has endured, for when Nicholas comes, he tells Eve, "I knew with the first word you spoke the other night that it had not changed for us." Having found that Christian is his own son, and that the boy really fears Gail, Nicholas plans to take the mother and son with him. Eve's love for him is as strong as it was on the night they spent on the laurel-covered river bank, but she sees that Gail will be a broken man if he should lose wife and son. To Hay's plea, "For years we have loved each other, and Christian is our child. That is the truth," she replies,

> No—those are the facts.—It may be that the truth is simply that I'm Gail's wife, and my place is here because he needs me. (III, iii)

She is silent as he questions, "Do you need no one?" but she seems to grow in stature, until, looking at her, he exclaims, "No—not any more, do you?—You have yourself, now." Her words, "That, too, you've given me," testify to the fact that their love affair, though a failure in its tangible satisfactions, has made her independent of the world around. As Nicholas takes her in his arms and kisses her tenderly, she murmurs triumphantly, "Oh my Nicholas—thanks—thanks—!" Her alienation from Gail and from nature and from all creativity has been dissolved by her realization of self through an overpowering love. She suffers loneliness no longer. The noise of the starting motor of the car taking Nicholas away brings her to the French windows, which she thrusts open with a bright face and no tears. Flinging out her arms, she says to herself, "Not changed. Complete." As the dark stage in the first scene testifies to her loneliness, the sunlit scene in the last reflects her happiness.

She rightly attributes her sense of belonging to the love affair, which she looks at as a thing apart from the two individuals involved. She could go away with her lover, she says, "If I didn't love us—you and me—!" Although she and Nicholas would derive happiness from living together, the us—the unity of the affair—would be spoiled because others would suffer. As Frankie in *The Member of the Wedding* speaks of the "we" of me, so Eve feels that the us to which she and Hay belong makes them members of the elect, "members of the whole world," as Frankie says. And through belonging to an us, each one belongs to himself to an extent otherwise impossible. Their love affair has resulted in the creation of a child, in a sense of the beauty of life, and in a self-realization for them both. It might seem to have been a failure in that they could never openly acknowledge their love and in that only in memory would they ever again experience the transport of love among the laurel blooms. But in reality the love affair which has been a failure is that between Gail and Eve. That between Eve and Nicholas has been a success because of the strength that both have gained from sacrificing their happiness for others.

What might have seemed to be a sacrilegious treatment of a holy prophet, Philip Barry has made a reverent love story. "Hail and Farewell," as it was originally called, would seem a more appropriate name than "Tomorrow and Tomorrow," which implies a kind of fatalistic cynicism not borne out by the play. Barry's forte is undoubtedly high comedy, and although *Tomorrow and Tomorrow* played more than two hundred performances on Broadway during the 1930-31 and 1931-32 seasons, it cannot compare in popularity with his lighter plays; it does, however, deal movingly with the theme of loneliness and its abatement through a love affair, with implications that loneliness for the lovers has compensations in the satisfactions derived from self-sacrifice. That such an affair as Eve's and Hay's has no relationship to social codes and is beyond time, Barry makes explicit by Americanizing the Biblical story in a love so vitalizing that the lovers are able to revive a child near death and to live apart with a deep sense of the beauty of the world.

Clifford Odets' *Rocket to the Moon,* which he subtitles "A Romance in Three Acts," might seem an irreverent treatment of love, not because, like Barry's play, it is a modernized dramatization of a Biblical passage, but because the characters are quite the opposite of "great," because the surroundings are inappropriate for romance, and because Odets' glib dialogue is not that traditionally associated with emotion. But in spite of these appearances, Odets writes with deep seriousness. In fact Edmond M. Gagey calls *Rocket to the Moon* a "paean to love in a dental office."[2] In many plays Odets protests against a stodgy existence, and appeals for an awakened understanding of life. In this one, it is a love affair which breaks the shackles of conventionality which bind a middle-class dentist. "In our youth," says the playwright, "we collect material to build a bridge to the moon; but in our old age, we use the materials to build a shack." Figuratively, it is in a lonely shack that Ben Stark, a forty-year-old dentist, lives with his wife, Belle.

As in Barry's play, the opening scene illustrates the separation of husband and wife. Belle's father wishes to set up his son-in-law with new equipment in a better office, but Belle forces Ben to refuse, for she believes his patients won't come to an uptown office. As they sit arguing in his hot waiting room, where the entire action of the play takes place, he admits, "You win, you win!" He closes the pages of the dental magazine which illustrates the new equipment he so strongly wants, and claims sadly, "I was a pioneer with Gladstone in orthodontia, once. Now I'm a dentist, good for sixty dollars a week." As he restlessly goes to the water cooler to get two paper cups of water for his window of drooping petunias, she advises him to take one at a time. Since he cannot fill a second cup with one hand full, she brings one herself, admonishing him, "Any day now I'm expecting to have to powder and diaper you." Stark does not answer, except presently, with a quiet, "I like flowers." The lack of sympathy between them permeates the air. Later in the play Ben tells her, "We're like two exposed nerves," a remark which is pointed up by the view of the dentist's chair and apparatus visible through the door beyond the waiting room.

There seems to be no subject upon which they can agree, no matter of importance on which they can feel an understanding of the other's viewpoint. Belle insists that Ben give up all thought of a new office, although she knows how much it means to him. She insists that his office girl, Cleo Singer, is incompetent and should be replaced. Belle cruelly reproaches the girl for not wearing stockings in the office and for choosing to come to work in a dress of angel-skin satin. Ben Stark knows she cannot afford stockings and has very few clothes, and that in spite of her boasting, she badly needs the job and the raise he has given her. Belle thinks her incompetency should be punished, not rewarded. Ben would like to have Belle's father, Mr. Prince, live with them, but Belle refuses to speak to him if she can help it and insists he would "be in the way." Belle tries to throw out the failing Dr. Cooper, who has not paid his share of the office rent for some months, but Ben feels sorry for him and wants to help him get on his feet. Belle wants Ben to spend long week ends at the beach with her, but he obviously prefers the office. The two are at odds on all matters and painfully isolated from each other.

Belle is a less sympathetic character than Ben, but her loneliness is made as real as his. "A woman wants to live *with* a man—not next to him," she says with recognition of their separation, and when he tells her to enjoy her week end at the beach, she almost sobs, "Don't be funny, Ben. A place is not a place. A place is who you're with." At another time, Ben admits to Belle's father, "She's very lonely since Momma died." The only baby Belle can have died at birth three years ago, and Ben forgets the anniversary. He does not want to adopt a child. She tries to hide her tears, but she lets the plea escape her lips, "Ben, you have to love me all the time. I have to know my husband's there, loving me and needing me." Unfortunately for Belle, however, she seems not to possess characteristics which make her lovable. Even her father, Mr.

Prince, in trying to get a particle out of Cleo's eye, remarks that it is "A glass splinter . . . from my daughter's heart." Poor, lonely Belle, longing for love, but not really of a loving nature herself! She comes into town from the beach because she "felt alone," but the coolness of her husband toward her sends her back to the beach, more alone than before.

Ben Stark is "a lovable being," according to his father-in-law, but he, too, is lonesome. For one reason, he has let Mrs. Stark run his life until, as Mr. Prince puts it, "Your nose is just the right shape to fit your wife's hand." He has always acceded to her wishes, so that, although he would like to have Mr. Prince live with them and would relish moving to a new office, he unhesitatingly gives in to her. For another, he has failed to reach his mark as a successful dentist. Applying the metaphor he had quoted earlier concerning the young man and a bridge to the moon, he scornfully tells Belle, "That's a shack on the beach, and this [office] is a shack." Failure to reach his expectations professionally has left him with a feeling of apartness of which he is painfully aware. For a third reason, Ben has some intimation that besides his unsuccessful marriage and career, he is missing the best that life should hold. "I'm sleeping," he says once, and at another time, "What I don't know would fill a book." Still again he remarks, "I'm not going to stay under water like an iceberg the rest of my life." Ben's lack of spiritual attainments is therefore, perhaps the greatest cause of his unhappiness.

Cleo Singer, trying to brazen her way through life by fabricating stories about her wealth and position, is lonely too. When Ben Stark urges her to tell the truth—"Life is so full of brutal facts . . . we all try to soften them by making believe"—she breaks down.

Nobody loves me! Millions of people moving around the city and nobody cares if you live or die. Go up a high building and see them down below. Some day I'll fall down on them all! (II, i)

Finally she admits that her family does not "have more money than they know what to do with," and that "my home life is fearful—eight in one apartment." Besides she has the awful feeling of being "unwanted" and laughed at by her family for wishing to be a dancer. Ben insists he understands. "You're an unhappy lonely girl," he says sympathetically, not laughing at all.

95

It is logical that Cleo and Ben turn to each other for love and comfort. Clifford Odets, however, having contrived the situation so that they might well fall into each other's arms, surprisingly enough makes Mr. Prince the instigator of the affair. The gallant old roué advises Ben:

> . . . make a motto for yourself: "Out of the coffin by Labor Day!" Have an affair with—with—with this girl . . . this Miss Cleo. She'll make you a living man again. (Act I)

Odets avoids sentimentality in favor of realism; although he sub-titles his play "a romance," he takes pains to make clear that he is not writing of moonlight and roses. The loneliness of life—the real loneliness—cannot be lessened by frivolous fabrications, nor do the lovers fall in love with the inevitability of fate. They set out to find love, because the American believes in working for what he wants. With Mr. Prince, Clifford Odets says, "Life is lonely, life is empty," but that is no reason for staying like an iceberg, mostly under water. The only way to combat the loneliness of life is to fight back. In *Rocket to the Moon* it is thus that Ben Stark and Cleo revitalize themselves.

Cleo is the aggressor in the scene in which they finally kiss and admit their love, but Ben is likewise swept away. He protests at first, until her enthusiasm becomes irresistible.

> Stark: I'm a married man.
> Cleo: Just because you're sad you can't make me sad. . . . I have too much in me!
> Stark: You're wonderful.
> Cleo: (*almost dancing*) : Talent!—I'm talented. I don't know for what, but it makes me want to dance in my bones. Don't want to be lonely, never left alone! Why should I cry? I have a throat to sing with, a heart to love with! . . .
> Stark: Cleo!
> Cleo: We're *both* alone, so alone. . . . Maybe I lie. You know why. Because I'm alone—nobody loves me. But I won't have it that way. I'll change life.
> Stark: You're wonderful. (II, i)

The stage directions at the end of the scene explain that the pair are together in a fierce embrace "in a swelter of heat, misunder-standing, loneliness and simple sex." There is no doubt that the motivating force behind their affair is the feeling of isolation of each one and the yearning to belong wholeheartedly to someone. At the end of the second act, as they again embrace passionately, she insists, "Hold me. Don't let me be alone in the world, Ben. . . . Don't let me be alone."

Obviously their affair is not destined for a felicitous conclusion. Ben is too much Belle's husband to kick over the traces, and Cleo is too much of an individual to accept half of him. In spite of their depth of feeling for each other Ben and Cleo soon realize that their sense of belonging in each other's arms is transitory. As Stark lovingly tells her of walking on the boardwalk and hearing each wave repeat her name, she counters with a demand to know whether he was walking with his wife. This, unfortunately for him, having been the case, she announces that she is going to have lunch in the office of Willy Wax, notorious corruptor of young girls. She has hurt Ben, as he has hurt her. They no longer belong to each other, and finally Ben admits, his voice trembling, ". . . facts are stubborn things, Cleo; I've wrestled with myself for weeks. This is how it must end." And end it does as an active love affair, but as in the case of Eve and Nicholas of *Tomorrow and Tomorrow,* its effects are more lasting.

Cleo makes her last exit alone, but as she says, "Experience gives more confidence, you know. I have more confidence than when I came here. Button my coat, Ben." She insists upon going home alone, knowing that in time she will find "a whole full world, with all the trimmings!" Love has made her aware of what life can be like. Love has taught her that she need not lead a lonely existence. For Ben, love has done as much. Insisting that now his life is beginning, he exclaims with eyes flooding with tears of emotion,

For years I sat here, taking things for granted, my wife, every-thing. Then just for an hour my life was in a spotlight. . . . I saw myself clearly, realized who and what I was. . . . for the first time in years I looked out on the world and saw things as they really are. (Act III)

The happiness of belonging to each other even for a short while has altered the outlook of both. The very fact that such a sense of union is possible brings them both a new understanding, even though the experience itself is not of long duration. According to Cleo, "Life is to live all you can and experience everything." The person who lives lethargically, unaware of the world around him,

Clifford Odets believes, might as well be dead. In *Rocket to the Moon* it is a love affair which arouses two characters to partake of the fullness of life, which must not be lived in lonely isolation, but with an understanding of the relationship of one man to all and a feeling of the unity of life.

As in *Night Music,* Odets enhances the theme of loneliness by including in the action a number of minor characters who are isolated. Mr. Prince, Belle's meticulously-dressed father, might seem to be a self-sustaining old gentleman, but he proves to be very lonesome. Completely alienated from his daughter, who claims he mistreated her mother, he keeps hoping to move in with the Starks because he is very fond of Ben. When Belle refuses to allow him in her house, "out of sheer respect for my mother's memory," Ben protests, "Your mother's been dead a year. He's an old man, lonely." But Belle is adamant. Mr. Pince makes more money than he knows what to do with, and does not want to leave it to Belle. In the end he proposes to Cleo. He sees youth and beauty in her which he feels would relieve his feeling of not belonging anywhere. He claims,

> You are clay, Miss Cleo, on the way to great womanhood. . . .
> You need a man who is proud to serve you and has the means
> to do it. . . . Every president of this great country is my age. Because this is the time he's at his best. (Act III)

In his ardent hope of possessing Cleo, he paints a picture of the money he will leave her when he dies, and of the fine life she can lead as a young wealthy widow. It takes only a word from her to dash his hopes. "But you forget one thing—I don't love you." Money cannot buy love. Mr. Prince is left blasé but disillusioned at the end. Ben's ardently expressed enthusiasm for his new-found enlightenment brings only the weary comment from Mr. Prince, "It's getting late." Having failed to find any satisfactory human relationship to appease his loneliness, he sadly announces that next week he will buy himself a dog.

Another pitifully lonesome character is the cynical Dr. Cooper, who cannot pay his share of the office rent, whose wife has died, whose child has broken his arm, and whose relief from his griefs is going out for a "drink of coffee, Scotch coffee." He has no patients and cannot borrow from the loan company. Despairing in his isolation, he recalls, "When I'm happy I'm a different person.

. . . everybody likes Phil Cooper." Feeling unwanted and useless, he sobs, "What did I do to my fellow man? Why am I punished like this?" Almost in hysteria, he throws his arms around Cleo, kisses her, and runs into his own office. Cleo is quite shattered by his display of emotion, but she tells Ben, "I understand his feelings. . . . He's all alone in the world. Nobody wants him . . . like an orphan." Cleo and Ben are drawn closer together by recognition that Cooper's loneliness corresponds to their own.

Even Willy Wax, who tries to entice Cleo with promises of a movie career, claims that his work with the movie industry requires hard work and means leading "a lonely life." Later he claims that his failure to remember names "comes from living alone. I have to admit I'm a lone wolf." Cleo is at first taken in by his sweet talk and admits, "You must be a very lonely man." Willy's insistence upon his loneliness may be used to gain sympathy from Cleo, but it is, obviously, the truth that his affairs with women give him little feeling of belonging. When she finally throws him out with, "No man can take a bite out of me, like an apple, and throw it away. Now go away, and we won't miss you," he is chagrined and angry. Although he tries to conceal his plight under a veneer of boastfulness about his power over women, he will never be other than lonesome.

The author's mouthpiece in some cases is Frenchy Jensen, a chiropodist with an office down the hall from Stark's. Frenchy has a deep affection for Ben, and tries to persuade Cleo that she is only making trouble. But he admits Cleo's attraction by exclaiming, "Cleo, you're like a magnet!" He doesn't see much happiness in marriage because it requires a whole balanced normal life. "In this day of stresses," he claims, " I don't see much normal life, myself included." Since a happy marriage is as rare as a dodo bird, Frenchy advises Ben to go back to his wife. He will not be able to do anything for Cleo by marrying her, and will find more permanent satisfaction with his wife. Frenchy is something of a universal cynic, having been given his name because he is a Swede from Utica, New York. Although he is lonesome, as are Cooper and Wax, he pretends to be satisfied with himself.

Since Ben and Cleo move in a world of lonely individuals, the love which inspires them for a brief moment shines the more brightly because of the somewhat allegorical connotations of the darkness of loneliness around them. It is difficult not to read into the name, "Cleo Singer," Cleopatra, for whom the world was well lost. Cleo is loved by Stark, kissed by Cooper, proposed to by Prince, flattered by Wax, and is tantalizing to Frenchy. But although Cleo may represent the perfect lover, she has not the self-sustaining characteristics which keep her from loneliness, until after her experience of loving Ben. Mrs. Stark and Stark represent what the name implies—an unbending and unadorned and even desolate pair, for whom love is a thing of the past. It is the more remarkable, therefore, that Stark through his love for Cleo comes to have a new vision of life. Mr. Prince is munificence itself, but his offers of money are not accepted, for to be truly loved he needs the best human qualities, not princely ones. Willy Wax is smooth and slippery as wax, and Frenchy, being American in all ways, is ironically dubbed Frenchy. Odets can justifiably call the play a romance. Although the characters do not live "happily ever after," it illustrates the beauty of love even in drab surroundings among ordinary people. As in *Tomorrow and Tomorrow,* the failure of a marriage results in a love affair which electrifies the two involved by a unifying experience that leads to their realization of the beauty of living.

In the popular play, *Golden Boy,* written by Odets in 1937, two years earlier than *Rocket to the Moon,* Joe Bonaparte attempts through a love affair to repossess his own soul, which he has sold for gold to the men who run the boxing game. But being unable to have Lorna because of her entanglement with his manager, he commits suicide with her by wrecking his speeding new automobile. The theme of the play is the battle of Joe—and by inference of every American—to find himself in a world in which material and spiritual values clash. Having broken his hand, he can no longer play his violin; but having attained great material success, he finds he has lost his true self. By contrast, his brother Frank, who is a labor organizer, belongs to himself because he is fighting for what he believes in. As Harold Clurman says, "Our hero fights as a lone ego; Frank fights, as he says, together with and for millions of others. Frank is a free man; our hero is destroyed."[3] Joe once protests at his manager's treatment of him: "What the hell do you think I am? A machine? Maybe I'm lonely, maybe . . . I want some personal life." His manager's reply, "Everybody's lonely. Get the money and you're not so lonely," represents the attitude of materialism which destroys Joe, until he soon discovers that

100

"he no longer belongs to himself, that the managers, gamblers, and gunmen who own 'a piece of him' have taken over his life."[4] His love affair might have been his salvation, but since it was ill-fated from the beginning, there is no way of reconciliation of his egotistical desire for fame and his love of art and of the simple life. Only in death can he belong. In *Golden Boy* the love affair is indeed a failure.

Strange Interlude is the story of a woman's attempt to bind herself to a series of men, who represent all the relationships which man can have to woman. Nina Leeds belongs at various times in her life to her father, her dead lover, her husband, her illicit lover, her son, and finally to her old friend, who represents her father. As in other plays, O'Neill proves himself America's greatest playwright by attempting more than a simple plot involving the eternal triangle, with which lesser playwrights are satisfied. As if Nina's life were a jewel which he turns in numerous directions to catch the light, he shows how her love for husband and for lover are affected by her former relationships to other men and how all the men in her life affect her. It is not only her love affair which is a failure, but also her relationships to all men. Failing to find more than a transitory sense of unity with any of them, she exclaims,

> The mistake began when God was created in a male image. . . .
> That makes life so perverted, and death so unnatural. We should
> have imagined life as created in the birth-pain of God the Mother.
> Then we would understand why we, Her children, have inherited
> pain, for we would know that our life's rhythm beats from Her
> great heart, torn with the agony of love and birth. And we would
> feel that death meant reunion with Her, a passing back into Her
> substance, blood of Her blood again, peace of Her peace! (Act II)

Aside from encounters with two women—her husband's mother near the beginning and her son's fiancée near the end—Nina's relationships are with men, and since they prove unsatisfying, it is perhaps no wonder that she can envision a state of true belonging only if God were a woman.

Actually, as she sinks into the arms of Charlie Marsden, her old friend, after her other men have died or left her, she may find peace there, partly because "good old Charlie" has "an indefinable feminine quality about him." There is one brief, moving moment in the play also when Mrs. Evans and Nina weep together united by the kind of grief which women share, for Nina must either suffer the daily terror that her child will grow into insanity, like so many members of the Evans family, or else she must make sure that it is never born. Mrs. Evans gathers Nina into her arms with tenderness: "You poor child! You're like the daughter of my sorrow! You're closer to me now than ever Sammy could be!" Perhaps in the last analysis Nina does not share such a sense of belonging with any of the male characters in spite of the intensity of her romantic ideal of love for her dead aviator lover, her sexual joy with Ned Darrell, her feeling of satisfaction in making Sam happy, her devotion to her son, and her peace with dear old Charlie.

As the play opens Nina is in the throes of grief for her beloved Gordon Shaw, whose plane has been shot down in flames. Her beautiful eyes "have a quality of continually shuddering before some terrible enigma, of being wounded to their depths and made defiant and resentful by their pain." The psychopathic nature of her grief is evidenced by the fact that it has continued for a long time and has taken various forms, from what appears a numbed sensation to a wild indiscriminatory burst of social activity; but always it is motivated by a feeling of guilt that she did not give herself entirely to Gordon or marry him before he left. She seems to live with a corpse and searches only for some way to punish herself for failing her dead lover. She thinks to herself,

> Ashes! . . . Oh, Gordon, my dear one! . . . oh, lips on my lips, oh, strong arms around me, oh, spirit so brave and generous and gay! . . . gone! . . . gone forever from me! (Act I)

As a means of expiation, she decides to give herself to the soldiers at the army hospital where she goes as a nurse.

> I must learn to give myself . . . for a man's happiness without scruple, without fear, . . . When I've accomplished this I'll have found myself. (Act I)

So alienated is Nina from father and friends that only by giving herself can she feel any sense of belonging again.

Nina's obsession concerning an ideal lover lasts through most of her life. At one time Dr. Darrell thinks to himself, "Gordon myth as strong as ever . . . root of her trouble still. . . ." and when Nina is carrying Sam's child, she loves it so much that she can almost

102

believe that Gordon came to her as she slept and was its real father. Insofar as Nina represents womankind, O'Neill is criticizing the female's tendency to romanticize love to the extent that she cannot accept happiness with any ordinary male. It is certainly true that for Nina the romantic ideal of love has a destructive influence on her life. It is her idea of love which has failed in the beginning rather than a true love affair, and it is therefore the more devastating to her life because the dream does not grow old. Poor Nina admits to herself, "when Gordon died, all men died." Since she insists upon attaching herself psychically to a dead man, how can she belong to any living man?

Nina's obsession with the idea of romantic love in reality motivates all the action. Ned Darrell, who later becomes her lover and who might have made a happy marriage partner for her in the first place, urges her to marry Sam Evans, a likable but unprepossessing young man, because he says, "In my mind she always belongs to Gordon. . . . And I couldn't share a woman—even with a ghost!" Her obsession likewise makes her turn to Evans for the reason that he too is a Gordon-worshipper, admitting readily with Nina that Gordon was a paragon in every way—in sportsmanship, judgment, courage, and physique. His admiration is as genuine as hers. "Even the Huns respected him!" marvels Sam. Although they do not seem well suited in other ways, Nina marries Sam because he reinforces the idea by which she lives. Indeed, Sam is perhaps the only kind of man she could accept, for even Charlie admits that it would be hard to share her with Gordon. "That species of dead is so invulnerably alive!" he exclaims. Nina is inevitably led along the path she follows by her prepossession with an ideal, which, being unattainable, results in her feeling an emptiness in her relationships with all men.

The intensity of Nina's feeling that she wronged Gordon first alienates her from her scholarly father, Professor Leeds, for she feels—with some justice—that it was he who prevented their marriage. Nina's father is misery itself as he explains that it was only for Nina's good that he had appealed to Gordon not to marry until he was established in the world. Nina's eyes constantly staring at him with hatred, however, bring from him an outburst which relieves his pent-up grief as he admits to her, "Very well. I was alone and I wanted to keep your love. I did my best to prevent your marriage." Nina says somewhat perfunctorily that she forgives him, but obviously father and daughter are unalterably separated. Professor Leeds muses: "If Nina's mother had lived . . . it's terrible to be so alone in this." And when the curtain falls on the first act, Nina is leaving for an army hospital and the old man sits in his study: "Oh, God! . . . I feel cold! . . . alone! . . . and I'll die in here some day . . . alone." His isolation is particularly touching because it is evident from the exposition during the act that the affection between father and daughter has been very real. That his loneliness was recognized by others is evidenced in the next act, when Nina has come home for his funeral and Charlie sits in the professor's study, thinking, "Poor Professor! he was horribly lonely . . . tried to hide it . . . always telling you how beneficial the training at the hospital would be for her . . . poor old chap!" Professor Leeds is the first to suffer because of Nina's obsession.

Nina is cajoled into marrying Sam Evans by Ned Darrell and Charlie Marsden, who recognize that her distracted state and promiscuity with a number of wounded soldiers will lead to her complete destruction, but that Sam's unselfish love might be her saving. Nina admits,

> Sam is a nice boy. Yes, it would be a career for me to bring a career to his surface. I would be busy—surface life—no more depths, please God! But I don't love him. (Act II)

One must wonder if any man will find happiness with a woman who does not love him, and indeed for a time it appears that Nina has destroyed Sam, but after the birth of young Gordon has restored confidence in his manhood, he becomes a success in the advertising business. Nina's cynicism is increased by seeing her husband revitalized through the birth of a son he has not fathered, and any sense of closeness to Sam which she might have felt during her former pregnancy with his aborted child is shattered. But since she prevents Ned Darrell from ever telling the truth about their child, she does preserve Sam's belief in her love. By "playing the game," however, she is isolated from her husband so that their life together from her point of view is, as she predicted, "a surface life."

At the point at which Mrs. Evans tells her daughter-in-law about the insanity in their family, Nina cries out, "I almost have [loved him]—lately—but only when I thought of his baby! Now I hate him." Nina plans to leave Sam until that "walled-in soul" who is Sam's mother—who at first feels: ". . . make her suffer what I was made to suffer! I've been too lonely!"—appeals to Nina with womanly sympathy to stay with Sam and by some means to give him a healthy child. Nina is moved and decides to play fair with Sam, but his gradual failure in business and his "pitiably harried" appearance as time goes on attest to his feeling that she does not love him. To himself he admits, "Lately, she jumps on me every chance she gets . . . as if everything I did disgusted her!" Nina's love for Ned alienates her with finality from Sam, but Sam is so unutterably overjoyed by the expected birth that he drops to his knees, thanking God "for our baby," and from that time to the end of his life is a new man. Utterly insensitive to her true feelings for him, Sam is unaware of the love of Nina and Ned, which is obvious to the child, and becomes so enmeshed in his successful pursuit of wealth that he feels the satisfaction of complete belonging.

Young Gordon, sensing something of dishonesty in his mother's attitude and recognizing that Sam, though unperceptive, is completely devoted to his wife, turns to Sam with great affection. The boy dislikes Ned and feels somewhat alienated from his mother because of her affection for the famous biologist. He says at the play's end, "It's funny how I got to care more for Dad than for Mother. I suppose it was finding out she loved Darrell." So Sam, loving and innocent, basks in his son's affection and benefits from his birth by a feeling of self-fulfillment which makes him a success in the business world. Through the machinations of his mother and then of Charlie and of Ned and Nina, Sam is guided into a life of happiness. Although he passes through a period of failure, he never suffers the depths of loneliness which each of them does. The fact that his ignorance results in a blissful state, however, is not an endorsement by Eugene O'Neill of such insensitivity, for Sam appears a somewhat foolish and unsympathetic character.

The love affair in *Strange Interlude* has none of the beauty and little of the remembered joy of those in *Tomorrow and Tomorrow* and *Rocket to the Moon*. Of the male characters Ned Darrell, who is the only one Nina ever loves with all her being, is, nevertheless, the most isolated through much of the play, and at the end he cries, "Oh, God, so deaf and dumb and blind! . . . teach me to be resigned to be an atom!" Although Ned, obviously designed as "the lover" of the play, dexterously fulfills his role, he is not entirely a sympathetic character. His self-sacrificing suppression of the knowledge that he is young Gordon's father does not overbalance his hesitancy in making Nina his wife. Using the excuse that Nina would always love Gordon and that her promiscuity has disgusted him, Ned purposefully guides her into marriage with Sam, although he does admit, "I felt a bit sorry for myself at their wedding . . . she always had strong physical attraction for me." Later, after they have spent afternoons of happiness together, she insists that they must tell Sam of their love so that after a divorce, she and Ned can marry. Ned to himself thinks,

> . . . marry! . . . own me! . . . ruin my career! . . . got me where she wants me! . . . then be as cruel to me as she is to him! . . . her body is a trap! . . . I'm caught in it! . . . she touches my hand, her eyes get in mine, I lose my will! (Act V)

He runs out of the house, and within the next few days sails for Europe, where Marsden later says he saw him "going the pace" and looking "desperate."

From the time that Ned escapes from Nina, he suffers a slow demoralization. He cannot escape from himself; his biological research suffers; his loneliness is overwhelming. A mistress in Munich is small satisfaction, and he longs to become like those one-celled specimens he studies, which cannot suffer his feeling of being useless. He comes back after the baby's birth to plead with Nina,

> Oh, it's been hell, Nina! I couldn't forget you! . . . those afternoons—God, how I've thought of them—lying awake—recalling every word you said, each movement, each expression on your face, smelling your hair, feeling your soft body—Nina! I love you so! (Act VI)

Ned is determined to take her and the baby away with him, but Nina, although wanting him as lover, will not leave Sam. Ned faces the alternative of leaving her entirely or of remaining to see Sam constantly with his beloved and his child. Cynically remarking upon his experiment of fathering Nina's child, he remarks,

> The ailing ones have been restored to normal function . . . only the other male, Ned, seems to have suffered deterioration. (Act VI)

Through the years Ned haunts the Evans household, pulled there by Nina's irresistible attraction for him and her desire for him. But, although she always greets his coming with joy, she welcomes his departure as a relief; for they always end up quarreling. She tells him,

> I'll send you away, and then after a time I'll call you back, be-
> cause I'll have gotten so lonely again living this lonely lie of my
> life, with no one to speak to except Sam's business friends and
> their deadly wives. Or else you'll get lonely in your lie a little
> before I do and come back again of your own desire! And then
> we'll kiss and cry and love each other again! (Act VII)

The central love affair of *Strange Interlude* is characterized by Nina in this passage. She and Ned are lonely in the lie of their lives, and no amount of physical pleasure can make them belong to each other—for one reason, their child dislikes Ned and turns against his mother because of her obvious love for the scientist, and for another they can never openly acknowledge their love. Furthermore, Ned is tortured by the urge to proclaim Gordon his son, whereas Nina is at pains to suppress the truth, even though she recognizes that both she and Ned suffer in the eyes of their son. At the end of the play, after Sam's death, she thanks Ned for keeping the secret. He says she can repay him by refusing his offer of marriage. The afternoons of long ago live only in memory.

When Ned is first introduced in the play, he is described as a man who has never been "close to anyone." His scientific interest in life itself and his lack of courage in not taking Nina when he might have had her, end in disaster. The part of "lover" cannot be sustained for a lifetime. Deep as is their joy, Ned suffers a sense of apartness within it and because of it and except for the afternoons with Nina never throughout his life really feels a relationship to anyone.

With the third of Nina's men—Charlie Marsden—the case is different. Sam mistakenly thinks he possesses Nina. Ned possesses her briefly and longs for the return of those romantic moments the rest of his life. Charlie knows he never possesses her until the end, when she curls up against him like a daughter, and he murmurs to himself. "God bless dear old Charlie . . . who, passed beyond desire, has all the luck at last." More than once throughout the play Nina herself recognizes the contribution of each of the three.

> My three men! I feel their desires converge in me! . . . to form
> one complete beautiful male desire which I absorb. . . . I am
> pregnant with the three! . . . husband! . . . lover! . . . father! . . .

and the fourth man! . . . little Gordon! . . . he is mine too! . . .
that makes it perfect! (Act VI)

It is not every woman who can have a representation of her father
to turn to after others have left her, but it is an ideal which Nina
achieves. "Good old Charlie," who always winces when that epithet
is applied to him, accepts it gratefully at the end as he and Nina
plan to live again in the old professor's house and she says, "home
again at last—to be in love with peace together—to love each other's
peace—to die in peace! I'm so contentedly weary with life!" Nina
can go home again, and Charlie will fit perfectly into the professor's
book-lined study. Charlie triumphs at last over a lifetime of
loneliness.

In mid-life he says that Nina's home is "mocking my loneliness,"
for the death of his mother has made his home "nothing but utter
loneliness." He has watched and waited through the time that Ned
was corrupted by sharing Nina, that Gordon left to be married,
and that Sam died. Now Nina is his. Both of them, having passed
beyond passion, can embrace with a relaxation impossible in the
young. Nina feels, "I am the only one who senses his deep hurt.
. . . I have wounded everyone," and so it is a double gratification
to her at the end to give her fading self to make him happy and
to avoid the lonesomeness of old age herself. Charlie pretends always that his love for Nina is pure—"I do not lust for her"—but
again he chides himself for pretending that he wouldn't give anything in life to see her beautiful eyes desire him. Therefore, when
he can finally say with honesty, "I do not lust for her," he feels at
peace with himself and can spiritually merge his life with hers.

The fourth of Nina's men, young Gordon, although he absorbs
much of her time and seems to be her "only man" after her love
for Ned has faded, dramaturgically plays a part like that of his
namesake. The memory of Gordon Shaw, as it affects Nina, and
consequently others, is all the audience ever knows of this character; the effect of Gordon Evans upon the others is what mainly
matters, as O'Neill has written the part of "son." Gordon was a
source of pride to Sam and made his feeling of fullness of life complete; Gordon broke the toy Ned gave him as a child and hit him
as an adult, thus embittering the lonely man who had fathered him.
Gordon provided Nina a human being all her own to cling to; but
even her desperate attempt to keep him by telling his fiancée that

there is insanity in the Evans family does not succeed, and so, like the first Gordon, he flies away, dipping his plane's wings in salute. To Nina,

> Having a son was a failure. . . . Sons are always their fathers. They pass through the mother to become their father again. The Sons of the Father have all been failures! . . . they could not stay with us, they could not give us happiness! (Act IX)

Her whole association with the Gordons had best be forgotten, Charlie advises Nina. There was something fantastic about it all. Nina could no more live a life ruled by the dream of romantic love than she could live a life attached to her son. All things change, says O'Neill. No one can escape a desperate feeling of apartness by trying to belong to one relationship through life. A woman must belong in turn to a number of men and finally give them all up to regain her own soul. And Gordon's function, as Charlie cynically remarks when he comes upon the boy and Madeline in a passionate embrace immediately after Sam's funeral, "is to love that life may keep on loving."

It is only after a bitter struggle with herself that Nina finally admits that peace with Charlie is what she wants. She has lived through moments of happiness, like her days of bliss with Ned and the months before she bore a child. Of the latter she says,

> Breathing in the tide I dream and breathe back my dream into the tide . . . suspended in the movement of the tide, I feel life move in me, suspended in me . . . no whys matter . . . I am a mother . . . God is a Mother. (Act V)

And she has lived through moments of loneliness like those when she regrets not having given herself to her hero, Gordon, for she says, "And now I am lonely and not pregnant with anything at all, but—loathing!" And when she finds out she must give up Sam's baby she cries bitterly, "But I'll be so lonely! I'll have lost my baby! . . . how can I keep on living?" Although she is lonesome without Ned, they quarrel when they are together. Her anomalous relationship to him makes her cynical remark from the beginning of the play seem true. "Say lie—L-i-i-e! Now say life. L-i-i-f-e! You see. Life is just a long drawn out lie with a sniffling sigh at the end!" From cynicism to passive acceptance is perhaps no great advance in the progress of a character to a state of belonging, but Nina's attitude at the end that "our lives are merely strange dark interludes in the electrical display of God the Father!" means that death brings, not the end of a lie, but of an interlude "in which our souls have been scraped clean of impure flesh." With Nina's realization of the fact that she could have each man in turn, but none permanently, and that now it is Charlie's turn, comes a sense of the wholeness of life which gives her a feeling of being a part of it instead of an alienated stranger.

There are two facets to the play which give emphasis to the theme of the loneliness of mankind in general and perhaps of Americans in particular. The first is the technical device of having each character speak his own thoughts aloud. His spoken words indicate a certain cooperation with other characters, but his thoughts indicate an apartness in feeling and understanding. As Hamlet's soliloquies define his aloneness, O'Neill's device of spoken thoughts, although overworked, signifies loneliness in every character.

The second theme, which has overtones of being peculiarly American, stresses fair play versus happiness and is reiterated at many points from the beginning to the end of the play. *Strange Interlude,* written four years before *Mourning Becomes Electra,* carries a like suggestion of the isolating effects upon human beings of a too stern devotion to duty with too little concern for the emotional side of life. In *Strange Interlude* the fair-play, square-deal, playing-the-game theme is epitomized in the first Gordon. As in the later play, it is the women who instinctively turn away from the suppression of feeling, whereas the men believe in playing the game of life with honor, regardless of conflicts with the emotions. Sam's mother insists to Nina, "Being happy is the nearest we can ever come to knowing what good is! Being happy, that's good! The rest is just talk!" Nina feels, whether justly or not, that it is the opposite philosophy which has wrecked her life from the beginning and made her always lonely. As the play opens, it is made clear that Nina's father has appealed to Gordon not to marry her because it wouldn't be "fair" to leave her a widow, possibly with a child to support. The "square thing" would be to wait until he is well established in the world. Nina claims that it was "only the honorable code-bound Gordon" who refused to take her on their last night together. Later she agrees to stay with Sam, in spite of not loving him, because she hears Gordon saying to her, "Play the game!" She finds it unbelievably hard to stay with him after the

110

operation which destroys his baby, and appeals again to Gordon's ghost.

> Oh, Gordon, I'm afraid this is a deeper point of honor than any that was ever shot down in flames! . . . what would your honor say now? . . . "Stick to him! . . . play the game!" oh, yes, I know . . . I'm sticking. . . .I'm trying to play the game. (Act IV)

As young Gordon inherits the name of Nina's hero, so he inherits his philosophy of life. Suppressing his dislike for Ned and recognizing that his mother has always loved the famous scientist and now, after Sam's death, will probably want to marry him, Gordon mutters, "And I'll have to wish them good luck. Dad would want me to. He was game." At a later time he is critical of his mother but reproaches himself: "but she made Dad happy . . . she gave up her own happiness for his sake . . . that was playing the game." There is of course much cynicism in O'Neill's reiteration of this idea, which he gives great prominence in the decisions of all the characters. At the end, as Gordon flies away, Ned, the man, with "grim fatalism," remarks, "Well, at least I've done my duty!" whereas Nina, the woman, calls up to Heaven, "Be happy, dear! You've got to be happy!"

No doubt good sportsmanship has been held as a virtue before the United States existed, but there is a concept of fair play which has a peculiarly American quality about it, and which to O'Neill is harmful. The American mother trains her child, according to Margaret Mead,[5] to fight belligerently if attacked, but she punishes him severely for attacking a smaller child. There is dishonor in fighting when the odds are on your side. The bully is despised. Americans, therefore, grow up sizing up each situation according to its fairness, without taking into consideration emotional and human values. Combined with a Puritanical background stressing devotion to duty, this ideal of fair play creates a sense of isolation, because the question of human joy is not given any weight. It is assumed that duty and pleasure are in conflict, and hence a character is isolated by accepting either. A theory much more calculated to make a human being feel a sense of belonging is Mrs. Evans' "happiness is goodness."

Nina's love affair with Ned did not bring lasting happiness because both were afraid to trust themselves with the idea that it was good. Hence it left each of them alone and sorrowful, striving to do his duty and to play fair with Sam and young Gordon and with life itself. Out of their loneliness Sam came to belong. He met no conflict between happiness and duty. In the beginning, it was Nina's attempt to belong to a romantic ideal of love which brought her grief, but through much of the drama, it is the concept of playing the game according to the rules rather than according to love which makes her life a lonely one.

O'Neill's artistry is apparent in a comparative analysis of *Tomorrow and Tomorrow, Rocket to the Moon,* and *Strange Interlude;* for, as was noted in regard to *Mourning Becomes Electra,* he has the power of elevating his best dramas above those of lesser playwrights. The presentation of "family" in *Mourning Becomes Electra* and of "woman" in *Strange Interlude*—Everymannon and Everywoman, according to Edwin Engel[6]—has a universal significance not found in plays dramatized about one incident or particularized characters. O'Neill's concern with the theme of belonging obviously motivates the inclusion of a number of his plays in this book, but a more important factor is the genius with which he endows the theme with meaning.

Although love plays a part in much serious American drama, a love story is little used as the main plot, but there are unhappy love affairs dramatized in Sidney Howard's *Alien Corn,* in Sidney Kingsley's *Men in White,* and in the dramatization of *Ethan Frome* by Owen and Donald Davis, as well as in Paul Green's *The Field God.* A few American playwrights have seen tragic implications of loneliness in the failure of every Jack to find his Jill unattached and adoring. As is illustrated in the plays in this chapter the love affair may evolve because a former relationship has already deteriorated. It may bring a spirit of elation after it ceases to have intensity, or it may cause a cynical bitterness in the lovers. In any case the effects worked by a love affair can never be erased, nor can the lovers ever regain their former emotional status. A love affair in the language of any serious playwright, whether it leads to a sense of belonging or to greater loneliness, is an ineradicable experience.

5

SOCIOECONOMIC FORCES

> Nothing ever turned out for Enoch Robinson. . . . He never grew up and of course he couldn't understand people and he couldn't make people understand him. The child in him kept bumping against things, against actualities like money and sex and opinions.
>
> —"Loneliness," Sherwood Anderson

The economic and social inequalities produced by the extensive industrialization of America have provided the background for many twentieth-century novels. After native American drama came into its own following World War I, a number of serious plays likewise dealt with the debilitating effects upon human character of the crushing forces of the capitalistic economic system. Arthur Richman's *Ambush* (1921), Gilbert Emery's *Tarnish* (1923), Sophie Treadwell's *Machinal* (1928), Elmer Rice's *We the People* (1933), Clifford Odets' *Awake and Sing* (1935), Sidney Kingsley's *Dead End* (1935), and Elsa Shelley's *Pick-Up Girl* (1944) are all examples of the drama of social protest. A number of Negro plays— for example, John Wesley's *They Shall Not Die* (1934), Paul Green and Richard Wright's *Native Son* (1941), and Philip Yordan's *Anna Lucasta* (1944)—and many labor plays, including Paul Peters and George Sklar's *Stevedore* (1934), Clifford Odets' *Waiting for Lefty* (1935), and John Howard Lawson's *Marching Song* (1937), likewise protest the social and economic order. In many of the plays of this kind propaganda outweighs characterization. The loneliness of the individual caught in circumstances beyond his control is subordinated to exposing the evil itself. In the three plays chosen for discussion in this chapter, however, the suffering of the characters involved, although portrayed against a background of social inequity, outweighs it. *The Hairy Ape* (1922) by Eugene

113

O'Neill, *Street Scene* (1929) by Elmer Rice, and *Winterset* (1935) by Maxwell Anderson, all artfully avoid the pitfall of being purely propagandistic even as they interweave scene and character so as to make implications of the effect of economic and social forces upon the characters inescapable.

Elmer Rice's *Street Scene,* written at the beginning of the depression of the thirties, in setting is exactly what the title indicates—a scene on a street in front of a tenement, not in the worst of slums, but in a very degraded neighborhood. There is a considerable amount of "window" conversation, but otherwise the playwright brings the life of the tenement dwellers to the front steps of the building. Although the audience is never led into any of the apartments, it is allowed to see the inner life of the inhabitants. The paradoxical loneliness resulting from never being able to be alone is a feeling which permeates the play. The formality of addressing their neighbors with the titles "Mr." and "Mrs." indicates some feeling of coldness toward those against whose shoulders they must almost literally rub each day. But a surface formality is no escape from the intimacy of each other's lives. The oppressive heat which makes their clothes stick to them—"I ain't got a dry stitch on me"—emphasizes the lack of "elbow room," a trite phrase which becomes accurately descriptive as any character tries to enter the building through those seated on the steps. Even when a character sits in one of the windows to cool off, someone from the steps below begins a conversation. It is almost as if all the people in the building live on the street. No move of anyone's is unobserved by others.

Rose Maurrant and Samuel Kaplan are harassed by their inability to talk together without interference. They dream about the chance of getting out of New York where they could "breathe and spread out a little," but the life of the tenement as they observe it discourages them from trying to begin somewhere else. Rose says she is going to leave by herself because all the people who live around them "start out loving each other and thinking that everything is going to be fine—and before you know it, they find out they haven't got anything and they wish they could do it over again—only it's too late." Even as Rose and Sam are locked in a farewell embrace, other characters pass in and out of the house, either staring at the young couple or intent upon their own business, but ever-present, like the city noises which rise and fall and

intermingle during the play. "The worst menace in the city's re-
morseless conspiracy against the young men and women who have
their own way to make within its gates, is the dreary loneliness of
its teeming streets,"[1] says a rhetorical editorial, but so says Elmer
Rice in more artistic form.

Many different nationalities and different types of characters are
represented in *Street Scene* but without any apparent allegorical
purpose. The play is a representation of a tenement's inhabitants
but not of the whole city's. Edmond Gagey, in remarking that the
villains of *Dead End* are poverty and the slums, points out that
"*Street Scene* merely depicts and the tragedy is mainly a personal
one, . . . the author remains in the background and ventures no
explicit thesis or propaganda."[2] Sam Kaplan, therefore, does not
represent "the lonely Jew," but it is made obvious that it is partly
because of his Jewish inheritance that he suffers loneliness. His
sister, a school teacher who is helping him to finish college, begs
Rose to stay away from him. You can get another fellow, she tells
Rose, "He's all I've got in the world. What else have I got to live
for?" Partly because of this appeal Rose refuses to let Sam leave
with her, because, aside from the fact that she sees the unhappiness
of couples around her, she sympathizes with the loneliness of Sam's
sister. Sam, himself, is among the loneliest of characters. His
weakness, demonstrated when he is knocked down while trying
to prevent Rose from being fondled by a ruffian who lives in an upstairs flat, makes his misery complete. He sits on the stoop sobbing
hysterically as Rose tries to comfort him. As the woman upstairs
cries out in childbirth, he exclaims,

> That's all there is in life—nothing but pain. From before we're
> born, until we die! Everywhere you look, oppression and cruelty.
> . . . life isn't worth it.

In the musical version of *Street Scene,* produced in 1947 with music
by Kurt Weill and lyrics by Langston Hughes, Sam sings "Lonely
House," in which he complains, "Lonely house, lonely me—funny
with so many neighbors, how lonely it can be." The people
constantly moving in and out and through the building furnish
no companionship. Even stray dogs find more friends than he. Rose's
compliment to him on his brains and ability brings only the
sorrowful thought, "What's the good of having brains, if nobody
ever looks at you—if nobody knows you exist?" The remarks con-

cerning the Kaplans' religion, though never complimentary, do not disturb Sam as much as does his feeling of being unwanted anywhere. He concludes his song in the musical version with, "I'm lonely in this lonely house in this lonely town."

Although Rose and Sam come nearer to belonging to each other than do the other characters of the drama, their understanding of each other's grief is not enough to inspire them with hope of a new life. Rose's sense of loneliness is acute, but she does not suffer the depressing sense of hopelessness which Sam does, and hence it is Rose alone at the play's end who sounds a note of self-reliance and freedom from the loneliness of the crowd. She tries to persuade Sam, "Believe in yourself. Because once you're sure of yourself, the things that happen to you aren't so important." And from years spent among so many people whose private living habits are exposed to all the others, she deduces a philosophy of belonging which includes in it a kind of isolation. In "The Case for and against Loneliness," Ernest Dimnet says that human beings really prefer "solitude with company near at hand, or the reverse. Hence our delight, a deep and primitive satisfaction, in situations where we are at the same time alone and in company; the concert, a reading room. . . ."[3] Rose, subjected to conditions in which solitude is never possible, refutes Sam's plea that they belong to each other.

> I don't think people ought to belong to anybody but themselves. I was thinking, that if my mother had really belonged to herself, and that if my father had really belonged to himself, it never would have happened. It was only because they were always depending on somebody else, for what they ought to have had inside themselves. (Act III)

Even in the midst of the tragedy of her father's shooting of her mother, Rose sees lucidly the impossibility of finding herself by dependence upon someone else. She has felt the suffocating effects of too many people around her throughout the play, and her dream of getting out of New York includes "being alone" so "you could sort of work things out for yourself." The playwright makes clear that the inability to "spread out" or to avoid bumping a neighbor if one as much as stretches, results in a feeling of frustrated loneliness for all the characters; but it is Rose who understands the need of being alone clearly enough to express herself.

Rose has even sensed that if the family could move to the suburbs, the tragedy, which she could see coming, could be averted, for Maurrant is driven to a crazed condition as much by the constant whisperings of the neighbors as by the affair of Sankey with his wife. As the police pull him away, he pleads with his daughter, "I must o' been out o' me head, Rose . . . all the talk that was goin' around. I just went clean off me nut, that's all." Maurrant has loved his wife, but as he says in the song, "I Loved Her Too," "There was always something inside of me . . . like a wall—seems like I never could break through." And Rose explains to Sam that, although her father means well, he makes "you freeze up, when you really want to be nice and loving." Maurrant is immovable as Rose begs him to consider moving to a house—"Queens or somewhere like that"—where "maybe if ma had a nice little home and some real nice neighbors—do you see what I mean?" Maurrant says the tenement suits him well enough. He is unaware of its effect upon his wife and Rose and upon himself as well. His loneliness—the wall he can't break through—he does not attribute to environmental causes, and indeed neither does the playwright explicitly, but the inference that such an individual may have isolated himself by a cold exterior as a defense against too close contacts is hard to avoid.

Mrs. Maurrant is a gentle, kind woman, "sort of gay and happy-like," according to her daughter. She spends the night with Mrs. Buchanan, who is suffering through the labor pains of her first child. Although thoughtful of others, she has found only loneliness in the life of the tenement. She explains to Rose that she likes Sankey because

> Every person in the world has to have somebody to talk to. You can't live without somebody to talk to. I'm not saying that I can't talk to you, Rose, but you're only a young girl and it's not the same thing. (Act II)

Rose shows understanding of her mother's need for companionship, but agrees with her that there is nothing either can do, especially since Mr. Maurrant refuses to consider moving and Mrs. Maurrant is too infatuated to resist Sankey. Mrs. Maurrant sometimes thinks she would be better off dead. The sense of belonging which she has found with Sankey is the source of jibes at her and her children almost every time any one of them enters the building. With sorrowful resignation, she admits the hopelessness of the circumstances. "It's just the way things are, that's all." Her loneliness has led her into an impossible situation, the melodramatic outcome of which is her death. Rose buys a white dress and white stockings for her mother (who, she says, looks as quiet and natural as if she were asleep) with an air of acceptance of what is past. But it is with determination that she refuses offers of help from her married boss, who has been pursuing her, and sets out to find a home for herself and her young brother in a neighborhood where they can breathe.

Besides the Maurrants and the Kaplans there are among others the Swedish Olsens, the Italian Fiorentinos, and the degenerate American Joneses who pass through the big center doors of the building and appear from time to time at their respective windows to comment or to pass the time of day with those on the steps. Yet in spite of the physical propinquity of the dwellers of the building, they are isolated in a sense from the outer world, for there is no phone in the building. In the case of the emergency calls—for the doctor for Mrs. Buchanan and for the police after the shooting of Mrs. Maurrant and Sankey—someone must be sent to the nearest phone in a neighboring warehouse. The lack of a phone in the building emphasizes the dependence of the inhabitants upon each other for conversational recreation and the blighting effect of being unable to communicate privately with anyone outside the building. Along with the frequent references to the stifling heat, the action which points up the lack of a telephone in the building makes clear that human loneliness can be caused by too close association with others. The impossibility of ever being alone or even of breathing fresh air which someone else has not already breathed creates tragedy in the life of the Maurrants and an enervating sense of loneliness in the lives of all.

The failure to be able to realize any sense of personal identity under slum conditions permeates the main characters of the play and has an obvious influence on the minor ones. It is not possible to say, "I am I because my neighbors know me," for the neighbors know each other so little that after the murders, in the musical version of the play, the victims are described as "the man from down the street and the woman who lived up there." The transiency of the lives of tenement dwellers is also pointed up at the end with the entrance of a dowdy, apartment hunting couple, who, noticing the black crepe which Rose has hung over the door, remark: "Somebody must o' just died." "Yeah, maybe that's why

118

they're movin' out." Tragedy in one family has meant little more than new tenants in the building and a public sensation—some nursemaids from a better neighborhood even wheel their charges over to look at the building pictured in the tabloids—and then continuation of the same lonely, crowded existence.

In *Winterset* Maxwell Anderson has apparently attempted to follow the pattern of great tragedy, in which he feels that the recognition scene, in which the hero makes a discovery about himself or another which alters his course of action, is the one fundamental touchstone.[4] And he has also followed his own dictum that in a three-act tragedy, such a scene should come toward the end of the second act. As the object of the action of *Oedipus* might be expressed in the infinitive phrase—to find the culprit—so the object of the action of *Winterset* might be expressed by the negative —to prove my father was not the culprit. Although Oedipus is a searcher after the truth, whereas Mio feels sure he knows the truth and wants proof of it for revenge, each hero stands alone, and each makes a discovery which ironically enough ends his search, but brings him misery. Mio's loneliness, however, is that of the revenger who has been battered socially and economically so that he is spiteful towards all humanity and toward God. Until he falls in love with Miriamne, he uses nothing but cynical epithets to respond to any argument about his father's unjust conviction. No faith that a God above will right all wrongs in the end or that there is any ultimate purpose in injustice sustains him. Crying that his father's voice rises to him from the quicklime where they buried him after electrocution and evisceration, he suffers in memory as well over the death of his mother and her quick, cheap burial by the county. Finally, he says, they turned to him and asked why the Romagna spawn—the son—could not have died with the mother.

> Well, ease him out of town,
> ease him out, boys, and see you're not too gentle.
> He might come back. And, by their own living Jesus
> I will go back, and hang the carrion
> around their necks that made it!
> Maybe I can sleep then.
> Or even live. (I, iii)

Mio has had to live homeless, obtaining food and shelter where he could, searching meanwhile for the real murderer, so he can make

119

those who condemned his father see the truth

till it scalds their eyes
and make them admit it till their tongues are blistered
with saying how black they lied! (I, iii)

Unlike Hamlet, Mio is driven to seek revenge, not for the sake
of his father's honor so much as for his own maltreatment by society.
He is bitter and recriminatory in his isolation. The gutters of the
world have been his home. The words in books are all he knows
of such things as freedom, heroism, honor, or enduring love—all
of which he needs because, as he tells Miriamne when she asks why
he wants them,

I'm alone, that's why. You see those lights,
along the river, cutting across the rain—?
those are the hearths of Brooklyn, and up this way
the love-nests of Manhattan—they turn their points
like knives against me—outcast of the world,
snake in the streets. (I, iii)

Mio belongs nowhere and to nothing except his idea of revenge.
He claims that he is one flame of the fire of truth, which will "burn
through and be seen/though it takes all the years there are." But
his feeling of the terrible loneliness imposed upon him as an outcast from society drives him to seek retaliation for his own wounds
rather than to expose falsehood. Recognizing that it is black revenge
and not the fire of truth which drives him on, he admits to
Miriamne, ". . . there's too much black/whirling inside me—for any
girl to know."

If, however, what Mio says of his treatment by school authorities
and townspeople is true, there is reason for his aim of revenging
himself upon them. He claims that he was thrown out of high
school for lack of a permanent address and ostracized from all
society by the town authorities.

When the State executes your father, and your mother dies of
grief, . . . and the authorities of your home town politely inform
you they'd consider it a favor if you lived somewhere else—that
cuts you off from the world—with a meat-axe. (I, iii)

It has not been Mio's doing that he is an outcast, nor is it his fault
that he is recriminatory; for he has nothing to call his own except
the voice of his father, to which he hearkens with ardor and which

120

he thinks bids him to devote his life to righting the wrong of the Romagna execution. The feeling that one has been "cut off from the world with a meat-axe" is a kind of loneliness perhaps inexpiable except by revenge.

With the advent of Miriamne into his life and, more important, into his affections, Mio undergoes a change. The love between them makes him an outcast no longer. He discovers a passion within himself unlike that which he has known. When he first learns that it is Miriamne's brother who will die if he makes known the truth, he berates the ironical gods who have given him his wish, and then have made it useless. But as he awaits death in the rain beside the tenement building, he pleads,

> Miriamne, if you love me
> teach me a treason to what I am, and have been,
> till I learn to live like a man! I think I'm waking
> from a long trauma of hate and fear and death
> that's hemmed me from my birth—and glimpse a life
> to be lived in hope—. . . (Act III)

Mio has passed through the period of isolation. He belongs to an ideal of love and forgiveness. By not exposing her brother, he belongs to Miriamne. The time is short, since Mio cannot live long with the knowledge he has. But the amount of time is nothing. "This half-hour is our eternity," says Mio. He has been seeking light in darkness, all the time running away from the dawn, but now has "stumbled on a morning." What Theodore Spencer says of the Shakespearean hero can be said of Mio:

> . . . to pass through the suffering and challenging period of isolation, to find at the end of the tunnel a new company, is to be a member of the elect. And it seems to me that this picture of isolation, the suffering which it involves, and the size and growth of soul which it indicates, is one of the things that Shakespeare shows us in his tragedies.[5]

Mio becomes a member of the elect. A lifetime spent in lonely hatred is wiped away by half an hour's belonging. He refuses the help of his friend, Carr, who thinks that Mio must be in trouble, "I'm not. Not at all. I have/ a genius that attends me where I go,/ and guards me now. I'm fine." Being saved physically would result in his being parted from Miriamne: ". . . if I should go on living we're cut apart/ by that brother of yours," he insists. Therefore Mio, with his new-found faith in love, welcomes death.

121

Mio is not the only one who has suffered for Trock's crime of murdering the paymaster, for which his father was executed. The Esdras family, consisting of Miriamne and her father and Garth, her brother, who had witnessed the murder, have all lived in degrading circumstances since the trial, hounded by the fear that Garth will be killed by the criminals or implicated if the case is reopened. Living in the cellar apartment of the building which abuts a huge river bridge, they resignedly endure the damp atmosphere, the cold cement floor, and the huge boa constrictor pipes that form the ceiling and dwarf the room. As outcasts from society, they, like Mio, have had to exist in miserable surroundings. Esdras explains to Mio,

> [Trock's] same crime that has dogged you, dogged us down
> from what little we had, to live here among the drains,
> where the waterbugs break out like a scrofula
> on what we eat—and if there's lower to go
> we'll go there when you've told your story. (Act II)

Their loneliness is perhaps more bitter than Mio's because all three know that if Garth had testified, Mio's innocent father would have been saved. Garth preserved his own life by silence, but he and his father and sister have had to hide in isolated anxiety ever since. Miriamne wonders if it were not better to tell the truth and die than to lie and live. But she protects Garth, for he is her brother. She cannot understand life, however, and as she sits crying in the cold rain, against the background of the huge masonry bridge, she represents youth shattered by forces beyond its comprehension and control. There is nothing in which she believes. "How can one?" she asks. What can anyone believe in, who, like Miriamne, has always suffered from a self-recognition of apartness?

Yet in the end Miriamne belongs in death to Mio. As he is shot trying to get away from Trock's men, she proclaims her love; and feeling guilty for sending him on the path between the rocks, she steps out the same way, crying to them to shoot her too if they do not want the truth revealed. The machine gun speaks again. As Capulet and Montague stand over the bodies of Shakespeare's famous lovers, the Prince declares, "See what a scourge is laid upon your hate,/ That heaven finds means to kill your joys with love." As Garth and Esdras look upon Miriamne and Mio, dead in the street, Esdras calls, ". . . forgive the ancient evil of the earth/ that brought you here." Both pairs of lovers could belong only in death. Either wished to live, but accepted death together, rather than life apart. Forces beyond them made isolation inevitable except in death, which Mio and Miriamne therefore accepted, according to Esdras, "standing, . . . implacable and defiant."

Esdras is an old man to whom life has become a torture, for he believes that "truth's a thing unknown/ . . . and as for justice,/ who has once seen it done?" Therefore, Esdras urges Mio to believe his father innocent but not to try to prove it. There is no title to land or life, he claims, which was not built on rape and murder a few years back. His cynicism alienates him from any kind of faith, as Garth's situation has alienated the family from society. Yet at the end he extends at least a half-hearted admiration to the dead lovers and wishes that he himself had died, "unsubmitting," long ago. His further utterance—". . . yet is my heart a cry toward something dim/ in distance, which is higher than I am/ and makes me emperor of the endless dark even in seeking!"—is only a "smoky mixture of romanticism and neo-stoicism," according to Theodore Spencer.[6] However, another critic, George Kernodle, sees in the same passage an expression of the "religion of emergent evolution,"[7] which he takes to be an example in modern drama of the healing of the rift which science made between Man and Nature at the end of the nineteenth century. The disillusioned old man does find proof of man's spirit in the bravery and love of the young couple, and to that extent he can no longer be ruled entirely by a deterministic philosophy which obliterates faith. Nature may be cold to man, but man's soul is made up of more than just atoms— this to some extent Esdras does acknowledge as the final curtain falls. And so even in his deep grief for his child, he, too, is less desolate than at the beginning.

Of the lonely characters in *Winterset* none is more isolated than Judge Gaunt—not by society but by his conscience. As Macbeth is said to undergo "an implacable progress into isolation,"[8] Judge Gaunt may be said to have already reached such a state when the play opens, but he too is driven there by the visions which a bad conscience arouses. The judge is not a central character of the plot, but his part enhances the theme of loneliness, for he who condemns unjustly suffers as do the guilty and the condemned. Trock, along with his henchman, Shadow, and Garth and Mio all meet in the cellar apartment of the Esdras family in the climactic scene of Mio's search for the truth. Judge Gaunt completes the picture to make the scene resemble that of thirteen years before, except that now he is distraught and irrational. Madly traversing the land, vociferously proclaiming that his decision was justified, he is like the lone, wandering Jew who is condemned to travel without ceasing. Trying to convince himself as well as Mio that he acted rightly, he insists:

> the verdict found
> and the precise machinery of law
> invoked to know him guilty—think what furor
> would rock the state if the court then flatly said
> all this was lies—must be reversed? It's better
> .... to let the record stand,
> let one man die. (Act II)

His argument is not good enough, and he admits, "I'm broken—broken across." There is symbolic significance in his final words as the police come to return him to his own city, "Yes, sir, I've lost my way./ I think I've lost my way." The isolating effect of guilt is perhaps nowhere better portrayed in modern American drama than in the character of Judge Gaunt.

In *Winterset* Maxwell Anderson has succeeded in the creation of a drama combining the influence of social forces with the suffering caused by their impact on individual human beings. With Harold Hickerson, the same playwright in 1928 wrote *Gods of the Lightning*, a journalistic play which protested the injustices of the Sacco-Vanzetti case with propagandistic vigor. Seven years later Anderson wrote *Winterset,* which has been called "an attack on a social wrong," but it is as well a dramatization of the lives of individuals made lonely by the forces of society, and as such far surpasses the earlier play in artistry and importance. Although it contains a certain amount of Shakespeare-like melodrama and echoes of Shakespearean speech in the dialogue, it is far from a mere imitation of the bard. It speaks to Americans because of the modernity of its subject matter and realistic setting as well as because of its truthful treatment of the universal theme of the lonely individual's search for justice.

In a play written shortly after *Winterset* and titled *The Wingless Victory,* Anderson portrays the isolated misery into which a New England sailing captain and his East Indian wife are thrust by the intolerance and prejudice of the world. With satirical vigor reminiscent of Shaw's in *The Devil's Disciple,* Anderson decries

the sanctimoniousness of the presumably good Christians and glori-
fies the good-heartedness of the captain's ne'er-do-well brother.
Having brought his wife—the East Indian princess, Oparre—and
their two young daughters to his home in Salem, Nathaniel is received by his minister brother and the townsfolk only because of
his wealth. But eventually Oparre and Nathaniel are parted by the
force of the prejudice of the people of the town. She would have
them go away together, but he plans to send her alone with the
children to the East. To Oparre

> There's such a thing as a love
> that holds the world well lost—I thought it was ours—
> perhaps it was only mine.

Nathaniel says:

> I love you still—but they've made
> our love a torment—it's the world that does it—
> it won't have us together. (Act II)

Nathaniel finally decides he cannot live without Oparre, but when
he arrives at the ship, he finds the children dead and Oparre dying
from poison. The loneliness of leaving without him has been more
that Oparre could bear, whereas the loneliness of living in a world
which shunned them and made their relationship seem "obscene"
had proved too much for Nathaniel. The play perhaps loses some
of its effectiveness because of its propagandistic denunciation of intolerance, and does not attain the artistic level of *Winterset,* but
it is another example of a play in which social forces kindle an
unbearable loneliness in the characters involved in the tragedy.

The Hairy Ape is ironically subtitled "A Comedy of Ancient and
Modern Life in Eight Scenes." Bernard Shaw in *Back to Me-
thuselah* purports to believe that in time man might become pure
mind, but O'Neill takes the view that up to modern times man
is more nearly pure body. Whereas the play is assuredly not a
"comedy," it is perhaps not correctly called a tragedy either because
of its symbolic nature. The idea of "belonging" is reiterated so
loudly and frequently by the ape-like stoker, Yank, that according
to Barrett Clark, he becomes more symbol than character. Clark
believes, "Yank cannot symbolize man and his efforts to 'belong,'
and yet remain a single individual."[9] O'Neill himself, however,
says, "The character of Yank remains a man and everyone recognizes

him as such."[10] In fact, complained O'Neill, the public at the produced play saw "just the stoker, not the symbol," and it is certain that O'Neill can be believed when he says he created the character from his acquaintance with a real Irish stoker. The play expresses, both symbolically and realistically, some philosophical ideas of O'Neill's about the nature of society in its treatment of man. The theme of individual loneliness—of the suffering self-recognition of not belonging—is paramount on both the realistic and the symbolic levels, and the drama thus attains a permanent importance which many contemporary plays dealing with social ills do not.

The eight scenes of the play include places frequented by representatives of the most exclusive society as well as those habitually visited by the lowest. On the ship the stokehole is contrasted with the promenade deck, and on land the rows of prison cells are contrasted with a portion of Fifth Avenue which includes an elegant jewelry establishment and a furrier's. The characters in the respective settings are as obviously contrasted, so that the effect is startling when a character from either level is placed in the inappropriate setting. The playwright insists that the treatment of the scenes in the cramped bowels of the ship, or any other scenes, "should by no means be naturalistic"; he is decidedly expressionistic in such scenes as that on Fifth Avenue, in which the elegant crowd coming from church appears as "a procession of gaudy marionettes," wearing expressions of "detached, mechanical unawareness."

Whereas socialites, even when they appear in their appropriate settings, never really belong, Yank, the stoker, as he appears at the beginning, imprisoned in the white steel in the depths of the ship, does belong. Arousing the drunken men to a pitch of excited pounding on their steel bunks, Yank proclaims:

> I'm smoke and express trains and steamers and factory whistles; I'm de ting in gold dat makes it money! And I'm what makes iron into steel! Steel, dat stands for de whole ting! And I'm steel—steel—steel! I'm de muscles in steel, de punch behind it! Slaves, hell! We run de whole woiks. All de rich guys dat tink dey're somep'n, dey ain't nothin'! Dey don't belong. But us guys, we're in de move, we're at de bottom, de whole ting is us. (Scene I)

Yank is not, however, representative of all of the men in the stokehole, for his mates, while admiring "their most highly developed individual," do not wholeheartedly agree with him. In fact, Paddy, the old wizened Irishman, grieving for the days of his youth, sorrowfully berates Yank:

> there was fine beautiful ships them days—clippers wid tall masts touching the sky—fine strong men in them—men that was sons of the sea as if 'twas the mother that bore them. . . . 'Twas them days men belonged to ships, not now. 'Twas them days a ship was part of the sea, and a man was part of the ship, and the sea joined all together and made it one. (Scene I)

Poor Paddy's vision of belonging is no longer possible in the day of steam. Mankind must search for new gods to replace those outmoded by science, says O'Neill in many of his plays. Paddy has not found any. That a great wave would sweep him over the side sometime when he is dreaming of the beauty of the past is his only wish. But Yank's god is steel, and he is a part of it as Paddy was a part of the ship and the sea and the sky when he was young.

Yank is disgusted by Paddy. "Yuh make me sick! Yuh don't belong." Charging Paddy with being nothing but fog, which the ship smashes through at twenty-five knots, Yank derides him for dreaming and thinking. "What's tinkin' got to do with it?" As is later evident, thinking is Yank's downfall, but as he leads the men in the regulated, mechanical rhythm of shoveling, it is indeed he and not Paddy who is at home in the world. Paddy's loneliness, to Yank, means that the old sailor has stopped living. "I belong and he don't. He's dead," claims Yank, entirely out of sympathy with Paddy's crazy dreams of the past. Today the man is "It" who is part of the engines and the smoke and the coal. Today the man who can take the hell of the stokehole, the roaring heat, the bending back is the man who belongs. Yank epitomizes the stoker who is a part of the machinery as the steel is a part of the ship.

Yank has no use either for the viewpoint of the stoker named Long, who calls the men slaves of the capitalist class. "What's dem slobs in de foist cabin got to do wit us? We're better men dan dey are, ain't we?" Deriding Long's "Socialist bull" and his arguments from the Bible about the equality of man, Yank calls him yellow and a shirker. For the man's job that is stoking the ship no speechmakers need apply. Yank believes that any man who does not throw himself wholeheartedly into the rhythm of shoveling and who does not enjoy the beat of the engines does not belong. Thinking and talking are not a part of the work, so that whoever

127

partakes of them does so because he is unable to meet the test of manhood required for the backbreaking work. Yank greets with utter disbelief the attempted persuasions by others that his immersion in his work is not all-satisfying.

In few plays is there such an instantaneous transition from a state of belonging as occurs in Scene Three of *The Hairy Ape*. As the men in the stokehole work amid the deafening noise of the roaring flames, the furnace doors, the throbbing engines, and the shoveling of coal, Mildred Douglas, the daughter of the millionaire owner of the ship line, comes in behind them. Although she has wished to see the seamy side of the ship's life, she turns almost as pale as the white dress she is wearing and shivers with fright at the sight of the hairy, sweaty men bending to their work. Yank, who does not see her, lets loose a barrage of blasphemous phrases as he brandishes his shovel murderously over his head in anger at the engineer's whistle bidding them stoke still faster. The other men look at the girl as at an apparition, while she stands paralyzed with terror at Yank's outburst. When he turns, snarling, toward the direction in which the men are staring, Mildred faints into the arms of the ship's engineers with the words, "Oh, the filthy beast." Yank is thunderstruck. In some unknown way his pride is shattered. As the iron door clangs shut behind her, he throws his shovel against it with a roar of "God damn yuh!" Confronted with the fact that the mere sight of him has aroused naked terror in another human being, Yank cannot feel himself a part of the engines anymore. Having once been looked on as a degraded specimen of the human race rather than as the force which runs the world of machines, he is lost.

From that moment he belongs nowhere. He can never feel himself a member of the race of beings of which Mildred is a part. But he cannot again be happy in the rhythm of the stoking. As Paddy baits him with the fact that Mildred looked at him as if he were a hairy ape, he swears to get revenge upon her. In the scene on Fifth Avenue, in which he taunts the elegant automatons—"Yuh don't belong, get me! . . . Steel, dat's me! Youse guys live on it and tink yuh're somep'n. But I'm *in* it, see!"—it is he and not they who recoil after each encounter. He cannot convince them that he is not beneath notice, and when the ladies hurry to the furrier's window to see the "monkey fur," he is driven wild and is clubbed by the police. In Scene Six in jail a still more bitter blow greets Yank, for he finds that Mildred's father is president of the Steel Trust: "makes half de steel in de world—steel—where I tought I belonged." It seems to Yank now that steel means the bars of the jail, and he wants to be fire which will melt it. Completely severed from his original feeling toward it, he now must destroy it. With massive arms he rends one of the bars, while the frightened guards turn the hose with full pressure on the cell.

In the next scene Yank goes to join the I.W.W. with the mistaken idea that it is a revolutionary organization with intentions of blowing up the capitalists and their machinery. He offers to dynamite all the steel singlehandedly if given that assignment. The blow to his morale at being thrown out of the union office is naturally greater than that when the police carry him off or the prison guards wet him down, for here he expected to be put to use. Out on the sidewalk, he sits mumbling bitterly, "So dem boids don't tink I belong, neider."

> Dis ting's in your inside, but it ain't your belly. It's way down—at de bottom. . . . I don't tick, see? I'm a busted Ingersoll, dat's what. Steel was me, and I owned de woild. Now I ain't steel, and de woild owns me. (Scene VII)

It is no wonder that in his desperation Yank finally turns to the ape for understanding. Having been alienated from man and machine, he goes to talk to a member of his club—"de Hairy Apes" —whom he finds in the monkey house at the zoo.

The entire object of the action of *The Hairy Ape*—to belong—is baldly and explicitly reiterated in every scene, but it is certain that O'Neill intended Yank's search to have a symbolic significance. Presumably man has lost his old animalistic harmony with the order of things, but he is not yet able to attain a mental and spiritual attachment which is satisfying. O'Neill himself explains the theme:

> The subject here is the same ancient one that always was and always will be the one subject for drama, and that is man and his struggle with his own fate. The struggle used to be with the gods, but is now with himself, his own past, his attempt "to belong."[11]

Perhaps more than he intended O'Neill makes society's forces of great importance in Yank's conflict with himself. The gods are replaced today in O'Neill's dramas by Freud within and environ-

mental influences without. Yank is first alienated from belonging
by the sight of the white-dressed girl; she overwhelms him, and
may represent a spiritual light to which he cannot attain; but she
also represents on a realistic level the high society which his work
enriches, but which despises him.

In his battle with himself Yank is willing to consider every hope
of finding a place into which he can fit. Although he has derided
Paddy's observations about Nature, he says in the last scene that
as he sat on a bench at the Battery and watched the sun come up,
he tried to feel the beauty around him.

> De sun was warm, dey wasn't no clouds, and dere was a breeze
> blowin'. Sure, it was great stuff. I got it aw right—what Paddy
> said about dat bein' de right dope—on'y I couldn't get *in* it, see?
> I couldn't belong in dat. It was over my head. (Scene VIII)

Yank comes to admit that Paddy may be right, but he cannot feel
it himself. Yank speaks like Thomas Wolfe, who, while recognizing that loneliness is not the best way of life, cannot accept any
other.

> The central purpose of Christ's life, therefore, is to destroy the
> life of loneliness and to establish here on earth the life of love.
> . . . I know Christ's way is better than mine, but I can't make it
> mine.[12]

Yank, however, tries valiantly. From the moment that his feeling
of unity is shattered he attempts to replace it by some means. His
anger first makes him revengeful, but he makes his offer to the
I.W.W. more in the hope of belonging to something else than with
the idea of destroying steel.

Yank is, therefore, justified in his complaint to the great gorilla
that he has tried everything.

> I ain't on oith and I ain't in heaven, get me? I'm in de middle
> tryin' to separate 'em, takin' all de woist punches from bot' of
> 'em. Maybe dat's what dey call hell, huh. But you, yuh're at de
> bottom. You belong! (Scene VIII)

Mankind is not in accord with the earth, and he has not yet attained the spirituality of heaven. But he is battered by both because
he has the insight to know that there is a life of the spirit which
would outshine that of the earth, but which only alienates him
from his old harmony with earth because of his inability to reach
it. As Yank lets the gorilla out of his cage, the mocking tone with

which he shakes the animal's hand enrages it, so that it wraps huge arms around Yank with "a murderous hug." As his crushed body slips to the floor, Yank bravely murmurs words about not squawking and dying with his boots on; but the tragic phrase which rings on after the end is: "Even him didn't tink I belonged." And as an especially tragic ironic touch the huge ape throws the body into the cage and shuts the door, so that Yank's dying words are from "In de cage." Man is not only not able to feel a part of anything, but he is caged as well. "Perhaps," says O'Neill, "the Hairy Ape at last belongs" in death. This is problematical, but it is certain there is nowhere he belongs in life.

The rich do not belong either. So far as the theme of the play goes, they are in the same predicament as Yank. On the realistic level Mildred and the elegant Fifth Avenue paraders furnish plot motivation for Yank's alienation from that to which he belonged before their attitude toward him is made explicit. But on the symbolic level, they are merely a variety of *Homo sapiens,* caught, like all of the species, between heaven and earth. In the second scene O'Neill makes clear in the stage directions that Mildred and her pompous, proud, fat, old aunt—"two incongruous, artificial figures, inert and disharmonious"—are not a part of the vivid life of the sea or the flood of sunshine upon the deck where they are sitting. Mildred admits,

> I would like to be sincere, to touch life somewhere. But I'm afraid I have neither the vitality nor integrity. . . . I am sired by gold and damned by it. . . . I'm a waste product in the Bessemer process—like the millions. (Scene II)

Yank must be given more credit than Mildred for his intense struggle; he valiantly tries to realign himself, whereas she, inert and bored, expresses hopelessness, and unlike him, refuses to admit any possible relationship to Nature with the words, "I don't like Nature. I was never athletic."

In the scene on Fifth Avenue the playwright again makes the point in the stage directions that the magnificently adorned shop windows with their glittering diamonds and expensive furs are "in tawdry disharmony with the clear light and sunshine on the street itself." Yank's sweeping condemnation of the displayed goods is justified: "Let her have 'em. Dey don't belong no more'n she does." So is his charge to the overdressed, rouged women and high-hatted men: "Yuh give me de eye-ache. Yuh don't belong, get me!"

In this scene too, Yank's courage shows to advantage against the background of the indifference of the aristocrats. As he deliberately lurches into one gentleman after another, he is greeted only by the affected reply, "I beg your pardon," from each one, while they all stalk by oblivious to his insults. They carry "something of the relentless horror of Frankensteins" in their detachment from all life. Yank wants to belong to something worthy of his allegiance; they are not even aware that there exists anything beyond themselves. He, therefore, has perhaps progressed farther than they on the road from earth to heaven.

Besides taking the "worst punches" from both heaven and earth, Yank finds himself lost in the realm of the mind. With a certain facetiousness the playwright places Yank, in the scene immediately after his shattering experience with Mildred, "on a bench in the exact attitude of Rodin's 'The Thinker.'" There is a kind of counterpoint between him and the other men acting as a chorus, which he begins by saying he wants to think and which they continue by jibes at the word and at his responses. To see the purely physical being who was one with his shovel, now sitting and attempting concentrated thought creates an aura of humor by its very incongruity. But think Yank does, although not very successfully, throughout the rest of the play. He is again seen as Rodin's "Thinker" with a bloodstained bandage around his head in the jail cell, and after being thrown out of the union office, he sits in the narrow cobbled street "in as near to the attitude of Rodin's 'Thinker' as he can get in his position." It is a final mockery that the gorilla in the zoo is discovered in the posture of the statue in the last scene; but it is not a negation of all the conclusions Yank has reached. "Tinkin' is hard," he tells the ape as he passes his hand across his brow with a painful gesture.

> Youse can sit and dope dream in de past, green woods, de jungle and de rest of it. . . . But me— I ain't got no past to tink in, nor nothin' dat's comin', on'y what's now—and dat don't belong. (Scene VIII)

He concludes that he and other members of the Hairy Apes will have to feel instead of thinking, but the gorilla puts too much "feeling" into his embrace of Yank and the stoker's body is crushed like his mind. If he perhaps belongs in death, that is the most mankind, as well, can hope for.

Of the three plays which attribute the loneliness of individual characters to socioeconomic causes, *Street Scene* is the most naturalistic. In Elmer Rice's play the actual push of people against each other illustrates the difficulty of anything except a lonely life amidst the crowd under slum conditions. The melodramatic incident of the shooting adds to, rather than detracts from, the realistic effect, for to the tenement dwellers it is just one occurrence in a life lived among neighbors who are yet strangers and who are quickly replaced by others. The insignificance of human beings in such conditions is made the cause of their overwhelming loneliness.

Winterset is realistic and melodramatic, like *Street Scene,* and the living conditions of the characters are even more degrading, but the theme of loneliness is made the result of a social injustice of thirteen years before. Each individual related directly or indirectly to the case has suffered through the years as an outcast from society through feelings of fear, hate, or guilt. Some aura of universality is given to the contemporary subject matter by means of blank verse and a certain heroism imparted to the characters by their grandiose reactions to the tragic situation. Maxwell Anderson says that the play "is largely in verse and treats a contemporary tragic theme, which makes it more of an experiment than I could wish, for the great masters themselves never tried to make tragic poetry out of the stuff of their own times."[13] Through his use of verse, Anderson has perhaps succeeded better than Rice in creating a drama of worth concerning individuals bested by social forces. Whereas Rice portrays the situation, Anderson interprets it as well by means of verse.

Eugene O'Neill writes realistic dialogue and creates some realistic scenes in *The Hairy Ape,* but he crosses the boundary, which neither Rice nor Anderson does, into what might be called superrealism, or expressionism. With purposeful symbolism he sets the highest in the social scale beside the lowest. Although on the symbolic level the various strata of society have little weight, one being no nearer a state of belonging than the others, on the realistic level they are all-important, for Yank's original alienation from his work comes from his encounter with a girl from the highest stratum. If it were not for the wider application which O'Neill makes of his theme, his play would be merely another one of socialistic propaganda. Like *Street Scene* and *Winterset,* however, *The Hairy Ape*'s portrayal of human loneliness has a meaning beyond the literal which gives it an important place in modern American drama.

It is also true that in the three plays discussed the characters rise above their environment. None obviously reaches the tragic heights of the great dramatic heroes of the world, but they are distinguishable from the mass as individuals with an importance of their own. To some extent Frank Hurburt O'Hara's comment on *Winterset* is true of *Street Scene* and *The Hairy Ape* as well.

> In so contemporary a tragedy Fate, as we would expect, lurks in the socioeconomic order. . . . Unrelenting, the same forces work on, not with the placable anger of the Gods, but with the impersonality of some vast, diabolical machine. And yet, for all the impersonality of this modern "social" Fate, it is man himself —today as with the Greeks—who rises through suffering beyond the reach of any disaster devised by Fate.[14]

Rose Maurrant and Mio and Yank all refuse to submit to the miserable isolation into which society attempts to thrust them. Rose decides to belong to herself, Mio to the idea of love instead of hate, and Yank to whatever his valiant search may guide him. Tragedy and violent death overtake them, but since each senses that there is more to life than what surrounds them, they all rate consideration in the ledgers of the gods.

IN THE SOUTH

Several American dramatists have made valuable contributions to the modern theatre in plays portraying the isolating effects of the particular socioeconomic conditions of the South. Tennessee Williams, frequently an interpreter of the lonely Southern female who lives in romantic dreams of the past but is lost in the modern world, has written two prize-winning plays on the theme: *The Glass Menagerie,* which won the Critics Circle Award for the season 1944-45; and *A Streetcar Named Desire,* which won both the Critics Circle Award and Pulitzer Prize for 1947-48. Although Lillian Hellman's theme in *The Little Foxes* (1939) and *Another Part of the Forest* (1946) is the rapaciousness of a family of rising Southerners, she contrasts them with the ruined aristocracy who now belong nowhere, but who play an important part in the dramas. Paul Green, in a number of plays, notable among which is *The House of Connelly* (1931), has portrayed the loneliness of decay into which the old Southern plantation owners have fallen. All three playwrights emphasize the changing social and economic structure as the basis for a kind of personal near-annihilation of those Southern aristocrats who cannot adapt themselves to changing conditions, and a sense of belonging to those who can.

Although no condemnation of the pre-Civil-War South is explicit in their plays, Williams, Hellman, and Green suggest that the wealthy plantation owners of the South had in them the germs of their own destruction before the Civil War with its aftereffects completed their downfall. Neuroticism or a destructive adherence to dreams and drink is displayed by those characters who do not enter into a healthy relationship with individuals adjusted to present-day society. The playwrights intimate, at least, that the way of life in the South contained elements deleterious to master and slave alike. "Man can adapt himself to slavery, but he reacts to it by lowering his intellectual and moral qualities," as Erich Fromm points out.[15] In a slave-owning society, man treats himself as his own slave, and becomes his own strict taskmaster, so that instead of developing a unified personality at home in the world, he becomes an isolated and haunted character, obsessed by feelings of guilt. Consequently, George Jean Nathan's complaint that a character like Blanche from *A Streetcar Named Desire* becomes so "psychologically, pathologically, and logically muddled that she gives the effect of three totally different women housed in the same body,"[16] may not be justified; for although it is true that Williams attributes the beginning of her downfall to the loss of the family plantation, which loss does not seem to account for all her psychological aberrations, nevertheless, her neuroses may logically be contained in a woman of her social and hereditary background.

The deleterious influence of socioeconomic conditions on Southern characters in American drama, therefore, includes the material loss of the plantations and the depletion of the land, as well as the destruction by the carpetbaggers, after the Civil War itself had wrought much havoc; but it also includes, by inference at least, the moral isolation inherent in the society before its material downfall. In Lillian Hellman's two plays about the Hubbards, they, the up-and-coming money-makers of the South, although filled with physical stamina, suffer as great a moral void as do the real "folks," for inasmuch as they are members of the same social order, they have suffered from its defects. Although the theme of tragic loneliness is carried by Birdie, at the end it is the powerful Regina who pleadingly asks her daughter to sleep with her because of fear of being alone. In *The Glass Menagerie,* only Tom escapes, and that by running away. In *A Streetcar Named Desire,* Stella adapts herself to a mode of living which might seem unacceptable, but one which removes her from the isolation of Blanche or Laura. In *The House of Connelly,* the remaining members of the family have deteriorated like the plantation. Only young Will is saved by marriage with the daughter of a family of soil-loving tenants. All these plays doubtless portray truthfully the terrifying loneliness of those clinging to a society of the South which has become so debilitated as to be almost nonexistent.

The symbolism of *The Glass Menagerie,* which is a memory play evoked in the mind of Tom, the son and narrator, is carried partly in the title; for the family is like the glass collection in the frowsy apartment, ill-adapted to its environment. The playwright says of Laura, the shy daughter who has a slightly crippled leg,

> Stemming from this [defect], Laura's separation increases till she is like a piece of her own glass collection, too exquisitely fragile to move from the shelf. (Author's Production Note)

Tennessee Williams further advises that the light, which should not appear realistic, should descend in a shaft upon Laura in several scenes in which she is only the onlooker, "with a peculiar pristine clarity such as light used in early religious portraits of female saints or madonnas." Laura's "separation" is thus symbolically illustrated by the lighting and staging. Nathan calls her "a creature crippled deeply in inner spirit,"[17] and it is certain that her physical disability is small compared to her psychological isolation.

It is no wonder that Laura suffers from a painful sense of loneliness, for from the first scene to the last, her mother makes her feel her lack of popularity with men and her inability to cope with any kind of social life. Laura's closing line of the first scene, "Mother's afraid that I'm going to be an old maid," is complemented by the closing scene in which the gentleman caller departs, never to return. In the intervening action Laura's pitiful inner apartness from the life around her is made overt by other incidents. Amanda's lack of sympathy of the girl's nervous sickness at business school elicits only Laura's reply of "I couldn't face it. I couldn't." Any contact with people is almost more than Laura can face. Seemingly her only sense of attachment is to her little glass figures, but this feeling of closeness to them is so intense that when Tom throws his coat and accidentally knocks some off the shelf, she cries out "as if wounded," and covers her face with her hands. Her devotion to so fragile a material object as the glass menagerie represents the enervation of her spiritual connection to anything. She substitutes playing the old phonograph records and dusting the figures in her menagerie for a healthy interest in living. As Tom says, "She lives in a world of her own," which is so unrelated to that of those around her that she seems "peculiar." When left alone with the gentleman caller, her speech is low and breathless from her paralyzing shyness. For a few moments with the young man, Jim, she comes into accord, as he displays a "warmth and charm which lights her inwardly with altar candles," but the scene increases the pathos of Laura's situation, for it ends by Jim's announcement that he is to be married to a girl named Betty. The humiliation of the rebuff would seem likely to stand in the way of her ever again even approaching a state of understanding with another individual.

To make Laura's sense of separateness doubly explicit, the playwright has inserted into the scene between Jim and Laura stage business with a little unicorn, her favorite figure. Since it has a horn and is different from all the horses, Jim remarks, "Poor little fellow must feel kind of lonesome." Although Laura insists he gets along well with the horses, it is with deep feeling that she says, after the horn has been broken by a fall,

He's lost his horn. It doesn't matter. Maybe it's a blessing in disguise. . . . The horn was removed to make him feel less— freakish! Now he will feel more at home with the other horses, the ones who don't have horns. (II, viii)

Laura's "horn" is the slight limp, which she has magnified to make her seem to herself "a freak," until she has become in a sense just that. Knowing how alone she is and always will be, Tom, although he must run away to save himself, is forever haunted by a feeling of guilt towards her and pleads that her candles may be extinguished in his memory. As the final curtain falls, Laura blows out the candles, and having thus apparently been forgotten by Tom, is left in black loneliness forever.

Laura has created around herself something of the atmosphere which Thomas Mann explains in "The Making of 'The Magic Mountain.'" Speaking of the tuberculosis sanitarium, he points out "the dangers of such a milieu for young people," and the idea expressed in his book "of the narrowness of this charmed circle of

137

isolation and invalidism," which makes the patient "become completely incapable of life in the 'flatland.' "[18] Laura lives in a mountainous retreat of her own making and has thus lived for so long that she is now incapable of life among the vale of people. Unlike Amanda, she has no past to which she can belong, and, as Tom recognizes, she obviously has no future to which she can look forward, so she exists from day to day, avoiding reality by withdrawing into herself, spending her lonely days dusting her little glass animals.

Amanda is a pitiful, even a tragic, figure according to Tennessee Williams. As Tom gives his closing speech of the play and the light is upon the pantomime of Amanda comforting Laura, the playwright says of Amanda: "Now that we cannot hear the mother's speech, her silliness is gone and she has dignity and tragic beauty." Her slow, graceful gestures indicate her upbringing in a genteel tradition. Circumstances have put her in a position that makes her reminiscences of the past ridiculous, but Jim, the gentleman caller, is sincere in toasting "the Old South" with her, for she has quite charmed him by her chatter, which although it seems affected to the audience, has an air of authenticity and warmth to the visitor. Amanda's taking out her feeling of dissatisfaction with herself upon Tom finally drives him away and leaves her alone with Laura, whose withdrawal makes companionship impossible. "Amanda," says Tennessee Williams, "having failed to establish contact with reality, continues to live vitally in her illusions." Since she is so removed from the world around her, Amanda is able, to some extent, to belong to the past, even going so far as to believe herself "girlish." Pitiful as is such adherence, however, she is not so alone as Laura, because of her ability to project the past into the present and be a part of it.

Amanda never sees the irony of her position. Although it is the charm of her husband which has led to his departure, the "cultivation of charm" should be Laura's aim in life. Even as the photograph of the smiling, but missing, head of the household is illuminated by a spotlight and as Amanda admits, "That's the only thing your father had plenty of—charm!" still she is urging Laura, "You have to cultivate charm—or vivacity—or charm!" Occasionally, though, her imagination fails, and Amanda feels lost, as when she appeals to Tom to help get a suitor for Laura. "In these trying times we live in," she pleads, "all that we have to cling to is—each other." "Clinging" best describes her relationship to her present life and "remembering," to her past. Whether the pathos of her life is important enough to be tragic is doubted by many critics. Alan Downer says of Tennessee Williams' plays that "though his themes are in possibility tragic, his plays are in actuality pathetic. Each of his characters passionately resists the moment of illumination, rejects the self-knowledge which might give tragic dignity to her failure."[19] If there is real tragedy in Laura and Amanda and others of Williams' characters whose world has been wrecked by changing social conditions, perhaps it is the very fact that they do not have any recognition of their failure. If their heredity is such that they not only cannot adapt to a different status in life but also cannot come to any understanding of their situation, the tragedy is perhaps one of the whole society from which they are derived. Is it not tragic that Southern society has produced such characters, who, whether typical of mankind or not, are apparently typical of their class? This is to ask, of course, whether Aristotle's definition of tragedy should be revised for twentieth-century America. Is "social tragedy" an anomalous term?

Tom is lonely like his mother and Laura, but he is not a pathetic figure and surely not a tragic one, except insofar as his escape from the "coffin" of his home is possible only in a physical sense. But on the literal level, Tom's escape is heroic and successful. George Kernodle cites it as one example of a happy escape from the strangling arms of home and family. This critic believes that the theme of escape is one of the most common in modern drama because of the deterministic cynicism of the twentieth century, which has left no other solution.[20] In the mind of the audience Tom, like his father, is more than justified in running away, for as he says, "I haven't got a thing, not a single thing left in this house that I can call my own." He complains justly about his "2 by 4 situation," which, like being nailed in a coffin, cuts him off entirely from all contacts. Tom has a recognition, too, of the family's plight, which the women lack, for he points out that Jim is "an emissary from a world that we were somehow set apart from." Tom does escape from the isolation which he feels in his home by going into the great world of reality—the Merchant Marine, and although his closing lines indicate that he does not find a sense of belonging in "motion," perhaps he has made an advance toward it by breaking the bonds which tied him to his mother.

Tennessee Williams' description of his scene for *The Glass Menagerie* might be that of *Street Scene*. Like Elmer Rice he makes explicit in the stage directions that it is the mass of humanity, which is unable to provide any sense of identity to its individual members, which makes tenement living so lonely. He explains that the Wingfield family lives in

> one of those vast hive-like conglomerations of cellular living-units that flower as warty growths in over-crowded urban centers of lower middle-class population and are symptomatic of the impulse of this largest and fundamentally enslaved section of American society to avoid fluidity and differentiation and to exist and function as one interfused mass of automatism. (I, i)

Amanda, it must be admitted, shows a certain courage in refusing to become one with the mass by maintaining her illusions, for there is perhaps more hope in living in the past than in being submerged in the present, and Laura likewise manages to keep some iota of identity through her glass menagerie. Tom escapes from this interfusion of mankind, as well as from his family, and attains some individuality by traversing the globe. As a whole, however, socioeconomic conditions have left all the Wingfields unattached to a satisfactory object of devotion and doomed them all to loneliness.

In Blanche DuBois, the leading character of *A Streetcar Named Desire,* Tennessee Williams is accused of having created a sexual pervert, who is insane by the end of the play, and whose portrayal is so particular as to have little relevance to life, or meaning to the American theatre. Williams, however, makes the point that it is the isolation resulting from social and hereditary factors which makes Blanche abnormal. Doubtless the accusation that Williams is strongly influenced by D. H. Lawrence is also true, but the playwright has made purposeful use of the sexual instinct by dramatizing its contrasting effect in two sisters and cannot be charged with mere sensationalism. The theme of the play, like that of Paul Green's *The House of Connelly,* indicates that members of the Southern plantation-owning class cannot exist in isolation. Stella is able to adapt herself to a new mode of living through her intense physical love for the Polish Stanley Kowalski, whereas Blanche cannot relate herself to any mode of life open to her in the modern age, and so perishes. Since, as Erich Fromm points out,

"Complete isolation is unbearable and incompatible with sanity," it is obvious that her end is the only possible logical conclusion to the drama. Fromm further explains,

> man cannot live alone and unrelated to others. He has to associate with others for defense, for work, for sexual satisfaction, for play, for the upbringing of the young, for the transmission of knowledge and material possessions. But beyond that, it is necessary for him to be related to others, one with them, part of a group.[21]

It is not enough for man to associate with others in those things which require cooperation; he must have a psychological sense of belonging somewhere, or else he suffers that self-recognition of apartness which is desolating. Whether or not the newspaper account is true that in Vienna, Austria, *A Streetcar Named Desire,* was called *Last Stop, Loneliness,* the appropriateness of such a title is evident.

As in *Street Scene* and *The Glass Menagerie,* the fact of the unbearable physical closeness of human beings to each other and their psychic separateness is dramatized with clarity in *A Streetcar Named Desire.* The isolating effect of crowded conditions is perhaps made even more explicit than in the other two plays, and the irony of the fact that the bathroom, associated with Stanley's vulgarity, is also Blanche's only place of retreat and relaxation is symbolic of the theme of the two sisters—one of whom belongs through the most physical of means, the other of whom cuts herself off from the life of the household. At the time the play opens, Blanche has failed at running the family plantation, at school teaching, and at keeping her good name. And her marriage of years before has been a failure, because her young husband proved to be a homosexual, who shot himself when she discovered the truth. In desperation she comes to her younger sister. The blows which she suffers there are enough to vanquish the spirit of a woman better equipped than Blanche to meet the loneliness of poverty and the alienation from all loved ones. Besides the recognition that Stella will not leave her coarse husband and besides Stanley's cruel present of a one-way bus ticket back to Laurel, Mitch fails to appear at her birthday party and then later comes to taunt her with her past and to thrust a glowing light bulb into her face. Added to these shocks, on the night when Stella goes to the hospital for the birth of her baby, Stanley rapes her. It is no wonder that she, like Tom in

The Glass Menagerie, speaks of her life in the apartment as "a trap." She has run like a mouse to a far corner and cannot escape. Reality is unbearable. Tom gets away by joining the Merchant Marine; but with every possible tie to life broken, Blanche can escape only into insanity.

Not a case study, however, Blanche's story is given wider application by Williams' use of symbolism throughout the play. For example, the varsoviana, which was being played when Blanche's young husband shot himself, rises intermittently with jazz from the saloon across the street, whenever Blanche tends to lose contact with reality. The contrast between the elegant past and the sordid present, which Blanche tries to conceal by covering the lights with paper lantern shades, is revealed in this use of music as well as by the chimes of the cathedral bells, which Blanche calls "the only clean thing in the Quarter." In *The Glass Menagerie,* Tom, coming home drunk, shakes a little toy noisemaker after each solemn tolling of the church bell to symbolize the foolishness of man in contrast to the Almighty. In *A Streetcar Named Desire* the chimes indicate the difference between paradise and the portrayed version of Elysian Fields. Other symbolism is meaningfully yet unobtrusively woven into the action, so that in truth Blanche's story takes on a significance larger than itself.

The character can be justified on the literal level as the dramatization of the progress of a woman into complete isolation. In the beginning Blanche admits to Stella:

> I'm not going to put up at a hotel. I want to be *near* you, got to be *with* somebody, I *can't* be *alone!* Because—as you must have noticed—I'm—*not* very well. (Scene I)

The fact that she has come to the Quarter in the finery she is wearing indicates at first glance that Blanche is very much out of place, and her frightened words indicate that she is appealing to Stella as a last hope. The next time she explains her loneliness is to Mitch. To his sympathetic ear she tells how she loved when she was young, how she accused her husband of homosexuality, how he shot himself, and how ever since, the searchlight which had been on the world has been turned off with only candles to take its place. "I understand what it is to be lonely," she tells him. It is almost impossible not to compare Williams' two plays in their treatment of the near-belonging of Laura and of Blanche. In each case the kiss of a man who seems to be sincere brings the girl to a sudden joyful sense of being one with a lover. After Mitch indicates his sympathy and kisses her, saying, "You need somebody. And I need somebody too. Could it be—you and me, Blanche?" She breathes with long, grateful sobs, "Sometimes—there's God—so quickly!" She is saved for the moment. But as in the case of Laura, this scene only makes her final isolation more devastating. Step by step she reaches the point of immutable loneliness until memory of the past and dreams of the future flood over her, mercifully to blot out the present.

Of course there is a question, as there is in Lillian Hellman's plays of the isolation of the families of the Old South, whether the rough characters who take over and compete successfully in the modern world really have a happy sense of belonging. At the moment the play takes place Stella seems to have adapted herself to a blissful relationship with Stanley. Even Blanche admits, "Maybe he's what we need to mix with our blood now that we've lost Belle Reve and have to go on without Belle Reve to protect us." But as they walk on to the restaurant, Blanche follows Stella, muttering, "The blind are—leading the blind!" and later when she tells her younger sister, "The only way to live with such a man is to—go to bed with him," the audience is inclined to agree. However, as the play is constructed, Stella loves Stanley. The two are one and by their unity highlight Blanche's loneliness.

In Lillian Hellman's two plays about the Hubbard family, the emphasis is upon the characters who in a material sense make a success of living, but who are as void of social or moral or spiritual values as a nest of vipers. Contrasted to them, as the DuBois family is to the Kowalskis, are those plantation owners who have been ruined materially by the war and its aftereffects, who are not reprehensible socially or morally, but who have not the stamina to compete in the world around them. Birdie has great similarity to both Laura and Blanche. Mistreated and unloved, she frequently drinks alone in her room as the only compensation for a life of otherwise unbearable isolation. The Hubbards, too, in battling each other for the family wealth, have lost all the affection which the ties of blood should give and the family as a whole is cut off from friendly contacts in the neighborhood.

Lillian Hellman wrote *Another Part of the Forest* in 1946, seven years after *The Little Foxes,* but the later play takes the Hubbard family back to the days of 1880, whereas the play written first begins the family history in 1900. Miss Hellman explains that, although she hated the Hubbards as much as anyone, she became annoyed at the display by the audience of moral superiority to them, and this, she says, "did make me feel that it was worth while to look into their family background and find out what it was that made them the nasty people they were."[22] In her second play she gives great emphasis to the social ostracizing of the Hubbards and their impulse to get ahead financially to compensate for their loneliness. The mother is driven out of her mind by the knowledge of her husband's treachery in aiding Union forces and turns to the Negroes and their church for comfort and understanding. She is loved by them and belongs to them. But the other members of the family compete for the favor of whoever has the upper hand and are mired in their hatred of each other and of the quality folks, who will not speak to them, as well as of the townspeople, who distrust them.

In *The Little Foxes* Regina, at forty, kills her husband and outwits her brothers to become the wealthiest of the Hubbards, but in the end loses the love of her daughter and stands frightened and alone as the final curtain falls. In *Another Part of the Forest,* Regina is portrayed as a girl who has learned at the age of twenty that the way to get along is coquettishly to flatter her father and to play her brothers off against each other. Since she loves John Bagtry, Birdie's cousin, she is anxious to have her father make the Bagtrys a loan to save their plantation, but she is also sincere in wanting to court their favor, for she says,

> I've been kind of lonely here with nobody nice having much to do with us. I'd sort of like to know people of my own age, a girl my own age, I mean—. . . (Act I)

When he questions her again, she still insists, "I been a little lonesome. No people my age ever coming here—I do think people like that sort of want to forgive you, and be nice to us." As Lillian Hellman probed into Regina's background, she found a lonely girlhood at least partly the cause of her later rapacity. Her lover, who feels he does not belong anywhere except with fighting men, leaves her, explaining her attachment to him with the words, "You're a lonely girl, and I'm the first man you've liked." When Ben contrives to send her lover away, she has nowhere to turn. No wonder the Regina of twenty years later knows only ruthlessness. She has suffered from a feeling of apartness since childhood days and has known nothing to make her appreciate the warmth of human affection.

So hardened has Regina become twenty years later that she says with sincerity of the northern industrialist, Mr. Marshall, "He seems a lonely man. Imagine being lonely with all that money." Lillian Hellman justifiably speaks of the Hubbards as "a nest of particularly vicious diamond-back rattlesnakes."[23] A comparison with the work of Franz Kafka, therefore, may be enlightening; for, in *Metamorphosis,* the story of a man's change into an insect, he interprets human psychology in terms of animal symbols. "Kafka's pathos is the pathos of loneliness and exclusion. . . . What it [*Metamorphosis*] represents objectively is the emotion of exclusion from the family and, beyond that, the estrangement of man from his human environment."[24] Although Regina has not the self-recognition of herself that the hero of *Metamorphosis* has, and so does not appear to herself as a despicable insect, it can be questioned whether in a sequel to *The Little Foxes* she might not have some self-revulsion, for there is a challenge in her young daughter's last words to her concerning "people who eat the earth," and certainly by this time she is suffering from a feeling of estrangement from everyone from whom she normally might expect affection.

Some critics have seen in *The Little Foxes* social implications beyond the story of the Hubbards. Richard Watts, Jr., says of the play, "Through its thoughtful indignation it becomes a scornful and heartfelt parable of the rise of the industrial South in all its ruthlessness, its savage sense of realism and its fine scorn for the older trappings of Confederate romanticism."[25] Although Lillian Hellman seems more interested in the devastating effects upon the people—both the old families and the wealthy new families—of socioeconomic changes, she does, nevertheless, indicate strongly the nature and importance of these changes. And assuredly she makes them the cause of the isolation of her characters. Miss Hellman's plays have special significance now that a second industrialization of the South seems underway. In "Second Chance for the South," Oscar Handlin points out: "The first New South failed because it could not cope with the problems it inherited from the past." He sees no disadvantage in the use of northern capital except

145

"when it obscures the true interests of the people and perverts public policy on behalf of the outsiders and of their local allies."[26] In the case of the Hubbards' use of outside capital, nobody's interests except their own were served, and the New South that they created ended in deep social inequalities. Miss Hellman's plays are not thesis plays, but the fact that she was interested enough in her characters to study their past and seek out the sociological and moral causes of their rapaciousness proves that she did not consider them mere figures in melodrama. Her further consideration of them also divulged a sense of loneliness, which, while not making them more sympathetic, at least made them better understood.

Marcus Hubbard, when Birdie explains that the people on her plantation are literally starving and that perhaps for a loan the families could be nice friends, replies: "Your mother hasn't bowed to me in the forty years I've lived in this town. Does she wish to be my nice friend now?" Granted that the suspicion about Marcus' war activities was well founded, nevertheless the man had a great love of music and Greek literature and seemingly might have been guided toward higher moral values if he had been helped and not snubbed. Marcus has something to be said for his viewpoint too, in his hot words to John Bagtry, who had been a Confederate soldier.

> Your people deserved to lose their war and their world. It was a backward world, getting in the way of history. Appalling that you still don't realize it. (Act II)

That the way of the Hubbards—the way of avarice, of robbing and cheating—was worse does not nullify the fact that Hellman and other playwrights suggest the degeneration of the aristocracy of the Old South before socioeconomic conditions brought about its ruin. In one sense Marcus is justified in questioning the tone of moral superiority which the Bagtrys have adopted toward him. He has not lived by the labor of others, nor has he inherited wealth or land. He has stood, in the best American tradition of individualism, on his own two feet.

It is his ruthless march toward wealth that has made him feared by his wife and hated by his children, and when tricked by Ben, "very, very, very—afraid." At one point, Ben appears to have failed and admits,

> I spent twenty years lying and cheating to help make you rich. I

was trying to outwait you, Papa, but I guess I couldn't do it. (Act II)

"Your tricks are getting nasty and they bore me," Marcus tells his oldest child; but in the end, he reaps what he has sown, and becomes Ben's slave. Brooks Atkinson's comment on Tennessee Williams' recent study in hatred among members of a Southern family— Cat on a Hot Tin Roof—applies to Lillian Hellman's two plays: "Essentially, each one of them [the family] is living in solitary confinement."[27] In another review Atkinson observes: "There seems to be something in the spiritual climate today that makes loneliness a universal theme. It underlies a good deal of the writing for the stage."[28] The "robber barons," whose rise was made possible during the late nineteenth century by social and economic conditions, apparently taught their sons, as did Marcus Hubbard, that any means to wealth and power was justified; and presumably they were as unloved by their progeny and as isolated finally as he. Ben profits by what he has been taught, however, and even accuses his father of getting soft.

> You were smart in your day and figured out what fools you lived among. But ever since the war you been too busy getting cultured, or getting Southern. A few more years and you'd have been just like the rest of them. (Act III)

Much has been made of the loneliness of Americans because of the conditions which fostered the competitive spirit and lent an undue prestige to wealth and power. Miss Hellman in her second play illustrates the cause of the rise of the bourgeoisie, for, as D. W. Brogan explains, American families from the beginning have risen and fallen according to their ability to compete, and those who made pretensions of surviving on ancient prestige deteriorated.

> The would-be gentry unlearned the idle lessons of gentility or sank into poverty. . . . There was no high plateau of effortless superiority to be attained, by Byrds in Virginia or by Saltonstalls in Massachusetts. A family or an individual had to have what it took to survive—and it took adaptability, toughness, perhaps a not too sensitive moral or social outlook.[29]

The Bagtrys became impoverished and failed, whereas the Hubbards, with a "not too sensitive moral or social outlook," took over.

Miss Hellman's two plays contrast the loneliness of the falling and the rising family, highlighting the two women, Birdie and

Regina. At the end of the second play it is hard to say whether Birdie, who must bear the abuse of the Hubbards and lose consciousness in drink, is more isolated than Regina, who, begging her daughter to sleep in the bedroom with her, receives the reply, "Are you afraid, Mama?" Birdie, like Amanda and Blanche in Williams' plays, lives in dreams of the past glory of the plantation, but Regina has no happy memories of the past and her future looks bleak. In warning the young Alexandra, Birdie says,

> In twenty years you'll just be like me. They'll do all the same things to you. In twenty-two years I haven't had a whole day of happiness. . . . And you'll trail after them, just like me, hoping they won't be so mean that day. . . . only you'll be worse off because you haven't got my Mama to remember. (Act III)

Birdie is so good-hearted that for more than twenty years she has not been able to believe that anyone could be so cruel as the Hubbards, and perhaps hardest of all to bear, her son has turned out to be like them. She admits ruefully that she likes even her husband better than she does her son. She has been told many times that Oscar married her for the plantation. Ben is frank to say, in front of her, "Lionnet now belongs to *us.* Twenty years ago we took over their land, their cotton, and their daughter." Birdie, living in this nest of rattlesnakes, is tragically lonesome, and has broken under the strain. But Birdie has the love of Alexandra, which Regina has lost so irretrievably that the girl hurls her a parting challenge after announcing that she is leaving her mother forever. Proclaiming that she is not going to stand around while the Hubbards eat the earth, she shouts,

> Tell him [Uncle Ben] for me, Mama, I'm not going to stand around and watch you do it. Tell him I'll be fighting as hard as he'll be fighting some place where people don't just stand around and watch. (Act III)

In Lillian Hellman's story a humanitarian with the tenderness of Birdie and the forcefulness of Regina arises to sound a new war cry.

To some extent John Bagtry and Ben Hubbard are contrasted as are the women of the two families. John has no place in the post-Civil War South, whereas Ben is in his element. Explaining that business is almost a religion with him, Ben frankly expounds, "A man ain't only in business for what he gets out of it. It's got to give him something here," as he places his hand upon his breast. But to John Bagtry, life on the failing plantation is torture. "I was only good once—in a war," he tells Regina, as he explains he is going to enlist in Brazil. "I want to be with fighting men again. I'm lonely for them." To the Hubbards he seems "A dead man, a foolish man, an empty man from an idiot world. . . . A man in space." Ben claims, "The Southern aristocrat can adapt himself to nothing. Too high-toned to try." John spends as much time as possible with Birdie and her mother because, as he sympathetically explains, "They are lonely," but he cannot feel he belongs to the plantation. John's loneliness is tragic, as is Birdie's; but Lillian Hellman convinces her audiences that there is also tragedy in belonging to nothing but business. The devotion of the Southern gentry to a way of life brings grief, but a deeper loneliness may be in store for those "who eat the earth," than for those who stand around and watch.

Some years before Tennessee Williams and Lillian Hellman wrote their dramas of the South, a North Carolinian, Paul Green, had made a reputation with his plays contrasting the old and the new South. Following his Pulitzer Prize winning tragedy of 1927, *In Abraham's Bosom,* he wrote *The House of Connelly,* which was produced in 1931. Williams and Hellman portray the effect of socioeconomic changes on those who have left the plantations, but Paul Green sets his figures among the rotting fences and cracked walls of the Connelly plantation. Deteriorated like the crumbling pillars, thirty-year-old Will Connelly, his mother, his uncle, and his two middle-aged spinster sisters wander through the mansion— his sisters "houseworn and tired," his mother dying, his lecherous uncle making cynical remarks, and Will "down, whipped, beaten." To the plantation as tenant farmers come Jesse Tate and his pretty daughter, Patsy—soil-loving, hard-working, farmers, who make the land productive again. But more important, Patsy makes Will himself productive again. When he exclaims, "I am nothing. Even the niggers laugh at me. My God! I'm done—done!" she pleads, "I'll help you—we'll do it—work—work—together. I know how to work with the earth. I know her ways." Will gradually becomes convinced: "With you—yes—I might do something—. But I'm numbed, cold, empty. I've stayed in this old house too long." (I, iii)

Since the Tates are, according to the Connelly family, poor white trash, while their own ancestry is impeccable, there is a deep reorientation which must take place in Will's whole being before he can make Patsy his wife. The play is the story of his successful but precarious advance to a happy relationship with Patsy, which rejuvenates his soul and body. In the beginning he might be said to be, like John Bagtry in *Another Part of the Forest,* "a man in space," and, like him, he wants to go away and leave the ruins to turn to dust without him. In this play the pictorial image of the decay is reflected in the looks and actions of the members of the family. The cracks through the plaster are indicative of the worn and weary bodies and minds of the last of the Connellys, and the condition of the land, grown up with weeds, washed away by rain, and crossed with sagging fences, likewise reflects the lack of stamina in the strain. It is made visually clear from the start that Will, as the youngest of the line, is doomed to failure.

His ability to adapt himself to a new way of looking at life might seem surprising were it not motivated by his desire to belong. He can overlook the fact that Patsy's nouns and verbs do not agree for the higher sense of compatibility which he finds with her. He can overthrow the indoctrination from generations of Connellys that their blood must not be polluted, and replace it with a recognition of a deeper human heredity which tells him that belonging to Patsy is his only hope of escape from loneliness and deterioration. The first step in his salvation is his growing consciousness of the degeneration of the Connellys, who have bred mulatto children for generations and who have led an otherwise lecherous existence.[30] He proclaims to the horrified family:

> There's something to search for—find it—a way to act right and know it's right. Father and Grandfather didn't do it, and we're paying for it. All the old Connellys have doomed us to die. Our character's gone. We're paying for their sins. (II, ii)

The next step which forces him to seek a solution to his dilemma is the poverty and actual hunger from which the family and the people of the plantation are suffering. In combination these factors lead him to the logical, but by no means inevitable, conclusion that the only way he can live productively is by union with Patsy. As Erich Fromm points out in *Man for Himself,* "Only if these two conditions, the subjective dissatisfaction with a culturally patterned aim and the socioeconomic basis for a change, are present, can an indispensable third factor, rational insight, become effective."[31]

The triumph of Will's action in marrying Patsy is that rational insight, more than sexual love, is involved. Their union would seem to have a better chance of permanent success than Stella and Stanley's, for mutual consideration and devotion to an ideal of rejuvenation of the soil join them. Will tells his young wife in the final scene: "It took me a long time to see it. . . . It gives me a sort of peace now. We're doing what's right." She asks, "You'll learn to love me, won't you?" "And you me maybe?" he replies. The couple, especially Will, suffer a shock upon finding that the two old-maid sisters have left the house to live with a relative in Richmond. Will feels he has been cruel in driving them away, but Patsy stands firm.

> To grow and live and be something in this world you've got to be cruel—. . . The dead and the proud have to give way to us— to us the living. We have our life to live and we'll fight for it to the end. . . . It's our life or theirs. It can't be both. They knew it—that's why they went away. (II, iii)

Will again regains his self-composure. "Yes, let them go. Let the past die. It's our life now—our house." Ordering the two fat lascivious, and impertinent old Negro women to obey Miss Patsy's commands, he makes her mistress of Connelly Hall.

In one version of the play, Paul Green had the two toothless sybil-like old Negresses kill Patsy in order to prevent poor white trash from becoming "folks." He finally decided against this version, and wisely, for since the theme of the play is Will's passage from isolation to a state of belonging, such an event would only add an extraneous note of tragedy and blur the purpose of the drama. These two Negro characters—Big Sis and Big Sue—serve in the beginning as expositors of some of the family history. Throughout the play, however, they illustrate the degenerative effect of slavery upon its victims. Vulgar, cynical, derisive of the Connellys—of the old judge, who hanged his own mulatto son; of young Will, who is no good at hunting or anything else; of Uncle Bob, with whom they crack dirty jokes—they yet denounce Will's marrying Patsy, for their attachment for generations has been to the Connellys, and they know no way of belonging except as slaves to the master.

Uncle Bob is Janus-faced in that, even though he is too far gone in lechery and cynicism to be able ever to lead a useful life, he continues, in a somewhat facetious manner, to urge Will to marry Patsy. Although he has attempted to fondle the girl himself, and although he and Big Sis and Big Sue dance suggestively after Will and Patsy walk to the fields together, he recognizes that Will's only hope is to become one with a girl like Patsy. In fact, he might be said to be Will's savior, for the young man has bought his ticket to Texas, and is prevented from leaving only by his uncle's suicide. Bob's face, which has been "set in an empty, desolate look" throughout Will's parting enumeration of his sins, becomes resolute, as he murmurs in a dull voice, "Marry Patsy Tate, Will. For now the proud days are ended," and leaves with his pistol, presumably to shoot a hawk in the cypress tree, but actually to aim it at his own head.

Uncle Bob is a representation of what Will is likely to become. A typical example of the isolation suffered by a member of an impoverished Southern family, Bob cannot bring himself to try to rejuvenate the plantation, or to mend his ways. He can live neither in the past nor in the future. It is his redeeming feature that there is in him the spark which lights the hope that the last of the Connellys can be saved, and so he gives his own life to prevent Will's running away, and with his last breath advises his nephew to marry the farm girl. A kind of heroism surrounds his action. Since he does not shoot himself in despair, but with recognition that his action might save Will, he attains a stature he never had in life. His remark, as he goes out looking at his shabby "best clothes," "Not much of a garb for a far traveller," indicates a kind of rueful, hereditary interest in clothing, as well as a certain cynical sense of humor, which he has cultivated through life to conceal from himself his own weakness of character. He has been more isolated than the women of the family, because of their ability to live in the past glory of the pre-Civil War times, but in his resolution to kill himself, he comes nearer to a feeling of belonging than they ever have.

Patsy, who enjoys getting out and hoeing in the fields, has such an obviously rewarding attachment to the soil that Will is inspired by her. Revitalized by her presence, he calls the tenants together to make plans for improving the plantation. The meeting is not a success, but the fact that he calls it indicates that he has found her influence the means of trying to stop the deterioration of the land and the tenants. His sudden springing upon Uncle Bob when he finds the old man trying to make love to Patsy is another step in his advance from his "numbed, cold, empty" disregard of all around him to a warm interest in the girl, and consequently in all life. Patsy comes by her love of the soil naturally, for her father, while grieving for the state of the plantation, "washed about and bogged up with briars and bushes," still would give anything to own it and to be able to make it productive again, for to him, "It's purty land, purty land and level as a table." And Patsy admits honestly, when Will accuses her of wanting the plantation rather than himself:

> All my people have wanted land, wanted land above everything. When we moved here I saw all this great plantation going to ruin. I wanted it, wanted to make something out of it. I loved you because you stood for all I wanted. (II, ii)

Out of her real devotion to the land comes her feeling of love for Will. "I think about the farm now and what we can do with it, but always there is something else there, you yourself. I want to belong to you." Nevertheless, she does not deny that the land is something to which she wants to belong as well.

Jeeter Lester of *Tobacco Road* (1933), much farther gone in poverty and degeneracy than the Connelly tenants, would literally starve upon the land rather than go to work in the city factories. The land is his religion, and one for which he is dying. "City ways ain't God-given. It wasn't intended for man with the smell of the land in him to live in a mill in Augusta," he argues with intensity. Even George Jean Nathan admits that in *Tobacco Road*, "Along with the theatrical smell of salacity there is here and there a whiff of the authentic smell of the Georgia cracker soil."[32] The Tates might make Jeeter's pronouncement of his belonging to the land:

> When the smell of that new earth turning over behind the plow strikes me, I get all weak and shaky. It's in my nature—burning broom sedge and plowing in the ground this time of year. . . . Us Lesters sure like to stir up the earth and make plants grow in it. The land has got a powerful hold on me, Lov.[33]

Perhaps it is unfair to compare the ambitious Tates with the lazy, filthy Lesters, but their attachment to the land is similar, and the comparison makes obvious what courage it takes for Will to cross his dying mother and drive out his sisters for a tenant girl. The fervor of Patsy's love of growing plants transmits itself to Will until rejuvenation of his plantation and of his line seems possible with her. Her sense of being one with the soil involves her emotionally with its owner. Thus she and Will belong to each other through the land.

The play portrays an old-line Southerner's progression from enervation and loneliness, on which he was far advanced, to the path of rehabilitation by his united attack with Patsy on the problems which confront him. The two other young men of fallen Southern families—Tom of *The Glass Menagerie* and John Bagtry of *Another Part of the Forest*—escape by running away to foreign climes; but neither escapes from the loneliness of failure and of being the last of the males of his line. The old Connelly sisters end like Amanda and Laura and Blanche and Birdie and Birdie's mother, dreaming of the past, cut off from the present by social, economic, and hereditary influences. Neither Stella's marriage, in which sexual attraction is the uniting force, nor certainly Birdie's, into which she was tricked by the Hubbard's greed for her land, is the successful union which Will and Patsy's appears to be; for the old-line families cannot be saved by mere physical junction with new blood unless a spiritual bond also exists. Of the plays of Williams, Hellman, and Green which portray the loneliness of the old Southern families juxtaposed with families of rising Southerners, none seems to portend a permanently happy conclusion except Paul Green's *The House of Connelly*.

6
CONFLICT BETWEEN THE
SPIRITUAL AND THE MATERIAL

The enemy has no definite name, though in a certain degree we all know him. He who puts the body before the spirit, the dead before the living; who makes things only in order to sell them; who has forgotten that there is such a thing as truth, and measures the world by advertisement or by money; who daily defiles the beauty that surrounds him and makes vulgar the tragedy.

—*Religio Grammatici,* Gilbert Murray

Modern drama, like other forms of literature in the Western World, has been concerned during the twentieth century with the loneliness of man because of his lack of faith in nonmaterial values. The writers of the time would seem to be reflecting the true state of affairs if David Riesman in *The Lonely Crowd* is correct in asserting that men exist today as antagonistic cooperators, selling themselves on the basis of marginal differences in personality, with the result that they become incapable of experiencing individual emotion or deep love. Riesman claims:

> If the other-directed people should discover how much needless work they do, discover that their own thoughts and their own lives are quite as interesting as other people's, that, indeed, they no more assuage their loneliness in a crowd of peers than one can assuage one's thirst by drinking sea water, then we might expect them to become more attentive to their own feelings and aspirations.[1]

The same cry is voiced by Norman Cousins in an editorial about Albert Schweitzer:

> We are swollen with meaningless satisfactions and dulled by petty immediacies. . . . Schweitzer's aim is not to dazzle an age but to

155

awaken it, to make it comprehend that moral splendor is part of the gift of life, and that each man has unlimited strength to feel human oneness and to act upon it.[2]

Men would be less lonely if they followed their own spiritual inclinations. They would conceive of the unity of all life instead of being involved in its competitive, marketable aspects.

In an essay, "The Problem of Moral Isolation in Contemporary Literature," Stanley R. Hopper points out that ours is a literature of "the lost." We experience "the dark night of the soul"; we are "waylost, wanderers"; we are "orphaned, alone, impotent." But he says, "We may now be approaching a time—a moment of recognition—. . . in which a character comes to understand the meaning of his dilemma and his true relation toward his fellow men and his world."[3] Many important American playwrights have written dramas in which characters suffering moral isolation attempt to come to some understanding of their situation and to resolve the conflict between material pettiness and spiritual elevation. Philip Barry's *Here Come the Clowns* (1938) is a semiallegorical play concerning a man named Clancy, who suffers almost as many tribulations as Job, but who is convinced by Pabst, the illusionist, that he has not lost all, according to Barry, for he "at last finds God in the will of man." Sidney Howard's *Alien Corn* (1933) tells of Elsa Brandt, whose consuming passion for music and all the finer things of life brings her into conflict with the people of the small, midwestern college town where she teaches. Susan Glaspell in *Alison's House* (1930) makes an effort to re-create the spiritual influence wielded by Emily Dickinson eighteen years after her death. In *Dinner At Eight* (1932) George Kaufman and Edna Ferber portray in a melodramatic but cynical play the tragic results of devotion to false ideals among a group of wealthy socialites and their acquaintances. Two years later Kaufman and Moss Hart in an even more bitter satire, *Merrily We Roll Along,* characterize a writer who has debased himself for public fame. Rachel Crothers in *Susan and God* (1937) has written a satirical comment on a woman who thinks she has found God in a policy of do-goodness for the world, but who discovers that true godliness is service to her own husband and daughter, who need and love her. All of these plays depict the loneliness of characters because of a conflict within themselves or in society between the ideals of the spirit and the satisfactions of the flesh.

156

Three outstanding examples of such plays are *Craig's Wife* (1925) by George Kelly, *The Great God Brown* (1926) by Eugene O'Neill, and *The Time of Your Life* (1939) by William Saroyan. The most recent of these is set in a San Francisco waterfront honky-tonk, through which twenty-six strongly individualized persons pass, each one of whom expresses one facet of the character of mankind. Every man at some time in his life might be like Dudley, who lives for love; or like Wesley, who considers life a battle between himself and the machine; or like Harry, sick at heart, but wanting to make people laugh; or like McCarthy, the muscular longshoreman who is a philosopher; or like his friend, Krupp, who likes people and hates his duties as a policeman; or like Joe, who is trying to find the answers to life's problems; or, unfortunately, like Blick, whose meanness makes him hated by all; or like the other characters who enter the scene. Although the idea was abandoned, Saroyan had wished to have the theme of his play announced over a loud-speaker before the curtain rises. It is, however, printed preceding the play, so that the reader is under no misapprehension as to the author's purpose. To add to its parable-like quality, Saroyan also originally intended the play to have six acts—one for each day of the worker's week. The statement of theme repeats the title—

> In the time of your life, live—so that in that good time there shall be no ugliness or death for yourself or for any life your life touches. Seek goodness everywhere, and when it is found, bring it out of its hiding-place and let it be free and unashamed. Place in matter and in flesh the least of the values, for these are the things that hold death and must pass away. . . . In the time of your life, live—so that in that wondrous time you shall not add to the misery and sorrow of the world, but shall smile to the infinite delight and mystery of it. (Preface)

Each character of the play, isolated in some degree from every other one, is trying in his own way to discover how to live in a way that life may seem filled with delight.

Not everyone succeeds. Blick is so misguided that his happiness lies in trying to make things worse instead of better; life for him is filled with evil and despair; Joe, on the other hand, does want to make life better for himself and for those around him, and says, "I don't understand things. I'm trying to understand them." A peculiar sense of the isolation of human beings is imparted by the modern plays which, like *The Iceman Cometh* and *The Time of*

157

Your Life, are concerned with characters unrelated by blood to each other. Even though bitter antagonism might exist among members of the families in Greek or Elizabethan tragedy, the ties of blood made a recognizable relationship between characters. In *The Time of Your Life* the only momentary suggestion of family life is made by the two-minute entrance of Nick's little daughter, and later, the walk-on entrance of his mother. The pleasure and pride which each of these two female characters evince toward Nick increase the sense of loneliness which pervades the characters who make use of the honky-tonk. The breath of family joy which blows upon Nick makes the atmosphere of his Entertainment Palace seem cold by comparison. The difficulty of "smiling to the infinite delight and mystery of life" is that each character is separated from the other by a wall of misunderstanding; yet a feeling of optimism pervades Nick's establishment from time to time and makes all the characters seem to be of the human family to which all mankind belongs.

Although the air of freedom which the place emits is provided by the kindly proprietor, Nick, the leading character is Joe, who sometimes spends as much as twenty hours a day sitting and drinking champagne while he tries to live a "life that can't hurt any other life." Joe claims that if he doesn't drink all the time, he becomes fascinated by unimportant things but that while drinking he "lives *all the time.*" Both he and Nick agree, after watching the performance of a young newsboy who wants to be a lyric tenor, ". . . people are so wonderful. . . . Every one of them is wonderful." And at another time he asks the prostitute, Kitty, to drink with him as he toasts, "To the spirit, Kitty Duval," to which, as she begins to understand him, she responds gratefully, "Thank you." In her defense, when Nick questions her story about being in burlesque, Joe answers, "I believe dreams sooner than statistics." The pettiness of life wiped from his mind by champagne, Joe concentrates on eternal truths, and according to the playwright's admonition, "seeks goodness everywhere."

But basically Joe is lonesome. Explaining to Tom where he got all his money, Joe reveals that, hard as he may try to live according to the spirit, the nature of the world and of his past prevents his reaching a state of fulfillment. He says,

If anybody's got any money—to hoard or to throw away—you can be sure he stole it from other people. Not from rich people who

158

can spare it, but from poor people who can't. . . . I hurt people to get it. Loafing around this way, I *still* earn money. The money itself earns *more*. I *still* hurt people. (Act V)

Joe has befriended Tom when the boy was down-and-out, just as he helps Kitty to a belief in her own virtue, but he does not belong to either of them, and it is only in a state of semiconsciousness induced by alcohol that he can recognize goodness in the world. So he admits, "You can't enjoy living unless you work. Unless you do something. I don't do anything. . . . Because I can't do simple, good things." Erich Fromm explains that man's loneliness can be allayed only by productive living:

> . . . there is no meaning to life except the meaning man gives his life by the unfolding of his powers, by living productively. . . . The mature and productive individual derives his feeling of identity from the experience of himself as the agent who is one with his powers. . . .[4]

If Fromm's psychology is sound, Joe obviously cannot feel an identity with his powers because he is afraid to use them. Although he has perhaps taken a step in the right direction in that he is attempting to live so that he does not hurt anyone he knows, he has not reached a point at which he can live creatively. Suspended in a kind of limbo, he would like to change the world, but fears to try. It is with astonishment that he learns that the evil Blick wants to change the world, too—though from "something bad to something worse." But he does not blame Blick. "It's not him, Nick. It's everything," he says, as he calls the gang around to watch his mechanical toy perform. By concentrating on trifles, Joe avoids the real battles of life; but he does not avoid loneliness, and one wonders when he sends Tom out for a revolver whether he plans to use it upon himself.

Around Joe in the friendly atmosphere of Nick's bar circulates a variety of characters, all of them striving toward some understanding of how to live with others while attaining a sense of personal identity. All except Blick are pleasant characters, but all have a self-recognition of separateness, of not being accepted or successful. Willie, the marble game maniac, sees the contest of life as himself versus the machine—Willie versus destiny. "He is the last of the American pioneers with nothing more to fight but the machine." Willie provides an element of humor, but he is deadly

159

serious about himself, and when he finally beats the slot machine, he imparts his elation to all the occupants of the place. As the red and green lights of the machine go on and off and the bell rings six times, announcing the sudden appearance of an American flag, Willie salutes the flag with, "I knew I could do it." Everybody who has watched the performance of the defeated machine rises to sing "America." Willie's triumph is that of spirit over matter. His inner self is now permeated with a sense of accomplishment. He is proud of being himself and of being one of his race. Pointing to the large "F" on his sweater, he proclaims,

> See that letter? That don't stand for some little-bitty high school somewhere. That stands for *me*. Faroughli. Willis Faroughli. I'm an Assyrian. We've got a civilization six or seven centuries old, I think. (Act V)

Willie is in possession of the field. He belongs. He has a past and a future and is triumphant as an individual in the present.

Dudley Bostwick, a swindled young man, because, although educated, he is "without the least real understanding," is nevertheless "a great personality because, against all these handicaps, what he wants is simple and basic: a woman." This desire, which elevates him from nothingness to greatness, indicates an innocent animal force and "a wholeness of spirit" which makes him confident that "he has a chance, as a person." Like Willie, he furnishes a humorous interlude, when, frantically trying to phone his beloved Elsie Mandelspiegel, he gets another girl by mistake, who proves upon arrival to be a hag. When Elsie finally comes, however, although Dudley is entranced, they go out together with reservations about love; for she is a nurse who sees death more often than love, and she asks with sorrowful pity, "You want to live. I want to live, too, but where? Where can we escape our poor world?" The streetwalkers joke cynically about the lovers, but since the relationship of Dudley and Elsie is so tentative, they need not be jealous of it. Love momentarily binds them together, but in the morning they will remember "debts, and duties, and the cost of ridiculous things," and be lonesome again.

Willie and Dudley are succeeded by Harry, whose theory is that the world needs laughter, that he is funny, that therefore the world needs him. But his "philosophy" is a result of his desperate need to feel a sense of belonging. According to Saroyan, he is "out of place everywhere, sick at heart, but determined to fit in somewhere."

As he goes into his act of dancing and patter, which nobody appreciates, he worries that the world does not want what he has to give. "Nobody knows me," he complains. The American experiences a feeling of satisfaction in his own identity according to his success in selling himself. No wonder Harry is lost in the world. His moment of elation comes when Nick asks him to stick around to give an evening show for the clients of the bar. "I'm on my way at last," he exclaims with the same kind of jubilation which Willie's beating the machine evokes and which Elsie's arrival elicits from Dudley.

Other characters who pass across the scene are the Arab ("No foundation. All the way down the line.") ; the starving Negro, Wesley, who sits at the piano and entrances them all with his music; the policeman, Krupp, who wants to give up enforcing the law and take a walk by the ocean; his friend, the big longshoreman, McCarthy, who is a gentle philosopher; and Kit Carson, teller of tall tales. They all are attempting to live in the time of their life so that there shall be no ugliness. Each tries to obey the admonition of the prologue: "Be the inferior of no man nor of any man be the superior."

With all these characters in the background Joe performs the feat of bringing Tom, the boy who is his "subject," and Kitty, the "spiritually crippled" prostitute, into a state of mutual love and belonging which may elevate and purify them both, and which makes him less lonely. Joe's treatment of Tom, although munificent in providing for his physical wants, is not entirely compassionate, for he expects Tom to run his errands promptly and without question, and quickly knocks the boy's hat off on one occasion when Tom hesitates. Tom indirectly indicates his own reaction to being a slave by pointing out that he loves Kitty because she, as he says, "makes me feel like *I'm* somebody." But Joe finally makes the transition toward human brotherhood which all the other characters make. As he and Tom sit in Kitty's room trying to stop her crying, Joe announces that he is going to hire an automobile so that they can drive to the ocean to watch the sun go down. Tom is too stupified to be able "to express his amazement and gratitude." "Joe," he exclaims, "You mean you're going to go on an errand for *me*? You mean you're not going to send me?" Giving Tom money and getting him a job so he can marry Kitty are as nothing compared to the service of running an errand for the boy. Whether Joe knows it or not this is the moment in the time of his life when he has placed "in matter and in flesh the least of the values," and has attained a spirituality which is deathless.

Kitty is among the loneliest of characters, but when Joe moves her to a decent hotel, she is more lost than she was in the cheap New York hotel. She feels she cannot wait there for Tom. "I can't stand being alone," she cries. "I know I don't belong there. It's what I've wanted all my life, but it's too late. . . . I wish I could tell you how it makes me feel to be alone." Tom is dismayed at the thought of her waiting for him in the new hotel where she knows no one, but Joe is adamant:

> I put her in that hotel, so she can have a chance to gather herself together again. . . . She'll get lonely. Sure. People can get lonely for *misery*, even. I want her to go on being lonely for *you*, so she can come together again the way she was meant to be from the beginning. Loneliness is good for people. Right now it's the only thing for Kitty. (Act V)

Before Kitty can belong to Tom, she must belong to herself. So Kitty must pass through a suffering period of isolation, which remakes her, and so Joe, too, is rewarded, for he has sensed that there is inner beauty in Kitty, where there seemed to be only ugliness and death, and it has shown him "how full of goodness this life is."

In one sense the isolation which each character of the play experiences is a necessary prerequisite loneliness to his becoming an individual who can belong to an ideal. Saroyan's thematic prologue is addressed to the individuals of the race and takes the viewpoint that each man must find salvation on his own. But on the other hand, it proclaims: "Remember that every man is a variation of yourself. No man's guilt is not yours, nor is any man's innocence a thing apart." Thus the cold-blooded shooting of the evil detective, Blick, at the end becomes not murder, but the destruction of the bad-heartedness of mankind. It is Blick's first entrance which shatters the state of happy belonging which has encompassed all the characters. Before his entrance, the playwright describes the scene:

> The atmosphere is now one of warm, natural, American ease. . . . Although everyone is dead serious, there is unmistakable smiling and humor in the scene; a sense of the human body and spirit emerging from the world-imposed state of stress and fret-

162

fulness. . . . Each person belongs to the environment, in his own person, as himself. (Act I)

As Blick's presence becomes known and his sharp words penetrate the air, "There is absolute silence, and a strange fearfulness and disharmony in the atmosphere now." It takes only a breath of evil to break the bonds of companionship, the feeling of alone-to-getherness, which Walt Whitman called ensemble individuality, and which Saroyan has so imaginatively pictured in the scene. Wesley stops playing; Harry stops dancing; Joe stops playing with his toys; Willie stops playing the marble-game; Dudley straightens up from the phone; the Arab is watchful; Nick, whose place has been invaded, is arrogantly aloof. A cold stillness permeates the air until Blick leaves, and then only gradually the pleasure in each other's activities revives and the first-act curtain falls on a scene of happy participation by all in the performance of each.

The hero of this semiallegorical play, in which evil is bested and virtue triumphs, is no mythical angel, but a good, solid, boasting American pioneer, Kit Carson. Although his tall tales are believed by no one but Joe, his last one vindicates him: "I shot a man once. In San Francisco. . . . Couldn't stand the way he talked to ladies." It is provable and noble, and makes whether he ever fell in love with a midget weighing thirty-nine pounds immaterial. Joe has said that he was willing to believe Kit's tales anyway, because "Living is an art. . . . It takes a lot of rehearsing for a man to get to be himself." Kit's moment of finally becoming himself is his action in eliminating Blick, who uses his force to hurt the weak and whose very presence is an isolating influence on all the characters.

Against a background of some of the paradoxical situations which life presents, Saroyan dramatizes the passage of numerous characters from a state of loneliness to one of belonging. There is the question of laughing and crying: Harry tries to be funny, but nobody laughs. He is sick at heart, but thinks himself a comedian. When the Arab plays beautifully on his harmonica, Wesley says, "That's crying. That's deep, deep crying." "I want to make people laugh," responds Harry. When Kitty is crying and crying in her room, Joe sends her toys to make her laugh, but they make her remember home and she cries more. Toys had made Joe stop crying when his mother died, and he wonders why. This sadness-versus-happiness theme is suggested in other ways, as in Nick's

163

narration of his hatred for Tchaikowsky because the playing of "None but the Lonely Heart" on the radio made him cry like a baby. There is also the question of living versus money-making, of spirituality versus materialism. Besides the battle of Willie versus the machine, there is the argument of Krupp, the policeman, that "It's wonderful just to be able to move around and whistle a song if you feel like it," so "why is everybody trying to get a lot of money in a hurry . . . wanting to make some kind of a killing?" McCarthy, his friend, who is fighting for the rights of the inferior, says that a man with brawn and sensitivity must be a heel or a worker, so not wishing to be a heel, he has become a longshoreman; a combination of goodness and physical prowess finds difficulty in being accepted in the world. Joe, who is trying to understand life, admits that he has reservations about the good he is accomplishing because he has made his money by hurting little people. And the cynical Arab insists that there is no foundation all the way down the line, so he will go for a walk and look at the sky.

As the play progresses, each character at least partially resolves some of the perplexities which keep him isolated, and becomes a part of the happy honky-tonk, which Nick's good nature provides. As Joe explains, when someone asks what the Arab means by "What. What-not,"

> That means this side, that side, Inhale, exhale. What: birth. What-not: death. . . . That man, in his own way, is a prophet. He is one who, with the help of *beer,* is able to reach that state of deep understanding in which what and what-not, the reasonable and the unreasonable, are *one.* (Act II)

A sensitivity to the feelings of others, which Blick utterly lacks, gradually permeates each other character, so that music, dance, and the rhythm of talk, while Nick shines his glasses, blend into a harmonious unity,[5] into which all pour their individualities and receive in return a sense of communication with the whole human race. Loneliness is dissolved as Joe makes his final exit to the accompaniment of friendly waves, and all "smile to the infinite delight and mystery of life."

Although George Kelly has insisted that he writes by inspiration rather than by plan, *Craig's Wife* is a masterfully constructed drama picturing the unmitigated progress of a woman into complete loneliness. Kelly has been quoted as saying, "I haven't any method.

... I follow no particular formula. ... I don't know anything about play construction. ... If a thing is true it can be acted."[6] If *Craig's Wife* was written without any design, George Kelly may be called a natural-born playwright; for, besides the main character, which while possibly overdrawn is nevertheless consistent and carefully delineated, he has dramatized the departure from her of five characters in succession so cleverly that the artifice of it is not noticed. So naturally is the audience led along that its astonishment at finding Mrs. Craig left tragically alone at the end is almost as great as that of the victim. The course she has pursued has led to this result as inevitably as fate led the Greek tragic heroes to their downfall, but the pity and terror evoked is combined with a kind of unexpected satisfaction that the mills of the gods grind so surely.

The characters are few, the setting realistic, and the action unmelodramatic; yet this Pulitzer Prize winning play, for all its simplicity, powerfully sets forth the plight of the American woman whose loneliness is the result of her fanatical devotion to things material. In contrast to Saroyan's long statement of the theme of the complicated, many-charactered *The Time of Your Life,* George Kelly prefaces *Craig's Wife* with a line from the play, which is, like the play itself, direct and unadorned. It is Miss Austen's line which reads; "People who live to themselves, Harriet, are generally left to themselves." Harriet's unswerving conformity to the course of action which drives first one and then another from her until she is left desolate might seem to argue too rigid a characterization, but the pity which one feels for Craig's wife at the end of the play is partly for her unawareness of the goal toward which she has been heading. Consummate loneliness, when she realizes its impact, leaves her with eyes "wide and despairing," but since she has never envisioned its effect, she has taken no step to save herself, and it is logical that her every action has been one which alienated others from her.

As a matter of fact, it is Mr. Craig who experiences what might be called a recognition scene in which he discovers the truth about himself and Mrs. Craig and the whole situation. Since Harriet never approaches such understanding, she cannot be called a tragic heroine, according to the definition of Maxwell Anderson and others, who insist upon a scene of recognition in every tragic drama. Even at the end, Harriet seems not to comprehend the cause of the defection of all family and friends. Although *Craig's Wife*

165

may not qualify as great drama, it is gripping and meaningful for the twentieth century in its presentation of loneliness. George Kelly obviously intends a universal application of the theme of his play, for he inserts remarks like that of the housekeeper about Mrs. Craig, "There's plenty like her—I've worked for three of them; you'd think their houses were God Almighty." The well-dramatized presentation of Mrs. Craig's fate makes *Craig's Wife* an important serious American play.

Drama being the visual art that it is, the setting is always of significance; nowhere is this fact more evident than in *Craig's Wife*, in which the highly polished, richly brocaded frozen grandeur of her living room reflects the character of Harriet Craig, who when she first enters, "appears to have been dressed for this particular room," in a fashionable fawn-colored ensemble suit with brown accessories. Mrs. Craig's propensity for meticulousness is first made known by the housekeeper's remark that the mistress might leave her dying sister and come home from Albany at once, "if she gets an idea that there's a pin out of place around here." When Mrs. Craig does indeed return unexpectedly, she complains about her sister's thoughtlessness, for, as she admits, she hasn't much patience with sick people anyway, and resents having to leave the house for a whole week, to go "racing up to Albany." When Mr. Craig enters, she allows him a kiss, but when he tries to get more affectionate she straightens her hair, asks him not to break every bone in her body, and makes him remove first his hat and then his newspaper from the side table where he has laid them. She then straightens the doily on the table and asks him not to lean against the piano, for he might scratch it. Later she points out to him the chair in which he may sit. Obviously it is with ironical truth that the scene of the play is laid in "The living room in the home of Mrs. Walter Craig."

Mrs. Craig is not long in revealing that, to her, material possessions far outweigh human beings in value. She strongly advises her niece not to marry the poorly-paid college professor whom she loves, even though her dying mother had hoped the girl might be settled soon. Harriet Craig argues that since Ethel has money of her own, she is foolish to consider such a marriage at this time. "Why does a person need anybody, dear, if he has money enough to get along on?" Harriet asks her niece with naive sincerity. Later, with unbelievable frankness she explains to the bewildered Ethel,

166

I had no private fortune. . . . So the only road to independence for *me,* that *I* could see, was through the man I married. I know that must sound extremely materialistic to *you.* . . . but it isn't really; because it isn't financial independence that I speak of particularly. I knew that would come—as the result of *another* kind of independence; and that is the independence of authority—*over* the man I married. (Act I)

After questioning the honesty of getting control of a man because the destiny of a woman's home is much "safer" in her own hands, Ethel wonders what will happen when her Uncle Walter discovers the plan. He never will, Aunt Harriet is certain, because "Mr. Craig is inveterately idealistic." Mrs. Craig has undoubtedly sized up her husband correctly, for a practical man would not have allowed himself to be cut off from all his friends by his marriage and still believe himself happy in the love of his scheming wife. Another man would not have listened to her talk of preserving her home and her question, "Well, what else has a woman like me *but* her home?" without asking sooner, "Hasn't she her husband?" But as his aunt, Miss Austen, tells him, "You're blinded by a pretty face, son, as many another man has been blinded." So Harriet Craig has continued for the past two years to succeed in "fixing" things for herself. The play is the story of her attempt to gain a house to worship, and her success in that aim with its attendant shattering disillusionment and loneliness.

Of the five people who are a part of or guests of Mrs. Craig's household as the play opens, Miss Austen is the first to announce her intention of departing. She has been heroically living with the Craigs, although she prefers to travel, because of a promise made to Walter's mother that she would live with her nephew. Since both older women had feared Harriet's alienating influence upon people, Miss Austen was willing to agree to attempt to ameliorate its effect. When Harriet sarcastically complains about the visit of a neighbor to Miss Austen's room, remarking that she seems to have returned to find her house "a thoroughfare for the entire neighborhood," however, Miss Austen can stand it no more. To her, a good neighbor is a fine thing to have. She resents the fact that Harriet has gone to every extremity to exclude people from what she calls "the Temple of the Lord. This Holy of Holies." She charges Harriet with having married the house and taken Walter Craig along with it as a regrettable necessity. Before leaving, she tries to enlighten her nephew as to Harriet's character:

> . . . she's a supremely selfish woman; and with the arrogance of the selfish mind, she wants to exclude the whole world—because she cannot impose her narrow little order upon it. And these four walls are the symbol of that selfish exclusion. (Act I)

With Harriet's frank admittance of her aims and Miss Austen's accurate analysis of Harriet's character, it seems strange that Walter is not enlightened until some time later when Harriet proves willing to sacrifice him to the police to save her own name and house. But Walter is gravely distressed at his aunt's leaving, and her words give him a glimpse of the truth.

Mazie, the parlormaid, is the next to leave. Mrs. Craig berates the girl for placing a club-membership card behind a favorite ornament upon the mantelpiece and dismisses her without notice. Mazie departs with unexpected haste, however, leaving Mrs. Craig surprised and angered to find the girl gone immediately after breakfast in the morning.

Shortly after Mazie is dismissed, Mr. Craig demonstrates his newly-dawned revolt by deliberately picking up the same ornament and smashing it to bits on the bricks of the fireplace, and then lighting a cigarette and throwing the match upon the floor. Mrs. Craig has gone one step too far in calling him a "romantic fool." He intends to smash all her ornaments—the gods she had been worshipping before him—for his recognition of the position she assigns him in the household rankles within him. As the middle one of five to rebel against Harriet's tyranny, Mr. Craig stands at the apex of the triangle which represents the climax of the play. That his revolt includes a "self-recognition scene" adds to the dramatic interest of the tense situation during which Harriet is exposed. To her claim that he was obviously out of his mind to have smashed her ornament, he replies:

> No, I was particularly clear in my mind, strange to say. You made a remark here last night, Harriet, that completely illuminated me; and illuminated you. And suddenly I saw—for the first time— everything—just as one sees an entire landscape at midnight in a flash of lightning. But, unfortunately, the lightning struck my house—and knocked it down; . . . (Act III)

Walter Craig, like the tragic hero, accepts the revelation of his situation stoically. He cannot go on in the old way, but he con-

168

siders himself more fortunate than many men whose wives have never made "a sufficiently illuminating remark." He continues.

And that other remark—when you said there were ways of getting rid of people without driving them away from the house, I saw your entire plan of life, Harriet, and its relationship to me.

The rest of the night Mr. Craig spends in littering up the "sanctum sanctorum" with cigarette butts and ashes to prove himself master of his home, but decides by morning that the role is not possible for him, that since he can play only a romantic part, his course must be to leave his wife. As Mrs. Craig stands staring at her husband, Ethel comes downstairs with the announcement that she has not been able to sleep all night and wishes to leave as soon as possible. "But you can't go immediately, dear," commands Mrs. Craig, with a slightly worried tone, still, however, putting in a word of warning to Ethel about marrying a poor man. While they are conversing, the sound of Miss Austen's trunks being taken out leads Harriet to tell her niece the lie that they are being removed to be mended. When Ethel asks: "Aunt Harriet, is Uncle Walter *leaving* you?" She replies, "Why, what on earth ever put that into your head, Ethel? . . . I'm sure I haven't the faintest idea what you're talking about." To complete Harriet's alienation from her niece, Ethel's fiancé arrives to complain about Mrs. Craig's refusal to allow Ethel to answer his long-distance call.

Fifth and last to announce her intention of leaving is Mrs. Harold, the housekeeper, who, when Harriet reproaches her for leaving without notice, points out that Mazie was given no notice, and also that the head of the employment agency is surprised she has stayed so long, since seven housekeepers before stayed less than a month.

Mrs. Craig's aloneness comes upon her suddenly and with terrible impact as the drama builds to its climax. There is some time between the announcement by Miss Austen that she is leaving and her actual departure, and there is some time between her announcement and that by any other character that he has come to the parting of the ways with Mrs. Craig, but the interval becomes shorter, both between the announcement and the departure and also between the announcements by the other characters. Mrs. Craig refuses to admit to herself that what she plotted and desired has happened so rapidly. As an anticlimax, Harriet, now alone in the house, receives a telegram announcing her sister's death. Her burst of tears comes as a recognition of the severing of all ties to family or friends. In desolation she wanders through the room and back again as the curtain descends very, very slowly.

Harriet Craig's isolation at the close of the play is perhaps more bitter than that of almost any other character in American dramatic literature. O'Neill's Electra of *Mourning Becomes Electra* shuts herself into the family mansion as a kind of a masochistic expiation of the family sins; and Maxwell Anderson's Mary of *Mary of Scotland* prefers the cold stone walls of a solitary cell to abdication of her throne. Although there is deep pity aroused as the curtain falls on each of these three lonely women, the feeling that both Electra and Mary are fulfilling an inevitable destiny elevates them to the realm of tragedy; but in the case of Harriet, there were no forces except her own character which imposed the final isolation upon her. Everything was propitious for the creation of a happy home around her. Therefore, the pity is for what might have been. George Jean Nathan quotes W. H. Auden as saying: "Greek tragedy is the tragedy of necessity; that is, the feeling aroused in the spectator is 'what a pity it had to be this way'; Christian tragedy is the tragedy of possibility, 'what a pity it was this way when it might have been otherwise.'"[7] If the first two border on classic tragedy, the third, *Craig's Wife,* is obviously a Christian tragedy, wherein Harriet's "despairing" eyes view the hopelessness of her plight. They express no ameliorating sense of fulfilling an expected and certain destiny, but only blank terror that the way of life to which she is addicted has brought her to this end.

There is strange irony in the fact that in a sense Harriet has attained exactly what she worked for: her own house unsullied by foreign fingermarks. In another sense, she has failed. As she tells Ethel in the beginning, she married to be independent of everybody, including her husband.

> I married to be on my own—in every sense of the word. I haven't entirely achieved the condition yet—but I know it can be done. (Act I)

That it can't be done—that she could not secure into her own hands "the control of the man" upon whom the security and protection of her home is founded—aggravates her appalling recognition that her deserted house brings only misery. Her intention of keeping a husband for the support and the name, while disparaging his love, has brought her to grief. When Walter Craig finally cries out: "There was more actual home in one room of my mother's house than there'd be in all of this if we lived in it a thousand years," she is defeated and from that point on descends rapidly to a state of permanent loneliness, which, because it is of her own making, is the more bitter.

Paraphrasing "the great God Pan," O'Neill, with the same cynicism with which he later paraphrased "the bridegroom cometh" in *The Iceman Cometh,* titled his play lamenting the suppression of man's natively-good spiritual nature *The Great God Brown.* Since both of the two leading male characters represent aspects of mankind, Barrett Clark is correct in assuming the essential conflict to be not between a spiritual protagonist and a materialistic antagonist but between the combined man they represent and his desire to belong creatively to the world of nature. Clark calls the play "a dramatic paean to man's struggle to identify himself with nature."[8] The superficial material prosperity which Brown enjoys leaves him inwardly empty and envious of Dion Anthony's creative life force, whereas in Dion the destruction of the creative nature by the Christian, ascetic nature makes him Mephistophelian. When Brown dies after having lived in the borrowed mask of the dead Anthony, Cybel announces to the police that the name of the deceased is Man. "How d'yuh spell it?" is the closing line of the play, asked by the police captain, who is writing in a grimy notebook with a very short pencil. As *Strange Interlude* illustrates all the relationships which a woman can have to men, so *The Great God Brown* pictures the various influences which alienate man from the natural world, from which he grew and to which he should belong. Looked at in this light Brown and Anthony are one man; Margaret is the eternal girl-wife-mother; and Cybel, the sensual prostitute, is Mother Earth, to which all men in the end return.

On the literal level, as the play is constructed, however, Dion Anthony is the hero—according to Edwin Engel, "a recurrent type of O'Neill hero—shy, lonely, misunderstood,"[9]—and Brown is the antagonist, the materialist, who receives credit for Dion's creativity. Brown is no less lonely than Dion, but he is a much less sympathetic character. In the eyes of the world Brown is the successful architect-businessman, who sells the public what they want. The suppression of Dion's natural life force makes him frustrated and

Satanic, but he cannot be condemned for Philistinism, as can Brown. He refuses to debase his talents merely to make a living, and hence leaves his wife and three sons poverty-stricken. Their obvious admiration for Brown and for his success only alienates Dion from them the more, and makes it possible for him to belong only to the prostitute, Cybel, whose sympathetic warmth seems to soothe his distraught nerves and to weld together his disunited soul. O'Neill's concept of man is not a simple Jekyll and Hyde characterization. O'Neill is distressed that in America the artist is repressed, not only by materialism but by puritanical Christianity, and perhaps the latter is more disastrous than the former. The pressure of the materialism of the world, represented in Brown, is not more destructive of the Pan in Dion than is his own increasing asceticism. Therefore, although Brown appears to be the villain of the play, he has none of that kind of malevolence which, during prohibition, was represented in the Volstead agent; whereas this same type of bigotry in Dion destroys the Dionysian joy in drink and productivity, and turns that joy to wickedness.

Dion proclaims: "When Pan was forbidden the light and warmth of the sun he grew sensitive and self-conscious and proud and re-vengeful—and became Prince of Darkness." So, the mask which Dion Anthony wears becomes, as time goes on, more evil as his un-veiled face becomes more saint-like. Compared to Dion, Brown, the materialist, is uncomprehending and passive. It is perhaps part of the cynicism of the play that the title bears his name. Although the loneliness of Dion is a result of the conflict of the spiritual with the material in American society, the play does more than state such a thesis. Also included in the same drama is a commentary upon the false ideal of spirituality which formal religious convictions have engendered in American society. Besides, there is portrayed by use of masks a third feature of human nature—the dichotomy in man's psychic make-up as a result of the conflict of his human-animal heredity with his social environment.

The first-named and most explicit of the controversies which make Dion Anthony's loneliness bitter and extreme is that between his own inner sense of spiritual beauty and the world's materialism as represented in Brown. He exclaims of their partnership,

> I've been the brains! I've been the design! I've designed even his success. . . . And this cathedral is my masterpiece! It will make Brown the most eminent architect in this state of God's Country.

172

. . . But Mr. Brown, the Great Brown, has no faith! He couldn't design a cathedral without it looking like the First Supernatural Bank! He only believes in the immortality of the moral belly! (II, iii)

In spite of Dion's cynicism, he is a sympathetic character as he calls out to Margaret, "I'm lonely! I'm frightened! I'm going away! . . . I'm a lonely man!" because even with his beloved Margaret it is impossible for him to be understood without his mask. In fact, she is so terrified of his naked face just before his death that she loses consciousness. But nevertheless, according to the playwright's own statement, Brown is as lonely, and much more empty and thus due his share of sympathy. It is because of American society that Brown is inevitably a success, and his inner lack of creativity makes him much to be pitied. In a public letter O'Neill explained,

Brown is the visionless demi-god of our new materialistic myth— a Success—building his life of exterior things, inwardly empty and resourceless, an uncreative creature of superficial preordained social grooves, a by-product forced aside into slack waters by the deep main current of life-desire.[10]

In spite of Dion's haunting sense of not belonging to anyone, of not being understood, of being utterly alone, he assuredly had Margaret's love, and he created three sons, and he was kindly treated by Mother Nature, called Cybel—none of which joys Brown had known. In *Man's Search for Himself* Rollo May, explaining that the feelings of emptiness and loneliness in modern man result in his alienation from nature, says:

People who have lost the sense of their identity as themselves also tend to lose their sense of relatedness to nature. . . . when a person feels himself inwardly empty, as is the case with so many modern people, he experiences nature around him also as empty, dried up, dead.[11]

Thus, Brown, although he tries to buy Cybel's love, does not even know her well enough to recognize her always, and is never loved by her, as is Dion.

O'Neill illustrates the fact that the exigencies of living in modern society make difficult, and probably almost impossible, that growth of the spirit which involves a sense of belonging to God and to Nature. Therefore, although Dion battles for his soul's progress against the materialistic William Brown, he finally gives in and

173

accepts a position in Brown's firm, crying the while, ". . . that
Ancient Humorist [God] has given me weak eyes, so now I'll have
to foreswear my quest for Him and go in for the Omnipresent
Successful Serious One, the Great God Mr. Brown, instead!" With
even greater cynicism he scoffs, as Brown takes his arm, "Lead on,
Almighty Brown, thou Kindly Light!" But the tragedy of the
conflict between the spiritual and material in the play is that Brown
is himself lonely, and longing for Dion's aliveness so desperately
that upon Dion's death, Brown assumes Dion's mask in the hope
of acquiring his spiritual quality; but by this time the mask has
become, not that of Pan, but of the devil. When Brown, driven to
distraction by his assumption of the mask, flees from the police
to the house of Cybel, he receives peace and comfort from her
presence; but it is too late, for he is accused of being the murderer
of Brown. Cybel calls him Dion Brown. He says he is both the
murdered and the murderer of William Brown. His attempt to
"belong" by the assumption of another man's mask has failed. As
he dies, Cybel gently removes Dion's mask. "You can't take this to
bed with you," she says as if to a child. "You've got to go to sleep
alone." Gratefully snuggling against her ample bosom, Brown
murmurs, "The earth is warm." Dion Anthony William Brown,
called Man, belongs to nature in death. But in life neither could
his spiritual side succeed against exterior material forces, nor
could his material nature become spiritual.

The second conflict and cause of loneliness—the discord between
natural goodness and the Puritanical ideal of goodness—is represented by the ever-increasing contrast in Dion's real face and the
mask he wears. In the beginning, the mask and the face of the
seventeen-year-old Dion are described:

> The mask is a fixed forcing of his own face—dark, spiritual, poetic,
> passionately supersensitive, helplessly unprotected in its child-
> like, religious faith in life—into the expression of a mocking, reck-
> less, defiant, gayly scoffing and sensual young Pan. (Prologue)

The mask, which at this time serves as an armor to protect the
sensitive boy from the world, becomes, seven years later, "more
defiant and mocking, its sneer more forced and bitter, its Pan
quality becoming Mephistophelian," whereas his real face, although
more strained and tortured, has in some queer way become "more
selfless and ascetic, more fixed in its resolute withdrawal from life."
As the qualities of St. Anthony take over Dion's real self, and his

religious faith in life becomes an ascetic withdrawal, his mask is no longer a representation of his face, but a reaction to it. The Dionysus in it, having been repressed, has turned devilish. Another seven years later and Dion's face is that of an ascetic, a martyr, furrowed by pain and self-torture, and his mask, having lost all "of its Pan quality," has become diabolically cruel and ironical.

As Dion Anthony dies in Brown's office, he proclaims, "My last will and testament! I leave Dion Anthony to William Brown—for him to love and obey—for him to become me—then my Margaret will love me—my children will love me." Ironically enough, although it is as Mephistopheles that Dion collapses, his mask falls off, and it is as a martyred saint that he kisses Brown's feet and pleads to be taught a prayer. In a trance Brown repeats for him "Our Father who art in Heaven." Brown in stealing Dion's mask believes he is acquiring the creativity which he always envied in Dion, whereas in reality he only gets "that creative power made self-destructive by complete frustration." This mask thus tortures him to a frenzy, until he, too, dies, his tortured Christian soul pleading with Cybel to teach him a prayer. "Our Father Who Art!" exclaims Mother Earth exultantly. The complete inability of either Dion or Brown to know anything but the most excruciating sense of isolation while torn between Pan and asceticism is changed as each dies, maskless and praying with a sense of fervent belonging to the God, who, each now feels, exists. Man's attempt to repress his natural good instincts and to impose artificial, Puritanical laws upon himself results in the frustration which leaves his soul faithless and lonely. Only death in the Mother's soft arms can heal the soul forced by a false idea of goodness into devilish wickedness.

The third conflict in modern man, according to O'Neill, is that between the biological impulses of his human nature and the demands of his social environment. The masks of the characters exemplify the fear in man of revealing himself to others. There is perhaps but one moment, aside from that of his death, when Dion Anthony reconciles his innate vitality with the exigencies of existence in society. When he finds that Margaret loves him, he is transfigured by joy and says to his mask, "You are outgrown! I am beyond you!" He continues ecstatically:

I am strong! I can love! She protects me! Her arms are softly around me! . . . Now I am born—I—the I!— one and indivisible— I who love Margaret! (Prologue)

175

Finding himself unacceptable, even to his beloved, without his mask, he turns cynical, and from the cry, "Awake! Live! Dissolve into dew—into silence—into night—into earth—into space—into peace —into meaning—into joy—into God—into the Great God Pan!" he changes to the call of a divided soul, "Learn to pretend! Cover your nakedness! Learn to lie! Learn to keep step! Join the procession! Great Pan is dead! Be ashamed." The contemplation of union with Margaret, the eternal girl-woman, makes union with all nature and with God seem possible. To her, "Dion is the moon and I'm the sea. I want to feel the moon kissing the sea." But since their mutual urge is frustrated by her reticence and his fear, Dion's whole life becomes neurotic and disunified. "Why am I afraid of love, I who love love? . . . Why must I live in a cage like a criminal, defying and hating, I who love peace and friendship?" he asks himself, and also "Why was I born without a skin, O God, that I must wear armor in order to touch or to be touched?"[12] Dion must always be lonesome, for he is caught between the desire to share in love and friendship and the inability to break through the barrier of apprehensive fearfulness, fostered by his having been repulsed by lover, family, and friend.

At one point Dion tells Margaret, "We communicate in code— when neither has the other's key." Even with his wife he has no sense of belonging, for they do not understand each other. Margaret, toward the end of the play, speaking to Brown, masked as Dion, whom she mistakes for her husband, says, "I knew you were so lonely! I could always hear you calling to me that you were lost, but I couldn't find the path to you because I was lost, too!" Dion's alienation from his father was as devastating to his child's heart, as that from Margaret was to his man's. He claims that he knew his father only at the moment of his conception. Idolizing his mother, he resented his father's treatment of her with true Freudian fervor. "I was the sole doll our ogre, her husband, allowed her," he explains. As a child he was betrayed by his friend, Billy Brown, who at four years old came up from behind and hit Dion on the head and destroyed his picture in the sand. Cries the grown Dion, the memory still vivid, "I had loved and trusted him and suddenly the good God was disproved in his person." So Dion designed a mask and wore it ever after to protect himself from hurt by society. And so his intimations of immortality were early wiped out, and as he is about to die, he mockingly tells his be-

176

wildered wife, "Tomorrow I'll have moved on to the next hell."

Through all his estrangement from those with whom he would like to feel a sense of belonging, however, Dion preserves a verve for living and a creative spirit which is never fully repressed; and so his life, though lonely, has compensations. Brown inquires of Cybel, "What is it that makes Dion so attractive to women—. . . Is it his looks—or because he's such a violent sensualist—or because he poses as artistic and temperamental—or because he's so wild— or just what is it?" With simplicity, Cybel replies, "He's alive," and nothing more. The life force, which surges through Dion, keeps him going in spite of the frustrations which society imposes upon him. He, himself, expresses his jubilation in having at least been true to his human heredity.

> I've loved, lusted, won and lost, sang and wept! I've been life's lover. I've fulfilled her will and if she's through with me now it's only because I was too weak to dominate her in turn. It isn't enough to be her creature, you've got to create her or she requests you to destroy yourself. (II, i)

It is the thesis of Erich Fromm's recent book, *Man for Himself,* that there is no meaning to life except that which man gives his life by living productively and by unfolding his powers. If this thesis is sound, Dion's loneliness is not so bitter as that of the man whose emptiness is due to his lack of resources. The neuroses which divide him do not completely stifle his inner self. Dion dies, alienated from wife, sons, and society, but not from life itself.

The theme of the whole play, *The Great God Brown,* might be said to be the loneliness of man, whose union with nature is thwarted by materialism, Christian asceticism, and socially-caused conflicts in the psyche. Mother Earth is ostracized as a prostitute in a world in which artificial, instead of natural laws, prevail. It is impossible to belong to her without leaving the socially accepted channels of life. Erich Fromm explains man's loneliness as in part his inability to feel close to nature:

> Self-awareness, reason, and imagination have disrupted the "harmony" which characterizes animal existence. He [man] is part of nature, subject to her physical laws and unable to change them, yet he transcends the rest of nature. He is set apart while being a part; he is homeless, yet chained to the home he shares with all creatures.[13]

By the use of masks, and allegorically suggestive names, by personifications of intangibles like Mother Earth in Cybel, and by settings such as a moonlit dock in June for the love scene of the Prologue and the Epilogue, as well as by the wallpapered scene in Cybel's parlor, in which flowers and fruits tumble riotously over each other, O'Neill has written a play which contains mystical and mythical overtones of the life of man in the modern world. The main dramatic conflict between the spirituality of Dion and the materialism of Brown is enriched by the other related conflicts, and all are wrought into a unity by the characterization of the cynical, suffering hero, the pretentious antagonist, the loving, faithful wife, and the sensual mistress.

Not so optimistic a play as *The Time of Your Life, The Great God Brown* is not so pessimistic as *Craig's Wife*. Although Dion Anthony William Brown, called Man, never comes into the feeling of close relationship with others that Saroyan's characters seem to experience, his loneliness is not so extreme as Harriet Craig's, and his battle through life has meant life is worth living, whereas her life has ended in utter fruitlessness. George Kelly's completely realistic portrayal of a woman's progress into isolation because of her absorption in worldly triviality contrasts with both Saroyan's and O'Neill's plays, which depart from realism and attempt by experimental and suggestive staging and writing to exemplify the aspirations which save man from an unbearable loneliness even in the face of serious conflicts between external forces and his own spiritual nature.

7

THE LONELY HERO

The hero is not fed on sweets,
Daily his own heart he eats.

—"Heroism," Ralph Waldo Emerson

In mid-twentieth century, when the belief is widely held that all acts are psychologically explainable and hence forgivable, it is frequently asked whether drama of high seriousness is possible, and it is inquired, as well, whether the apotheosis of the common man makes heroism in life or in art unlikely. If man is viewed as a biological specimen, he cannot be held responsible for his actions, and if every individual is the equal of every other one, no hero can emerge above the throng. Is the common man too common even to conceive of heroic deeds? Has mediocrity become, not only a virtue, but an aim? Arthur Schlesinger, Jr., decrying the decline of greatness, prophesies: "If our society has lost its wish for heroes and the ability to produce them, it may well turn out to have lost everything else as well."[1] Francis Henry Taylor in an article, "Modern Art and the Dignity of Man,"[2] insists that so-called "modern" artists should not be condemned for meaninglessness, because they are not the cause, but merely the effect of "an age which does not believe in the dignity of man and does not seek, therefore, to assign him his place and prescribe for him his purpose in the developing scheme of a purposeful universe." According to Mr. Taylor, "If he [the artist] has ceased to be a spiritual leader, it is only because he has no Gospel to impart."

In an editorial in *Life*, entitled "Untragic America," the same idea is expressed in regard to modern American drama.

He [modern man] cannot esteem himself highly enough for high tragedy. He can appraise, analyze, respect and belittle himself, but he cannot regard himself with awe.

179

Without awe tragedy cannot achieve its greatest impact. And it may be that our belief that all men are equal, our refusal to admit the very concept of aristocracy, debars us from ever feeling the awe that the Athenians felt toward Oedipus or the Elizabethan groundlings toward Lear.[3]

Americans, nevertheless, have their heroes, and like other aspects of American life, those heroes have been portrayed in serious plays of merit. Like traditional, mythical dramatic heroes, they partake of a form of loneliness inextricably connected with the leaders of men. The very fact of deification which sets the hero apart from other men is a cause of his loneliness. In a sense the hero should not be lonely, for he must have within himself the spiritual qualities of self-sustainment which prevent his isolation from being psychologically devastating. He has, however, a deep, suffering self-recognition of apartness, which he accepts as inevitable. Thomas Wolfe insists that, although the total import of Christ's teaching is that "the life of loneliness could be destroyed by the life of love," still, "Christ himself was as lonely as any man who ever lived."[4] Christ's loneliness stemmed, according to an editorial in the *Outlook,*[5] from the fact that he had reached a perfect knowledge of himself and saw other men as ignorant of themselves. Although the tragic hero, pagan or Christian, is impelled by the search for something greater than himself to which he can belong, his feeling of loneliness in the struggle is acute, for it is impossible that he be accompanied by friends. His sense of responsibility to himself and to humanity isolates him from dependence upon others. His loneliness, therefore, although of a different cause is not different in kind from that of the common man who fails to enter into companionable relationships because of hereditary or environmental factors, and his loneliness is as painful as that of those who have less spiritually sustaining faith within them.

Three American plays which set forth characterizations of the modern hero are *Men in White* (1933) by Sidney Kingsley, *Abe Lincoln in Illinois* (1938) by Robert E. Sherwood, and *Command Decision* (1947) by William Wister Haines. As is obvious from the titles, *Abe Lincoln in Illinois* is a dramatization of America's favorite mythical hero,[6] which corresponds to the dramatizations of *Oedipus, Agamemnon,* or *Antigone,* whereas *Men in White* and *Command Decision* make heroes of the doctor and the soldier in American life without reference to any individual who has become a representative idol in either profession. These latter two dramas are of the serious type which has caused modern critics to question whether or not the Aristotelian concept of the tragic hero as a great man should be revised. Even in the case of *Abe Lincoln in Illinois* it is of course a nobility of spirit rather than an inherited aristocracy which can be claimed for the hero. In spite of other differences as well, there are many similarities in the dramatization of the ancient and modern hero, to both of whom the adjective "lonely" applies.

Abe Lincoln in Robert Sherwood's play is driven by an inexorable fate as surely as is Oedipus. The gods will not be placated until Abe has fulfilled the function in life provided for him. With uncharacteristic callousness Abe, on the very day which was to have been their wedding day, refuses to marry Miss Mary Todd, because, as he says, "I don't want to be ridden and driven, upward and onward through life, with her whip lashing me, and her spurs digging into me!" But Billy Herndon, like a choric voice interpreting the speaker's motivation, claims

> You're only using her as a living sacrifice, offering her up, in the hope that you will thus gain forgiveness of the gods for your failure to do your own great duty! (II, vi)

Later, after the self-recognition scene, in which the hero comes to an understanding of his true destiny, Abe appeals to Mary to be his wife with the stoical avowal:

> The way I must go is the way you have always wanted me to go.
> Mary: And you will promise that never again will you falter, or turn to run away?
> Abe: I promise, Mary—if you will have me—I shall devote myself for the rest of my days to trying—to do what is right—as God gives me power to see what is right. (II, viii)

As the curtain falls upon Mary's protestations of love, Abe, holding her in a loose embrace, stares down at the carpet. The American predilection for the happy love affair has never altered the view that Abe's relationship with Mary was not a happy one for him personally. As Oedipus destroys himself to save his country, so Abe Lincoln renounces personal happiness to become the savior and uniter of his country.

If Abe seemed a lonely figure before his acceptance of his duty, how much more so he appears from that time on. Only in his love for Ann Rutledge had Abe ever found any true sense of belonging. Of her, he says:

> I used to think it was better to be alone. I was always most contented when I was alone. . . . And then—when I saw her, I knew there could be beauty and purity in people—. . . When I took hold of her hand and held it, all fear, all doubt went out of me. I believed in God. (I, iii)

After her death, he cries with frenzy, "I've got to die and be with her again, or I'll go crazy! I can't bear to think of her out there alone." With the death of the only person in the world who had ever given Abe a sense of happy relationship to others came an accentuation of what Nancy Green calls his hypochondria—"He listens too much to the whispers, that he heard in the forest where he grew up," she says. Even so, the loss of the one woman he had ever loved resulted perhaps in not such a lonely situation as that of attaching himself by marriage to one he did not love, especially since the admitted purpose of the attachment is to goad him on to greatness. Thus isolating himself from the few close friends he has had, Abe receives in return no affectionate communion with a wife. When, on the eve of his election to the presidency, he curses Mary—"Damn you! Damn you for taking every opportunity you can to make a public fool of me"—he gives vent to long years of resentment, not so much of her, as of the fate which has condemned him to greatness as well as to loneliness.

Mary is in the anomalous position in the play, as in the myth, of being honored by a grateful country for prodding Abe into the presidency while being disliked for her lack of understanding and inability to inspire him with love. Like Jonah, who tries to escape the duty God imposes upon him, Abe refuses at first to submit to Mary's whip; but, like Jonah, after he comes to a recognition of his fated course, Abe accepts with fortitude the obvious means provided to carry it through. Mary Todd thus becomes not so much a character in her own right as the *deus ex machina* of the drama. Since it is impossible for the hero to combine love with duty, Abe Lincoln could not have attained greatness if Ann Rutledge had lived to become his wife. It has been said that if a character like Abe Lincoln had not lived, it would have been necessary for Americans to create him.[7] Likewise, if Mary Todd had been beloved by Abe, it would have been necessary to alter the facts to make her, instead, his goad. The hero's is a lonely road. Mary Todd's function is not to alleviate, but to enhance, Abe's isolation. She accomplishes this purpose perfectly because her own selfish ambition is the motivation which makes her drive her husband to success. Abe recognizes that Mary's goading is not for the high, idealistic motive of his friend, Billy Herndon, that he save the Union and keep it free. But Billy does not succeed; therefore Abe is in the position of attaining greatness to satisfy a selfish woman's ambition. Before the entrance of Mary Todd, Abe says of the Civil War, "There seems to be one going on inside me all the time." How fierce the civil war within after Abe submits to Mary!

Robert Sherwood has subtitled his story of Abe Lincoln, "A Play in Twelve Scenes," apparently wishing to indicate that, in spite of the divisions into three acts, the continuity of the hero's life flows unbroken by dramatic technique. The playwright is, however, in agreement with the dictate of Maxwell Anderson[8] in making the recognition scene the climax of his play, with the preceding scenes all building toward this moment, and the following ones all dramatizing the hero's fulfillment of purpose. The scene in which Abe perceives his obligation to his people takes place on a moonlit night on the prairie near New Salem. Around a campfire, Abe is talking with an old friend, Seth Gale, who with his wife and sick child is traveling westward by covered wagon. The scene is as unpretentious as the hero. Seth's fears that the new country to which they are going will become slave country or else will secede from the Union are quieted by Abe's reassurance:

> You mustn't be scared, Seth. I know I'm a poor one to be telling you that—because I've been scared all my life. But—seeing you now—and thinking of the big thing you've set out to do—well, it's made me feel pretty small. It's made me feel that I've got to do something, too, to keep you and your kind in the United States of America. (II, vii)

After this Abe says a prayer for the sick child, and the short scene ends; but in the few moments of giving comfort to an old friend, Abe gets over being scared himself and sets out to devote his life to his country.

There might seem to be a certain grim humor in the fact that in the next scene, a few days later, Abe is seeking admittance to the parlor of Miss Mary Todd. But Americans do not laugh. Although Abe desires Mary no more than before, he has reached that resolve within himself which will enable him to stand alone, to succeed in his mission in life, and to accept his isolation as inevitable. As Fishwick explains,

The hero must turn within himself for the support and solution he needs. Then, like the boonbringer, he can return to the outside world and aid those in it. The hero is a man first of self-achieved submission and then of action. His path is like that represented in the rites of passage; separation, initiation, and return. This cycle is exemplified in the careers of Prometheus, Buddha, and Aeneas, as well as of many who have followed them.[9]

Abe's failure, up to the time of the scene on the prairie, ends with his initiation there into the true meaning of his life; and from that time on his path is a straightforward one of service to his fellow man. He is willing to sacrifice himself for the idea he envisions as surely as is Antigone for her brother's honor.

Lincoln's life follows most closely of all, perhaps, that of Christ, with its humble beginning, unpretentious rise, and martyr's death. Sherwood's drama covers only the middle span of Lincoln's life, but the audience's knowledge of his beginning and tragic conclusion adds weight to the significance of the action portrayed. Lincoln's "If I live," when asked if he would continue his law practice after serving as President, indicates his own premonition of his death; and his expression of his real sense of relief if he should fail to be elected President likewise arouses the sympathy of the audience for the beloved hero whose loneliness in his fated path is recognized. The whole drama, as well as the Lincoln myth, would seem to refute the opinion of Dixon Wecter that, to Americans, "the hero must be a man of good will and also a good neighbor, preferably something of a joiner. Of the solitudes and lonely isolations of a great man like Lincoln the public has little conception."[10] Of Lincoln's lonely isolations the public would seem to have a conception, and for them, a sympathy. Lincoln's fear that in a city as big as New Orleans the people would not be friendly causes his friend, Mentor, to accuse him of misanthropy, explaining to Abe that a misanthrope distrusts men and avoids their society. Lincoln himself claims that he likes people one by one, but not in crowds; but it is only Ann Rutledge who makes him feel closely akin to humanity. Nancy Green's exclamation, "Poor, lonely soul," as Lincoln grieves for Ann's death, expresses the reaction of the audience to this hero. Loneliness is intrinsic to the character of

184

their idol. In E. P. Conkle's *Prologue to Glory* (1938) Lincoln, after the death of Ann Rutledge, walks out alone into the twilight and on toward Springfield as the final curtain falls. In Sherwood's play which covers a later period of Lincoln's life, as well as some of the same period, Lincoln still walks alone.

As a contrast to his treatment of America's hero, in *The Petrified Forest*, written three years earlier, Robert Sherwood does some satirizing of American hero worship within an exciting melodramatic plot. No less lonely than Lincoln, Alan Squier is the opposite to the President-hero in that he has no ideals to live by, no thought of service to his fellow man, and nothing but disillusionment about life in general. He expects to walk straight west to the Pacific Ocean and drown there. An intellectual, literally in the desert wasteland of Arizona, he is enchanted by a young girl who, while helping her family run an isolated filling station, hopes to travel to France where her mother lives. When the place is held up by the killer, Duke Mantee (a caricature of America's shooting heroes like Billy the Kid), Alan, having undergone the hero's rites of initiation through his spiritual transformation in loving Gabriele, and also being slightly drunk, persuades Duke Mantee to kill him, so that his insurance money may send the girl to Paris. Fittingly enough, he will be buried like a hero, in the petrified forest. Had Sherwood's play about Abe Lincoln been as dramatically effective as this semisatirical portrayal of the lonely hero, it might well be the mainstay of little theaters through the years; episodic and constricted perhaps by the use of excerpts from Lincoln's own speeches, it does not attain dramatic heights. Thus far, however, no better play than Sherwood's has been written about Lincoln, but it is likely that in time a greater will be and that in it Lincoln's loneliness will be intrinsic to his character.

The mythically heroic character of the doctor is emphasized by Sidney Kingsley's inclusion of excerpts from the Hippocratic oath as the frontispiece of his Pulitzer Prize winning *Men in White*. Beginning with "I swear by Apollo, the physician, and Aesculapius, and Hygeia, and Panacea, and all the gods and all the goddesses," and ending with "if I shall fulfill this oath . . . may I be honored of all men for all time," the antiquity and solemnity of the oath give a stature above that of common men to him who takes and keeps it. He who takes the oath also assumes a burden of loneliness in his dedication to his profession. He swears, ". . . hallowed will I keep my life and mine art." Kingsley's plot involves the struggle of George Ferguson, young intern at St. George's hospital, to choose between a life of economic, social, married happiness and one of consecration to medicine.

The opening scene of the play, all of which takes place in some part of the hospital, is in the library of St. George's, where, niched high in the wall, presides a bust of Hippocrates. The dominating figure of the scene is the quiet, dignified Dr. Hochberg, chief surgeon of the hospital, who represents overtly the forces pulling George Ferguson toward dedication to medicine, as Laura Hudson, a wealthy society girl to whom he is engaged, represents the forces which impel him toward an easier way of life. Throughout the play George attempts to avoid the loneliness inevitable to the life of a great surgeon by making plans to marry Laura and to take her to Vienna with him when he goes to study there. But it becomes more and more certain that surgery is a demanding mistress and will require all the talents and energy of the capable young doctor for many years to come and perhaps for all of his life. When he must finally make a choice between the woman he loves and the profession represented by Hochberg, he decides in favor of the latter. Alone at the end, with tears of emotion running down his cheeks at Laura's departure, he answers the phone with professional assurance and explains to a hysterical mother that her son will live.

Although George is very much in love with Laura and she with him, his work separates them constantly. The playwright logically provides for Laura's presence at the hospital in visits to her sick father. It follows logically as well that the most touching love scenes are interrupted by calls on the loudspeaker for Dr. Ferguson. If it were not for the meaningful theme and for the drama inherent in the activity of a modern hospital, the situations might seem contrived and the explicit action indicating George's inner struggle too obvious. As it is written, however, audience sympathy for both the lovers is mixed with admiration for the doctor's final resolution to dedicate his life to the work of saving human lives.

George's loneliness reaches a peak, when, after he has had to break a second date with Laura because of an emergency at the hospital, she refuses to go out with him later in the evening. He is sitting alone in his hospital room when Barbara, a young student nurse, comes to ask him for some notes for an examination she is

186

to take the next day. There is a bond of sympathy between them, for George that afternoon has saved the life of a child whom Barbara has been nursing. With deep admiration for him and understanding of his mood, she commiserates with him.

Barbara: You work very hard, don't you?

Ferguson: Work? Sure! What else is there but *work*—and *work!*

Barbara: You know, when I thought Dots was going to die . . . I got the feeling like I . . . I . . . God! . . . I can't put it into words!

Ferguson: I know. I know that feeling. . . .

Barbara: You, too?

Ferguson: Me, too? (*Clutching his throat.*) Up to here, Barbara! Right now! Christ! I'm tired of work, and blood and sweat and pain! And the chap in 341 is dead! And Levine's wife is going to die . . . and one begins to wonder where in Heaven's God, and what in Hell's it all about, and why on earth does everything make any difference.

Barbara: Yes, that's the feeling . . . and you get so lonely . . . and you feel . . . tomorrow it's me. . . . (I, iv)

Through pure loneliness they turn to each other that night, with tragic death resulting three months later for Barbara and an ineradicable sense of guilt for George. As he later explains to Laura,

I wanted you more than anything else in the world that night Laura. But we'd quarrelled and—you wouldn't even go out with me. . . . I didn't want to give up Hocky [Dr. Hochberg] . . . and I didn't want to give you up . . . and I was fighting you . . . and. . . . (III, i)

Three months later George is on the point of accepting a well-paid position on the staff (which he is to receive because of a large financial gift to the hospital from Laura's father) and of giving up any further study of surgery.

At this point in the play, he, like many another hero, is forced to reverse his plan of action. Although he had not seen Barbara Dennin since the night they spent together, when he hears that she is critically ill from a septic abortion, he comes gradually, with shocked chagrin, to acceptance of the blame for her condition. With the inevitability of fate, the operation which Dr. Hochberg has prepared Laura to witness in order to increase her understanding of medicine is the hysterectomy upon Barbara. After the operation, George, having persuaded himself that only by marrying Barbara

187

can he live with his conscience, makes plans to go into practice somewhere so he can support a wife. Dr. Hochberg has no success in trying to persuade him that there is no happiness that way for either George or the young nurse. And Laura herself, who comes to some understanding of how it all happened, is unable to persuade George that marriage with Barbara will bring him disaster. It appears that both Hochberg and Laura have failed. George will devote his life neither to medicine nor to a full, happy existence, but instead will throw away his chance of success in medicine and in life by setting up a meagre practice and living with a woman he does not love.

Barbara's sudden death releases George from this necessity, but he thinks only of the fact that she was pleading to live, and that Dr. Hochberg, with all his experience, could not save her. Feeling abandoned and helpless, he cries out against the failure of medicine. But the ordeal through which he has just passed has purged him of selfishness and worldliness, so that he is receptive to Dr. Hochberg's reply:

> . . . you're right. We are groping. We are guessing. But, at least our guesses today are closer than they were twenty years ago. . . . there's so much to be done. . . . that one life is never long enough. . . . It's not easy for any of us. But in the end our reward is something richer than simply living. Maybe it's a kind of success that world out there can't measure . . . maybe it's a kind of glory, George. (III, i)

In the last moments of the play, therefore, the hero comes to the unmistakable revelation of his course. To Laura's plea that they leave the hospital and go somewhere to talk, he answers, "No, Laura. This is where I belong!" She hurries out as the hospital loud-speaker repeats a call for Dr. Ferguson, and he moves to the phone to answer.

No historical doctor is the inspiration for Kingsley's hero. Minor characters illustrate varied degrees of successful attainment in medicine in order to emphasize the nature of the sacrifice involved in a life of dedication. For example, Dr. Levine, who has been disowned by his wealthy Jewish mother for marrying a gentile, has struggled and starved with a tenement practice, only to discover that his wife has tuberculosis. Smiling sadly, he asks George, "Burnt offerings! Jehovah and Aesculapius! They both demand their human sacrifice. . . . Medicine! Why do we kill ourselves for

188

it?" And it is not strange that Kingsley's characterization of the doctor-hero revolves about the fictitious George Ferguson, for Dixon Wecter is stating the obvious in his comment: "No physician, for his work in medicine, has ever become a first-class hero to the American people. Walter Reed and William Gorgas as victors over yellow fever, . . . have received less personal adoration than Lindbergh or Jack Dempsey or Babe Ruth."[11] Even in Sidney Howard and Paul de Kruif's *Yellow Jack,* Dr. Gorgas and Dr. Reed do not appear more heroic than the men who volunteer to be subjects for the experiments. In *Men in White,* however, the course of George Ferguson is that of the typical, mythical hero, with its final disclosure that deification is the only compensation for the loneliness involved.

Like a choric voice the passage of nurses, doctors, and patients through the halls and rooms of the hospital adds to the emotional effect of the play by its steady flow and intrinsic tension. As the drama reaches its climax in the operating-room scene with the discovery by Laura that George has been the cause of Barbara's condition, the rhythmic beat of the surgical process is like a mechanical dance composition, with doctors and nurses acting silently, swiftly, and proficiently in ministering to the patient. The necessary conversations are very brief, the drama of the scene being conveyed mainly by pantomime. Barbara's few words to George, as she is wheeled to the operating table, his reassurance, Laura's frantic and impulsive seizure of George's arm as she realizes the truth, his ripping off the gown she has contaminated and calling for another—all these brief actions fit into the background of rhythmic preparations for the operation. Laura's sobbing exit is noticed only by two nurses, who assume she is a beginning "med-student." As the curtain falls, the doctors at the operating table are surrounded by the sterile nurses, and these by unsterile nurses, and all are bathed in the 'fierce, merciless, white brilliance" of the operating light. Dr. Hochberg, who had hoped to convince Laura of the importance of George's work, has, as chance would have it, convinced her that she has been a fool to love him; but the whole regulated series of motions of the hospital staff, with their culmination in the final tableau in which the doctor is enthroned as the hero-savior, exclude her and isolate George Ferguson, Doctor of Medicine, from the rest of humanity as surely as the bright light excludes in shadow the rest of the stage.

To that man who is suited for medicine there is no true happiness elsewhere. As George admits to Dr. Hochberg,

> I love Laura so much. She's so full of life and fun, and all the things I've missed for so many years. . . . I kidded myself that I could have that, and still go on. And last night, I realized I kidded myself out of the most important thing that ever happened to me, a chance to work with you. . . . (III, i)

When tragedy enters his life, George is brought to the realization that nothing can mean so much to him as trying to save lives, even though he must shut himself away from what the ordinary man considers a satisfying kind of existence. Laura pleads with him not to become so devoted to one cause that he is a caricature of a man, flat, colorless, with no outside interests. She wants their lives together to be rich and full. Obviously the hero is not intended to lead a rich, full life, but to devote himself to what he conceives to be his duty; and so it is with George. Thus, although he suffers from the recognition of the loneliness to come, he receives compensation for his heroic abnegation of happiness in service to mankind.

Of all the heroes of the nations, undoubtedly none has been more revered and honored than the military. So it was that Washington, during the Second Continental Congress, by virtue of his uniform, wielded an influence far greater than that with which his few words endowed him; so it was that he became commander-in-chief of the army of the colonies and later first President of the Republic. In the twentieth century, two world wars furnished American military heroes the opportunity of becoming legendary. Although the first world war produced its share of temporary heroes, the reaction of the public and of playwrights to the war to end wars was, during the twenties and through much of the thirties, that it had been a degrading farce. Maxwell Anderson and Laurence Stallings ended *What Price Glory* (1924) with the words, "What a lot of goddam fools it takes to make a war." Robert Sherwood's *Idiot's Delight* (1936) expressed much the same philosophy. And Paul Green's *Johnny Johnson* (1936) portrayed a simple man of good will who is considered insane in the modern world of warmongering. At the end of the thirties and in the early forties, however, a large number of anti-Nazi heroes emerged in the work of prominent American playwrights,[12] and as America herself became involved in the war, several war front plays made heroes of the common

190

fighting man. Maxwell Anderson covered three battle fronts of the world: the Spanish civil war in *Key Largo* (1939), the Pacific war in *The Eve of St. Mark* (1942), and the African campaign in *Storm Operation* (1944). Robert Sherwood's *Rugged Path* (1945), like the first two of Anderson's dramas, is involved with a story on the home front as well as on the battle front. *Mister Roberts* (1948) by Thomas Heggen and Joshua Logan created a naval hero whose modesty and bravery have endeared him to Americans on the stage and on film.

No war play, however, has so well dramatized the loneliness of the high-ranking officer, whose word means life or death to thousands, as has William Wister Haines' *Command Decision*. Brigadier General K. C. Dennis is no less a democratic hero than are the dozen or so common-man heroes of the other important American war plays; for, although he does not have to die like the common soldier, he must live through the shattering experience of sending others to death, and unlike the aristocratic or dictatorial commander, he feels the worth of each individual life. He is therefore in the position of sacrificing that which he holds most sacred, and as it happens, in such fantastically large numbers that the high command has to remove him from his post. Unified as to place and time—the entire play is set in the office of Brigadier General K. C. Dennis at the headquarters of the Fifth American Bombardment Division in England during twenty-eight hours' interval—the drama also has a classical unity of action: Dennis strives unremittingly to effect the destruction of three targets.

General Dennis has become convinced by incontrovertible evidence that three German plants which are beginning to make jet fighters must be destroyed if the allied air forces are to remain aloft and if the ground forces are to succeed in advancing on the continent. Having himself tested, against his doctor's advice, a German jet fighter in which a Czechoslovakian engineer has escaped to England, General Dennis knows that it surpasses allied fighters in many ways and can, as he says, "run us out of Europe in sixty days." At the time the play opens *in medias res* the bombers are nearly due to return from a mission to the second of the jet-manufacturing cities. The first one has been destroyed the day before to the accompaniment of the loss of almost one fourth of the planes and men whom General Dennis has ordered to make the run. Expected cloudy weather necessitates bombing the three cities on consecutive nights. Having waited a month for the weather to clear, Dennis is determined in spite of the losses, of the complaints from higher officers, of protestations from the press and visiting congressmen, to execute his plan. Through the play his loneliness increases as he alienates himself from men, officers, and dignitaries; and when his friend, Squadron Leader Ted Martin, is killed on the second try to bomb objective number two, Dennis is left desolate.

Although Martin had insisted upon going, to make up for his mistake in bombing the wrong target the night before, and had urged Dennis to complete his plan in the face of opposition from all quarters, claiming, "You're the only Commander in this hemisphere with guts enough to see it through," nevertheless Dennis takes full responsibility for his friend's death. Alone and grieving, he remarks bitterly that he will tell Helen, Martin's wife, "and then," he adds, "I'll tell Claude Minter's wife. . . . tell her I sent Claude to Fendelhorst tomorrow." With his announcement that he intends to bomb the third objective on the next night, Dennis is relieved of his command. Therefore he has sacrificed hundreds of men in vain, for with one plant still working, the Germans can attain air supremacy. No feeling of consolation that he has only done his duty sustains Dennis. His bitter words to the new general in command convey a sense of his isolation. Claiming that he has done one thing for the new General Garnett, he adds, "I've killed Ted. You won't have to do that." And in response to General Garnett's sympathetic remark, "You've hated this, every minute of it, haven't you?" Dennis answers cynically, "I got paid for it."

The sarcastic juxtaposition of the two ideas—the wracking torment of making the decision, on one's own, which sends men to die, and the monetary remuneration—indicate how isolated Dennis is from sympathetic human contact. And General Garnett's appeal that Dennis stay and help him make the first decision as to whether to give the men a "milk run" that night or to go ahead and bomb Fendelhorst indicates that the new commander is already feeling the isolation which surrounds whoever holds the position. "If you'll help me just this once. . . ," he pleads. "When *you* first came over here you had Ted and Joe Lucas to talk to." Joe Lucas, Dennis' predecessor, never talked, insists Dennis, but one day he counted in the planes, added up the losses, took a hotel room, and shot himself. How he could have done it, Dennis explains:

Wait till you've counted in a really bad one that you've ordered

192

yourself. Wait till you start noticing the faces of those kids on the trucks from the replacement centers—the new ones, coming in. Wait till you start waking up in the afternoon—and wondering what it is that makes *those* faces look so much like the faces of the ones you're already killing, that same afternoon. Then go out and puke up your powdered eggs and then take veronal to get back to sleep—and then have them wake you up and give you benzedrine to keep you awake while you count in your stragglers and plan your next mission. . . . I've wanted to do the same thing, five or six times when I've signed those field orders—and so will you! (Act III)

General Garnett is aghast, having understood that Joe Lucas was killed in an air raid; nor is he comforted by Dennis' assurance that he too has thought of suicide more than once, and has been deterred only by the idea that it would help only *one* guy. From the moment he has assumed the command he coveted, Garnett has been made aware of the overwhelming loneliness of the responsibility involved in it. Part of the art of Haines' drama is that the experience of Casey Dennis as commander is reinforced and highlighted by the revelation, at the end, of the fate of his predecessor and by the dramatization of the suffering of his successor. With a great deal of success the playwright has characterized the loneliness of the individual hero, while making the point that the condition of loneliness is inseparable from the position of commander. In the typical classically unified play the main concern is for the fate of the individual hero. So it is in *Command Decision,* but since the aristocracy portrayed is not one of heredity, but of ability, it is possible to indicate that the forces which make isolation of the hero inevitable also act on whoever holds the post of command. There is in this concept perhaps a very modernized version of the Greek idea of fate.

It is highly ironic, in view of the suffering which the command imposes on its holder, that General Garnett's question as to how the men will take to a new face is answered by his aide, "All generals look alike to them, sir." The men hope only that a new general will not send them on hazardous missions. It is as illogical to them as it is to the small boy whose father says, "This hurts me more than it does you," that the master of their fate endures any pain. And perhaps there is a democratically modified version of the hero in the anonymity with which the men view the commander,

193

for Homer implies that during the Trojan war there was no difficulty in distinguishing Ajax from Agamemnon, or either from Achilles, but if, as Edith Hamilton claims,[13] the test of the true hero, and of tragedy itself, is whether or not the hero is capable of suffering, then *Command Decision* meets the test of tragedy and Casey Dennis the test of the tragic hero. There is perhaps, as well, a democratically modified concept of the loneliness of the hero in Casey Dennis in that part of the torture of holding the post of command lies in the necessity of making every decision entirely upon his own. In a community socially and politically organized to make joint decisions and to carry them out through a government which represents everyone, there is a peculiar loneliness in having to make decisions of moment without aid or advice from others. In the Greek or Shakespearean hero, who has in a sense inherited the right to make such decisions, loneliness is part of his fate, his apotheosis being the reward for his isolation.

The democratic hero in command, however, is less apt to be apotheosized than the common-man hero. In *Command Decision* the priggish pilot, whom the Air Corps has exploited and the press glorified for his moderately successful exploits, refuses to make the highly dangerous run far into Germany to bomb the jet plane factories. Having cleverly named his bomber the Urgent Virgin and being a personable young man, the amount of publicity which he has gained for the Air Force has made him overvalue his own importance to such an extent that he believes he can defy orders with impunity. The playwright implements the theme of the heroism of the commander by this contrasting minor theme of the conceited cowardice of the publicly honored hero. This minor theme is also clearly woven into the plot as well, for since the pompous Congressman from the home state of the defecting pilot, Jenks, is arriving to inspect the post, and since this same Congressman may be able to influence the Air Force appropriation, General Dennis' superior orders him to stop the court martial proceedings against Jenks. To climax the irony of the false-hero theme, the Congressman manages to maneuver himself into a publicity shot with Jenks being decorated for bravery. Still more ironical, the concession which Dennis gets in return for giving in on the Jenks affair is the dreaded privilege of ordering a second night's run at the target which was missed the night before. And furthermore this privilege is granted with the warning that he will probably have to be "jettisoned" if he makes use of it. And *so* he is.

Shades of Billy Mitchell and the loneliness of his fight for air power hover over Casey Dennis, who holds the same theory that battles cannot be won without aerial supremacy. Casey also feels in the present instance that without the destruction of the three targets, the Germans will have aerial supremacy. In his driving aim to carry out his plan—the aim which motivates all the main actions of the play—Casey Dennis' loneliness is increased by several factors, both physical and mental. Pure exhaustion overcomes him to such an extent that when no one is in his office he slumps over his desk, face down and almost sleeps. Since he has not had his clothes off for three days, it is no wonder that the visiting General Garnett finds him "so strung up—so tense." Besides being too physically fatigued to be in communication with those around him, he is emotionally involved in the life of Ted Martin, his squadron leader; for he was best man at Ted's wedding, and Ted's wife in the States is momentarily expecting the arrival of their first baby. Dennis' outward placidity during the visit of the Generals Garnett and Kane falls from him with their departure, as he lifts the phone and in a "voice racked with fear and nervousness" pleads, "Haley, haven't you *anything* on Ted yet?" Of minor personal concern to Dennis are the frequent threats through his commanding general, through Washington dispatches, through the visiting Congressmen, and through the newsman, Brockhurst, that he will be demoted if the staggering losses continue; but they are of intense concern in consideration of the success of his plan. Through the characterization of Dennis the factors which isolate the modern hero-commander in a democratic society are superbly dramatized.

At the end of Act II, Dennis is removed. In Act III, General Garnett has taken his place. Through Garnett's reactions as commander, the playwright makes even more vivid the nature of the loneliness which Dennis suffered. Garnett assumes that the commanding General Kane will give the order for the next day's run. Already he senses the isolating burden of making the decision upon his own. "Any word from General Kane?" he asks early in the act; "Anything from General Kane?" a little later; and in response to the announcement that there is a message for him, he jumps to the hoped conclusion, "From General Kane?" Then he asks again later, "And you're sure there's nothing from General Kane?" At another time he announces, "Of course that depends entirely on

195

General Kane's orders." Toward the end of the act, he faces what Dennis had long ago faced, that no orders are coming from General Kane, that in the absence of such orders, "Division Commanders will exercise their own discretion," that the decision, which he knows is a momentous one, rests upon him *alone.* He appeals to the medical officer; he appeals to the weather officer; he appeals to the officer who interprets the reconnaissance photographs; he even appeals to Casey Dennis. He gets information from them all, but when he asks about the next day's target, "Would you attack Fendelhorst?" he receives some variant of, "Sir, I'm thankful I don't have to decide that!"

The hero can rely on no one but himself. His feeling of separation from others is intense, because of the impossibility of his sharing the responsibility which he has assumed. In this modern day in which, according to Rollo May, "the opposite to courage is not cowardice, but automaton conformity," the hero, like those of old, is heroic by virtue of being himself. "Maturity and eventual overcoming of loneliness are possible only as one courageously accepts his aloneness to begin with" is the thesis of *Man's Search for Himself.*[14] Don Marquis expresses the similar idea that the man who is able to stand alone is also the most able to belong to another. "And here is one of the paradoxes of the universe: the more trenchantly individualized is the personality the stronger is the impulse and the better is the equipment for overcoming the obstacles to this blending of spirit with spirit."[15] The courage which enables the hero to rise above the crowd is, nevertheless, an isolating factor in itself. Be the hero statesman, doctor, or soldier, no matter how solely he depends upon himself, no matter how individualized his character, he suffers from a self-recognition of separateness which he cannot overcome. In modern drama, although it is the character of the hero which has elevated him, not his royal inheritance, his self-imposed loneliness is none the less inevitable.

CONCLUSION

> The loneliness you feel has come to you because you are no
> longer a child. But the whole world has always been full of
> that loneliness. The loneliness does not come from the War.
> The War did not make it. It was the loneliness that made
> the War.
>
> —*The Human Comedy,* William Saroyan

Of the plays examined in this book, it is not strange that six of
the twenty-six were written by Eugene O'Neill. O'Neill's constant
theme has been that of man's search for something outside himself
to which he can belong, and since many of his characters do not
succeed in attaining a mystical union or an ideal state of belonging,
they succumb to loneliness. O'Neill, both in the number of successful dramas and in their excellence, as well as in experimentation
in new dramatic forms, is the outstanding American playwright of
the modern theater. It is not strange either, therefore, that, since
loneliness seems to be a common theme, he made much use of it
in attempting to express American life in dramatic form. As an
illustration of O'Neill's versatility it is noteworthy that each one
of the six plays falls under a different chapter heading—a fact
which indicates that the loneliness he saw in American life he
ascribed to a number of causes. For all the above reasons it is
logical that, although only three other playwrights are represented
by as many as two plays, O'Neill is represented by half a dozen.

If merit in playwriting be judged according to the Pulitzer and
Critics Circle awards, it is evident that most of the best playwrights
of serious dramas since 1920 have used the theme of loneliness in at
least one of their plays, for all but five[1] of the winners have written
plays included in this study. Of these Thornton Wilder is probably the only one of importance and seems to be something of
an exception among playwrights in that whether he looks at the
world in microcosm, as in *Our Town,* or in macrocosm, as in *The*

197

Skin of Our Teeth, he sees man at home in his environment—without much margin to spare, it is true, but still at home and belonging. As it happens, only two playwrights who have not won either of the two awards are included—Philip Barry and Clifford Odets. Since so many major playwrights have utilized the theme of loneliness, it is assuredly a pervasive theme and not the affectation of a coterie or the forte of one or two practitioners for the stage.

To exemplify the theme, these playwrights have used the various techniques of realism, naturalism, expressionism, impressionism, surrealism, and symbolism. It is increasingly difficult to classify modern dramas inasmuch as experimentation with the dramatic form since 1920 has led to the combination of many techniques. For example, *Death of a Salesman,* which is basically realistic, borders on expressionism in those scenes in which Willy recalls his past, and on symbolism in the setting, in Willy's digging in the dirt as an approach to reality through contact with the earth, and in the flute music, which at the beginning and the end signify Willy's desire for parental comfort. In a scene like that in which Willy is left babbling in the men's room of the restaurant, from which his sons have departed with two "floozies," the drama becomes naturalistic. Obviously, therefore, the present classifications are not rigid.

Of the traditional, drawing-room type of realism, *Craig's Wife, The Silver Cord,* and *The Little Foxes* are the best examples. It is perhaps most logical that it is the loneliness of women which is emphasized in these realistic plays; for since the days of Ibsen's Nora, Mrs. Alving, and Hedda Gabler, the true-to-life drawing room has frequently been the dramatic realm of women. Examples of plays which are essentially realistic but which border on naturalism at times are *Come Back, Little Sheba, The House of Connelly,* and *Anna Christie.* All these include elements of sordidness which extend the plays into the naturalistic area by the inclusion of gross rather than realistic elements—for example, Doc's drunkenness, during which he tries to cut away some of Lola's fat; the depravity of old Uncle Bob and the house with its falling plaster; and Anna's inescapable past life of prostitution.

Realistic plays which lean toward symbolism are those involving a love affair. *Tomorrow and Tomorrow* modernizes the story of the miracle of a son born to the presumably barren Shunemite woman; *Rocket to the Moon* suggests that love in even the most drab surroundings may elevate a man, symbolically, moon-high; *Strange Interlude* portrays Everywoman, who ruins her life through addiction to a false ideal of love. Markedly symbolic plays are *Mourning Becomes Electra, Night Music,* and especially *The Great God Brown.* The first expresses the impossibility of man's overcoming the influence of his heredity; the second, the opposite thesis—the possibility of overpowering fate or bad luck by will power; and the third symbolizes man's alienation from nature by the specific use of masks, symbolic names, and the submerging of the individual characters into types.

Naturalistic plays include *The Iceman Cometh, Of Mice and Men, Street Scene, Winterset,* and *A Streetcar Named Desire.* In all, the effect of the staging, the characters, and the dialogue is to portray the grossness and degradation of segments of humanity. In the surrealistic play *The Time of Your Life* loneliness is made one of the important characteristics of the *dramatis personae,* who, in this type of play, imitate mankind's subconscious dreams. *The Hairy Ape* is expressionistic in attempting to portray man's inner feelings through stylized setting and action. According to W. David Sievers much of the American drama since 1920 should be included under the term, "motivationism,"[2] to indicate its concern with the question of human motivation; but to illustrate their critical interest in the causes of and compensations for loneliness, the playwrights have employed techniques which are not enough alike to be classified under one term.

Regardless of the dramatic medium, however, the theme of loneliness in general affects the dramaturgy of many plays in certain recognizable ways.

The forward movement of a play in which loneliness is the theme is in general impelled by the desire of the lonely ones to belong. *The Hairy Ape* illustrates this method of development in a more explicit way than does any other play analyzed. From the moment in which the white-dressed society girl exclaims of Yank in the stokehole, "Oh, the filthy beast!" his entire concentration of thought and action is upon finding the place where he fits in. He no longer belongs as a stoker, but neither does he belong as an assailant of the plutocrats on Fifth Avenue nor as a destroyer of industry through violence in a labor organization, and so he is driven on by his compelling need, to end up crushed to death by the ape, of which Yank says, "Yuh're at de bottom. You belong!"

The entire play is given direction and each coming scene forecast by the explicit reiteration of Yank's overwhelming aspiration to belong.

In other plays the progress of the action is not so transparently manifested by speeches of characters, but the direction of the play is set by the willfully conceived desire of the lonely ones to belong. Frankie in *The Member of the Wedding* lays plans to join with her brother and the bride on their wedding trip with such fervor that the whole plot revolves around her attempt and its aftermath. In *Winterset* Mio's search for justice seems at first only indirectly a desire to belong; after the direction of his search is changed by his love for Miriamne, he says, however, "I came here seeking/light in darkness, running from the dawn/and stumbled on a morning." From that time on he no longer seeks revenge, but escape, because his need to belong to someone is satisfied. In other plays, as well, the desire of the lonely characters to belong furnishes the plot motivation in varying degrees and impels the action forward.

In the plays discussed the inner conflict of the lonely characters is explicated in overt action. Doc in *Come Back, Little Sheba* furnishes an example of this dramatic technique in its most obvious terms when, distressed by his wife's approval of the shady love affair of Marie and Turk, he reaches for the bottle of whisky, at the end of Act I. He restrains himself with difficulty, but by the end of the next scene, when it is obvious that Marie and Turk have spent the night together, he succumbs. His leaving with the bottle symbolizes the complete alienation of Doc from Lola and his retreat from loneliness into drink. Likewise his fondling of Marie's scarf is symbolic of his inner emptiness. In *Death of a Salesman* Willy's psychic deterioration and eventual isolation from all around him are made explicit in his actions. From the moment at the beginning when he objects to the kind of cheese his wife has bought, until that at the end when he tries to plant seeds by flashlight, his inner perturbation is evident in his actions. Coming soon after the loss of his job, the desertion of his sons in a restaurant leaves him babbling incoherently on the floor of the men's washroom and climaxes his alienation from those about him. His inner longing to belong somewhere leads him then to the soil, which, having failed him as well, leaves death the only solution to his loneliness.

Anna Christie, having finally found a home on the boat, indicates by her appearance and actions that her loneliness is lessened. Not alcohol but the stimulating sea air now makes her cheeks glow. And Eve Redman in *Tomorrow and Tomorrow* indicates the depth of her love for Nicholas Hay by going with him to see the laurel in bloom—although she had since childhood feared to look at it. In many other instances in the plays considered, indication of a character's progress from or toward isolation is given by his overt actions.

The inability of characters fully to communicate with each other is in some cases made the direct cause of their loneliness and in others a contributing cause. In *The Great God Brown* the failure to communicate is made doubly clear by the use of masks, which prevent the true features of one character from being revealed to another. Dion's wife, Margaret, is terrified at the sight of his real features, and Dion once says to her, "We communicate in code—when neither has the other's key." In *Street Scene* the very press of people puts a "wall" between Mr. and Mrs. Maurrant, so that she is unable to make him understand her need of getting away from the crowded environment. And in *Strange Interlude* O'Neill exemplifies the difficulty of communication by interposing the characters' inner thoughts between their oral speeches. Loneliness in all of these cases and in many others is partly a result of the inability of speech to convey inner thought to other characters.

The play in which loneliness is the theme illustrates the progress of one or more characters into a state of complete isolation or from some degree of isolation toward a state of belonging. In *The Glass Menagerie* Laura, who is lonely to begin with, ends in a state of irreparable isolation through her devastating experience with the gentleman caller. And Blanche in *A Streetcar Named Desire* likewise passes from a semi-isolated situation to one so overwhelmingly lonely that she loses sanity. The same is true of Willy in *Death of a Salesman*. Harriet Craig of *Craig's Wife* and Regina of *The Little Foxes* attain their goals materially, but end, unexpectedly, in distressing states of loneliness. George, in *Of Mice and Men*, gives up the dream of a home with Lennie and accepts loneliness as inevitable. On the other hand, Dr. Stark in *Rocket to the Moon* progresses toward a new understanding of himself and of his wife. Will Connelly in *The House of Connelly* becomes united with Patsy Tate to begin a rejuvenation of the estate. And the characters of *The Time of Your Life* pass from alienated entities to a homogeneous group bound together by the removal of Blick, the isola-

201

ting agent. In most of the plays, the progress of the lonely characters, as in the above, is mainly in one direction—toward either isolation or belonging. In *Anna Christie*, however, Anna passes from isolation to a joyful state of belonging and back again to loneliness, as her father and lover leave her. Perhaps this change of direction is the cause of the weakness of the play, as it is of the varying interpretations of the ending.

In modern American drama the theme of loneliness is sometimes reinforced by the loneliness of minor characters somewhat analogous to that of the leading characters. In *The Member of the Wedding,* the middle-aged Negress, Berenice, is alone in the world except for her brother, who kills a white man and hangs himself in jail. At the end of the play, as Frankie leaves with her new-found friends, Berenice sits alone in the empty kitchen. Here loneliness, although its cause is very different from Frankie's, adds to the poignancy and significance of the theme through the whole play. In *Night Music* glimpses of lonely characters, such as Homeless Man on the park bench and Mr. Nichols, forever trying to reach someone on the telephone, reinforce the loneliness of Suitcase Steve and his girl, Fay. Even Steve's guardian angel, Rosenberger, is alone in the world. In *Of Mice and Men* the other ranch hands suffer as do George and Lennie. The companionship of the two men and their fervent dream of a home of their own inspire the other hands with disbelief and wonder. Homelessness being the lot of them all, an analogy to the situation in which George and Lennie exist is presented by each of the others as well. In *Street Scene* the loneliness of the Maurrants is duplicated by that of the Kaplans, the Fiorentinos, and the dispossessed Hildebrands. In *The Little Foxes* and *Another Part of the Forest,* the loneliness which Birdie and her family experience, through the inroads which the Hubbards have made on them economically and psychologically, is partly revenged by the fact that in the end Alexandra loves Birdie but hates her mother, Regina. In *Winterset* studies in loneliness comparable to Mio's are those of the Romagna family and Judge Gaunt.

Loneliness in the plays studied may seem pitiful in some cases and truly tragic in others, but it is always a painful condition for its victims and those around them. That loneliness is painful is one contention of Colin Wilson's study of twentieth-century man, *The Outsider.* "The Outsider's chief desire," he says, "is *to cease to be an*

202

Outsider."³ But it is no true solution for him to go back to becoming an "ordinary bourgeois"; his problem is how to go forward to a self-realization and an acceptance of life. Some of the lonely characters portrayed make an attempt in this direction, and verge on the tragic; others do not and are merely pitiful. In a play like *The Silver Cord* the emotion aroused is one of pity, for her sons and for Mrs. Phelps as well. How sad, one remarks, that a woman should think it happiness to keep a grown man at her breast like a baby. How deep is her need for the understanding that emotional maturity brings. And how lonesome is the lot of the sons so bound. But of tragic catharsis the audience experiences very little, for Mrs. Phelps drives herself into the morass of irremedial personal isolation without recognizing her own predicament. And one son remains lost forever in his mother's arms, whereas the one who escapes does so only through the extremely forceful persuasion of his pregnant wife. The situation, Sidney Howard tries to emphasize, has tragic consequences through what he believes is its widespread extent among Americans, but as for the characters of his play, they do not show the depth and courage necessary to make their failure tragic.

In *The Glass Menagerie* Amanda is a ludicrous, but also a pitiful, representation of the Southern belle, living in the past and unable to adapt herself to the present. Her daughter Laura, crippled in body and spirit, is an even more pitiful figure. Their fate is not tragic, however, because neither attempts to face reality, but rather to avoid it. And, as Wolcott Gibbs notes of *A Streetcar Named Desire,*

> Altogether Blanche is one of the most tragic figures in the modern theatre, but there is no grandeur in the remnant we are now permitted to see. There is nothing, in fact, except desperate affectation, terror, and weak and futile rage.⁴

In *Come Back, Little Sheba* Doc and Lola are innocent of malice against anyone. But as in the case of the characters of *The Silver Cord* and the two plays of Tennessee Williams, they never come to that understanding of themselves which, in great tragedy, leads the audience to experience an elevation of soul through the recognition of man's courage to face adversity. In *Strange Interlude,* although Nina, with a certain degree of heroism, supplies her husband with a healthy child, fathered by another man, she mainly drifts with life's tide. Dominated always by a false ideal of what love is, she searches for it in various ways, but without the direction and steadfastness of the tragic heroine. In these plays the emotion aroused by the presentation of the lonely characters on the stage is that of pity, but not that of the deeper fear or terror, or whatever that emotion may be called, which truly evokes a tragic catharsis.

In *Death of a Salesman* Arthur Miller has consciously made an effort to write what, according to his definition, is a tragedy, and to some extent he seems to have succeeded in making Willy's downfall a subject of tragic consequence. According to Miller, "the tragic feeling is evoked in us when we are in the presence of a character who is ready to lay down his life, if need be, to secure one thing—his sense of personal dignity."[5] Miller would like to believe that in total effect the story of Willy expresses "the indestructible will of man to achieve his humanity." Willy's self-examination alone makes his fate more meaningful that that of Mrs. Phelps or Doc or Amanda, none of whom try to analyze the situation in which they find themselves. Even though it is belatedly and with mistaken interpretation, Willy valiantly attempts to discover why he has not succeeded in being well liked. The realization that his sons' failures are attributable to him, but that he can no more analyze them than he can his own, is the crowning blow, from which he turns to the soil and then to death for balm. Willy succeeds partially in evoking the tragic emotion of the world's great dramas.

The use of an ancient Greek plot in *Mourning Becomes Electra* perhaps makes the play merely seem to reach great tragic heights. O'Neill must be credited, however, with a modernization of the Electra story which brings to life the struggles within the Mannon family in a way to arouse more than mere pity. Some of the horror and grief which Electra feels for the murder of her father, which Lavinia feels for the murder of her lover, and which Orin feels for the suicide of his mother permeates the audience. And Electra's final immersion of herself for life into the darkened family mansion seems a mode of expiation worthy of a tragic heroine. *Winterset* is another American play which rises above the commonplace. Mio's discovery that love is of greater force than revenge and Miriamne's sacrifice of her life to prove her love give the characters a stature which makes their deaths tragic. In the three plays in the chapter entitled, "The Lonely Hero"—*Abe Lincoln in Illinois, Men in White,* and *Command Decision*—a tragic elation of soul is aroused by the portrayal of the hero suffering for an ideal of service to his fellow man. Lincoln's final good-by to his friends and neighbors from the platform of the Washington-bound train is symbolic of his departure from life in the role of savior of his country. The doctor who sacrifices his own happiness in his devotion to duty and the soldier who performs the harder-than-death task of sending others to death call forth the feeling of awe through which great tragedy endows human life with dignity and significance.

In *The Iceman Cometh* O'Neill portrays a group of characters who are merely pitiful and a salesman who comes near to reaching tragic significance and may truly achieve it. The men who live on dreams and drink at Hope's bar are figures perhaps allegorically representative of mankind but not of great importance individually. In the salesman, Hickey, however, O'Neill has created a character who attempts to reform the misguided lot, who comes to a sudden recognition that he himself is misguided, and who, finally, by claiming himself insane, mercifully allows the men to return to their state of insensibility. If Edith Hamilton is right, that "Tragedy's one essential is a soul that can feel greatly,"[6] then *The Iceman Cometh* perhaps qualifies through Hickey's suffering and self-recognition of the cause of his own downfall.

Those plays in which the theme of loneliness is prominent tend to be unified in action, form, and purpose. By "action" of the play is meant the particular object which the playwright is trying to illustrate and which the actor must remember if he is to keep his direction. The "form" of the play is related to the plot, but is not synonymous with it. Here the word is used broadly to encompass the setting, the method of plot development, and the means of dramatizing the object of the action. Although the ultimate purpose of all drama is to arouse an emotional response from the audience, here the use of the term "purpose" is to indicate that particular aim of each play through which each playwright hopes to gain an emotional reaction.

In *Command Decision* the purpose—to illustrate the loneliness of the commander—is accomplished through the action—to hasten the end of the war by destruction of three German plane factories—in a form embodying the unities of time, place, and action appropriate to the military precision required for the mission portrayed. In *Craig's Wife* Harriet Craig step by step isolates herself in action which enhances the purpose of the play—to show the desolate plight of a selfish woman. In the form of the play there is not an exces-

205

sive or irrelevant motion on her part. As there is no speck of dust in her perfectly-appointed drawing room and no hair out of place upon her head, so there is nothing extraneous to detract from the perfectly-plotted form of the play. The object of the action in *Of Mice and Men* is "to find a home." The purpose of the playwright—to portray the loneliness of the transient ranch hands—is accomplished by the action and by the form of the play, which begins on a river bank, a temporary home for the night, includes scenes in the impermanent home represented by the bunkhouse, and concludes again on the river bank, the only home Lennie will ever know. In *Death of a Salesman* the purpose of the playwright to present the lonely situation in which the characters find themselves is served by the object of the action—Willy's attempt to be well liked—in a form by which flashbacks explain the cause of the situation while at the same time illustrating Willy's aim.

The purpose, action, and form of *Mourning Becomes Electra* are clearly unified; to show the pernicious influence of Puritanism in repressing normal emotions, O'Neill adapted the Electra story in the light of his understanding of Freudian theories of psychoanalysis. Electra's final isolation is the logical result of the action and of the form with its three parts ending, one, in the father's death, two, in the mother's death, three, in the brother's death and her immersion in the deserted house. In *The Time of Your Life* Saroyan wishes to show how to live so that life may hold no ugliness. By means of characters illustrating the various faces of human nature, he makes this heterogeneous group homogeneous by the elimination of an evil member within it. The object of the action—to overcome the isolation among the characters which makes for misery—is finally completed by the forthright shooting of the villain by Kit Carson. The form, which includes much apparently erratic movement on the part of the characters, in reality is an appropriate contrast to the end, at which time all move in harmony. Of all the plays studied perhaps it is *Abe Lincoln in Illinois* alone which does not show a typical unity of purpose, form, and action, but which succeeds rather by the eulogizing of America's hero, partly through speeches of his own composition. The purpose being patriotic, however, a pageant-like form is appropriate for the portrayal of the action—expressed in the phrase, to do one's duty.

Besides various dramaturgical devices, plays dealing with the theme of loneliness have made use of modern techniques of staging to reinforce the theme. Since this book does not deal with technicalities of production, no more than passing mention has been made of this important aspect of theater. Nevertheless, it should be noted that through lighting particularly, and through setting and sound, as well, the plays described have been increased in effectiveness by modern staging. *Men in White* makes the role of the doctor of more import than that of the common man by means of the scene in the operating room. As the nurse hands over the scalpel, which cuts a gleaming arc through the air, all the lights on stage dim down except the fierce, merciless, white brilliance which bathes the operating table. *The Glass Menagerie* points up the misery of living isolated, crowded amongst a mass of people, by its inside-outside setting which portrays Laura, alone in the dingy apartment, and Tom, encompassed by buildings and a dance hall on the outside stairway. The use of lights to cause the picture of the missing but ever-smiling father to glow at appropriate points and the use of spotlights to emphasize Laura's isolation also add to the purpose of the play.

In *Command Decision* the sound of the planes roaring in for landings or faltering and crashing contrasts the isolation of the commander in his office with the participation of the men who are doing the fighting. O'Neill's studies of two families—*Mourning Becomes Electra* and *Desire Under the Elms*—are appropriately staged, with the Grecian temple portico and its six pure-white, tall columns standing rigid and forbidding in the former and the enormous old elms hanging over the farm house in the latter "like exhausted women resting their sagging breasts and hands and hair on its roof." In *The Time of Your Life* effective and symbolic use is made of mechanical contrivances—toys, slot machines, and juke boxes—of the sort which have their influence on all Americans. The great contrast in social levels is symbolized in *The Hairy Ape* by the scene in the black stokehole and the scene in brilliant sunlight on the ship's deck. In *Death of a Salesman* Willy's memories of the past are dramatized by lighting of particular stage areas as he moves from one to another. His loneliness seems to be the greater in the present as scenes in the past bring with them the effect of fluttering leaves of trees instead of towering buildings around the house. In Arthur Miller's play, as in many others, modern stage practices have made possible an enrichment of the emotional experience and an enhancement of the theme of the play.

The causes of loneliness as portrayed in American drama vary from a personal to a social basis, several being a result of both. In an age in which man is considered only partly responsible for his actions—his heredity and environment being inescapable deterministic factors—it is not strange that perhaps the only personal classification is that of the failure of a love affair. Personal failure, as well, however, is made out to be far more an individual responsibility than a social matter. Homelessness and the conflict of the spiritual with the material represent the forces of society and the individual about equally. Socioeconomic conditions put emphasis upon the social and economic causes rather than upon personal accountability. Abnormal family relationships presuppose a certain fatalistic concept in that the individual cannot choose the family into which he is born. There is something of the same inevitability about the loneliness of the hero, whom chance, heredity, and the times in which he lives thrust into the isolation which goes with deification.

Perhaps the most deep-seated of the causes of loneliness today have not been exhumed; however, modern playwrights like Tennessee Williams and Eugene O'Neill have attempted to explain man's psychological predicament by the modernization of ancient myths. In *Orpheus Descending,* Williams asks the audience to supply implications of the timelessness of human behavior by making an analogy between an appealing vagrant guitar player and the God Orpheus. Lack of audience approval of the play may have been due to lack of knowledge of the myth. Undoubtedly more to their understanding is the character of the socially-ostracized Carol Cutrere, who says of her promiscuity, "The act of lovemaking is almost unbearably painful, and yet, of course, I do bear it, because to be not alone, even for a few moments, is worth the pain and the danger." More mythological truth as well may lie in her character than in that of the singer, for as Erich Fromm points out: "Rites of communal sexual orgies were a part of many primitive rituals. It seems that after the orgiastic experience, man can go on for a time without suffering too much from his separateness."[7] Williams dramatizes Fromm's further contention that in modern society the feelings of anxiety and guilt produced in the individual seeking to escape loneliness through sexual orgasm result in "an ever-increasing sense of separateness."

O'Neill in *Mourning Becomes Electra* and *The Great God Brown* likewise intimates that pagan practices relieved the bitter isolation which Christian dogma and social codes have made inevitable. And in *Strange Interlude,* Nina's recurring cry that God should have been a woman is authenticated by Robert Graves in his study of poetic myth. According to him the medieval attempt to move nearer and nearer to deification of the Virgin Mary as a primitive Goddess was thwarted by the Reformation, which strengthened the unnatural deification of the Son and Father. Graves believes "there can be no escape from the present more than usually miserable state of the world until . . . the repressed desire of the Western races, which is for some practical form of Goddess worship . . . finds satisfaction at last."[8] Instead of worshipping the all-embracing Mother-Goddess, modern man, according to O'Neill, sees life only as a strange interlude in the electrical display of God the Father. Although some modern dramatists may, therefore, be reaching toward mythical explanations of man's present loneliness, it is doubtful that they will find wide acceptance, for with the present emphasis (superficial as it may be) upon America as a "Christian" nation, public favor will probably go to the plays conforming to the quasi-official creed.

It is not to be assumed, of course, that the playwrights went through the process of deciding to write a serious play on the subject of loneliness, debating within themselves the possible causes, and then creating a set of characters to fit the plan. This would be as mechanical a means of playwriting as Maxwell Anderson describes. According to him a recognition scene is the one touchstone of great tragedy. He therefore advises the playwright: "If the plot he has in mind does not contain a playable episode in which the hero or heroine makes an emotional discovery, . . . then such an episode must be inserted. . . . it must be made central, and the whole action must revolve around it."[9] It is impossible to believe that this important playwright has succeeded by "inserting" an episode—and that the crux of the whole play—into his plots. A seemingly more reasonable explanation of the method of the playwright is that of Rachel Crothers. There comes to her, she says, "first the idea, then the story which will concretely develop this idea, then the characters which spring instantaneously with the story because they are the story and they are the idea—. . ."[10] It is with something like this assumption of the process of dramatic creation that twenty-six plays have been analyzed in chapters based on the causes of loneliness.

Although the playwrights, therefore, in conceiving the ideas for their plays perhaps did not conceive of loneliness as the theme or a particular cause as the plot, when the idea had coalesced into dramatic form, such was the effect. Elmer Rice, in commenting on Sievers' recent study, *Freud on Broadway*, notes that, like Moliére's hero who discovered to his astonishment that he had been speaking prose all his life, America's playwrights are astonished to find they have been expounding Freudian psychoanalysis during the past three or four decades.[11] Likewise many a playwright might be surprised to discover that he has written a play dealing with the theme of loneliness. If Sievers is correct about the number of characters of arrested maturity presented on the modern stage, it is not strange that some of the psychological phenomena displayed emerge in the presentation of the theme of loneliness.

There are certain compensations suggested by the dramatists which are a result of the feeling of separateness, which is itself the result of a personal or social cause. In those plays in which loneliness results from personal failure, the characters compensate by dreams and drink. Lola engages in dreams, Doc in drink, Willy Loman in dreams, and the characters of *The Iceman Cometh* in both dreams and drink. The characters who are homeless dream of and struggle to attain homes. Those in unhappy families engage in abnormal desires and succumb, or mature and escape. Those characters involved in an extramarital love affair compensate for the loss of the loved one in memories of past joy. Those pitted against social and economic forces are overwhelmed except in the cases in which individuals can adapt themselves to a new order. Those confronted with a conflict of the material and the spiritual compensate by devotion to one or the other and thereby either succeed or fail in life. In *The Time of Your Life* the characters succeed by devotion to the spiritual. In *Craig's Wife* Mrs. Craig fails by compensating entirely by devotion to the material. In *The Great God Brown* man's only compensation for involvement in the conflict is return to Mother Earth. The compensation of the hero for his loneliness is his apotheosis.

In view of the broad scope of the theme of loneliness in modern American drama—in the number of playwrights treating the theme, in the great variety of characters portrayed, and in the many causes and compensations which make up the plots of the plays—some conclusions may be drawn as to its importance to today's audience. Sievers believes that the therapeutic value of modern American drama is the same which Aristotle attributed to the Greek. Besides the achievement by the audience of an awareness which implies an "intellectual perception of *wholeness*," Sievers believes that modern drama accomplishes "an emotional release of repressed fears, wishes or anxieties which parallel those of the characters on stage."[12] If it is true that an emotional release is possible, the audience finds balm for whatever loneliness it feels by viewing that emotion dramatized. Furthermore, if it is also true that the audience achieves an intellectual perception of wholeness from the portrayal of the theme of loneliness, then an added comfort results. The opinion of dramatic historians that modern American drama closely reflects modern American life would seem to find verification in Sievers' thesis that the audience responds to dramatic expression paralleling its own suffering.

Modern drama has been accused of being such a critical imitation of modern life that it has been, to some extent at least, propaganda rather than art. No doubt it is true that plays on juvenile delinquency, economic inequality, race prejudice, political corruption, and many other such subjects have veered too near the former of Horace's precepts for poetry—to instruct and entertain. Arthur Miller in *Death of a Salesman*, O'Neill in *The Iceman Cometh*, Lillian Hellman in *The Little Foxes* might be accused of delivering a social message. The theme of loneliness as it is presented in modern American drama, however, is undoubtedly a reflection of life rather than an expression of zeal for reformation of the world.

If it seems doubtful that the plays in which loneliness is the theme rise to the tragic heights of great literature, perhaps the fault lies in inartistic playwriting or in the social and moral environment of the times rather than in the theme itself. Possibly the lack of mythologically significant plots and the absence of figurative imagery make them undistinguished. It may be that the modern tendency toward psychiatric interpretation of character and emphasis upon social improvement rather than upon individual salvation make the creation of supremely great drama difficult. According to Alfred Harbage, it is not the theme of loneliness *per se* but the "spiritual poverty" of the treatment which it is given in modern literature that makes it a failure. He claims:

211

> Loneliness is an ancient theme in literature, and its treatment, usually muted, has often been very beautiful. . . . Loneliness is the most exclusively human of the forms of suffering, the most closely related to the capacity for love; but it loses its beauty and great promise if treated frivolously or petulantly, if reduced to frustration, if expressed as the plaint of the persecuted or the whine of the rejected. Instead of a universal emotion shared, we get an individual *malaise* communicated.[13]

Perhaps there is a lack of faith in the temper of the times which makes lasting art impossible and pessimism as to human fate inevitable, so that modern drama becomes the "plaint of the persecuted" rather than the "universal emotion shared."

Loneliness as a phenomenon of modern life, with its reflection in the drama, may be a result, and possibly a cause of the nihilism of today. Eric Bentley believes that there cannot be great theater without what Walt Whitman called "great audiences," and that, because of the isolation of individuals from one another, there cannot be great audiences today. He complains: "You get insight into the modern audience as you sit in a New York theater listening to the comments of those around you, . . . you get insight into the modern audience, the modern population, as you sit, or, more likely, stand, in the New York subway. Boredom everywhere, and isolation of each from all."[14] A great audience, Bentley believes, is "an assembly of fully human beings with something in common, something relevant to the occasion." He regrets the want of common understanding among people. "Lack of community is a problem not of our arts but of our whole civilization." If loneliness is the touchstone of the modern audience, those plays dealing with loneliness may bring a common response and a cohesion among its members which may lead in time to greater drama. The multifeatured view of numerous dramatists may coalesce into the work of one, who, inspired by the theme, expresses the age.

NOTES

INTRODUCTION

1. "The most original playwrights of the 1920-30 period were coming to realize that American audiences were readier than ever before to see and study American types, to hear American themes and ideas discussed—in a word, to become conscious of and excited about their Americanness. The same impulse that lay behind Henry Ford's mania for collecting American furniture, books, and glass, that spread through the country in the craze for the acquisition of American rather than English or French antiques and precipitated the floods of historical novels and biographies, that brought foreigners to our shores to tell us about our own land and our future destiny, drove our playwrights—and continues to drive them—to compress into dramatic form the colors and shapes of American life." (*A History of Modern Drama*, eds. Barrett H. Clark and George Freedley, p. 683).

2. Ernest Dimnet, "The Case for and against Loneliness," *American Magazine*, CX (July 1930), 33.

3. In collaboration with Reuel Denney and Nathan Glazer.

4. Abram Kardiner and Associates, *The Psychological Frontiers of Society*, 1945.

5. *The Human Mind.* In Chapter II, the author includes among seven "personality types predisposed to failure" the "isolation type," which results in the "lonely personality." The "lonely personality" suffers from a sense of inferiority, self-preoccupation, self-criticism, a feeling of being unappreciated, perfectionist tendencies, and an unwillingness to put himself to the test in overt situations.

6. "Loneliness: its Relation to Narcissism," *Atlantic*, CLXI (January 1938), 50.

7. The quotations and paraphrasing of Thornton Wilder are taken from two articles, "Toward an American Language," *Atlantic*, CXC (July 1952), 29-37, and "The American Loneliness," *Atlantic*, CXC (August 1952), 65-69.

8. "The Anatomy of Loneliness," *American Mercury*, LIII (October 1941), 467.   9. P. 488.

10. "The Loneliness of the Modern Man," *Current Opinion*, LXXII (May 1922), 670.   11. *Sewannee Review*, LII (1944), 313-331.

12. *The Sandburg Range*, opposite p. 255.

13. *Theory and Technique of Playwriting*, p. x.

14. "Two by Rattigan," New York *Times* (May 22, 1955), Sec. 2, p. 1, col. 1.

15. "The recurrent themes of our plays are loneliness, rebellion against parental authority, incest-longings, emotional starvation, escape mechanisms, juvenile delinquency, crimes of violence, homosexuality, terror fantasies, sadism, and schizophrenia." ("American Theatre and the Human Spirit," *Saturday Review*, XXXVIII [December 17, 1955], 41.)

16. *Revolution in American Drama*, p. vii.

CHAPTER 1

1. *The American People*, p. 107.   2. *America as a Civilization*, p. 164.

3. Gilbert Seldes in *The Great Audience*, pp. 236-237, lists some characteristics of women who listen to the daytime serials. It is obvious they apply to Lola. They include "reduced imagination and personal resources, fear of not succeeding, apprehension of the unknown, a distrust of imaginative expression, and an existence in an atmosphere of disillusion and frustration."

4. D. W. Brogan, *The American Character*, p. 46.   5. See note 3.

6. *The Lonely Crowd*, pp. 37-38.   7. *The Tower and the Abyss*, pp. 41-42.

8. Henry Steele Commager, *The American Mind*, p. 7.

9. *The Burns Mantle Best Plays of 1948-1949*, ed. John Chapman, pp. 48-49.

10. Further illustration of Willy's contradictory state of mind is found in the remark of Happy: "He stops at a green light and then it turns red and he goes."

11. Gilbert Highet in *The Art of Teaching*, p. 183, attempts to explain on psychological grounds the ruin of a son's own life to revenge himself upon his father.

12. See note 7 of the "Introduction."   13. *The Idea of a Theater*, p. 231.

14. *The Burns Mantle Best Plays of 1948-1949*, p. 54.

15. *The Theater Book of the Year 1946-1947*, p. 95.

16. Thornton Wilder, "Toward an American Language," *Atlantic*, CXC (July 1952), 33.   17. New York *Post*, Oct. 10, 1946.

18. *In Search of Theater*, p. 242.

19. It should be noted that the love-hate theme involves the hatred of a man for a woman in each case and is carried over into the truth-illusion theme, for Harry Hope unexpectedly admits that he hated his presumably beloved dead wife, and Jimmy Tomorrow's wife has been unfaithful to him. The only women in the play are three prostitutes. The play would seem to say that only sex, not love, can exist between man and woman, a fact which perhaps augments mankind's loneliness.

20. Eric Bentley (*In Search of Theater*, p. 242) apparently has no evidence that Hickey " (as it turns out) is a maniac." O'Neill has made it clear that Hickey makes the claim to relieve the men of the burden of facing reality. Later Parritt, in reference to Hickey, says that he betrayed his own mother. "And I'm not putting up any bluff, either, that I was crazy afterwards when I laughed to myself. . . ." Parritt recognizes, as does the audience, that Hickey is not really insane!

21. "The Isolation of the Shakespearean Hero," *Sewanee Review*, LII (1944), 315.   22. *Op. cit.*, p. 231.

23. Maxim Gorki, *The Lower Depths*, in *A Treasury of the Theatre*, ed. John Gassner, p. 245.   24. Gassner, *op. cit.*, p. 228.

25. *The Haunted Heroes of Eugene O'Neill*, p. 282.

26. Gorki, *op. cit.*, p. 220.   27. *Ibid.*, p. 231.

28. "The Anatomy of Loneliness," *American Mercury*, LIII (October 1941), 473.

29. *"Modernism" in Modern Drama: a Definition and an Estimate*, p. 118.

CHAPTER 2

1. Anson Page in his review of the Hamilton Basso novel, *The View from Pompey's Head*, in *New York Times Book Review* (October 24, 1954), says, "Usually the homeward call is largely irrational; the home town would seem to have little to offer the voluntary exile except what is sometimes called 'the indefinable' and sometimes 'roots.' . . . The pattern has been that the hero either can't go home again or can do so only at the expense of falling into outgrown habits of mind. . . ."

2. In the "Introduction" to *Night Music*, p. viii, Harold Clurman says, "Whether or not *Night Music* is the best of the Odets plays I cannot say, but I am sure that among his longer plays it is the most integrated in its feeling and the most completely conceived. The play stems from the basic sentiment

that people nowadays are affected by a sense of insecurity; they are haunted by the fear of impermanence in all their relationships; they are fundamentally *homeless,* and whether or not they know it, they are in search of a home, of something real, secure, dependable in a slippery, shadowy, noisy and nervous world."

3. "Patterns of Belief in Contemporary Drama," in *Spiritual Problems in Contemporary Literature,* ed. Stanley Romaine Hopper, p. 202.

4. Introduction to *Night Music,* p. ix.

5. Stanley Romaine Hopper, in *Spiritual Problems,* p. 161.

6. In speaking of her home in Philadelphia Fay calls it "a dead place." According to Steve, "The place where you live is always dead." Both realize they can't go home again.

7. Kernodle, who sees allegory in *Night Music,* says of Rosenberger, "Compassion as a guardian angel seems to me definitely a religious concept," in *Spiritual Problems,* p. 202.

8. If Walter Kerr is right, the lack of action may be the cause of the play's poor success. He believes that the modern theater is hostile to the idea of activity. "What happens next," he says, has been thoroughly discarded. "Killing Off the Theater," *Harper's Magazine,* CCX (April 1955), 55-62.

9. Since the cricket is frequently associated with the hearth, Fay may be unconsciously expressing her desire for a home in this speech, but the playwright does not make this point explicitly.   10. *In Search of Theater,* p. 356.

11. Roy considers himself imprisoned by loneliness, as is evidenced from the song he hums on the bench.   12. *Narration,* p. 11.

13. Although *Of Mice and Men* appeared first as a novel, it had dramatic qualities, and the novelist himself has made the adaptation of the play, so that the Drama Critics' Circle, which awarded it the prize as the best play of 1937-38, and other critics have never considered it as an adapted novel, but as a play in its own right.   14. *The Best Plays of 1937-38,* p. 31.

15. O'Neill makes ruthless fun of this American sentimental desire for life on the farm in *The Iceman Cometh,* in which Chuck, the pimp, and Cora, the prostitute, dream of getting married and living on a farm. Both dreams are obviously as unattainable as those of the other characters. Neither Chuck nor Cora is quite so removed from reality, however, as to dream of a home in the West. As Cora explains: "He says Joisey's de best place, and I says Long Island because we'll be near Coney."

16. *The Haunted Heroes of Eugene O'Neill,* p. 41.

17. According to Barrett H. Clark, *Eugene O'Neill: The Man and His Plays,* p. 99, O'Neill originally called his play *Chris Christopherson* and described it as "a sea play—a character study of an old Swede." In this form it failed. Rewritten around Anna it was a success, but it is obvious that Chris's theme is not subordinated as it would have been if the playwright had begun with Anna as the major character.

18. See Joseph Wood Krutch, "Modernism" in Modern Drama, p. 118.

19. *A Treasury of the Theatre,* ed. John Gassner, p. 788. A review of the musical version of *Anna Christie, New Girl in Town,* in *Theatre Arts,* XLI (July 1957), 15, indicates that O'Neill's fear that his ending would be considered a happy one was justified, for according to the writer: "There actually has been little tampering with the basic details of the original story, other than moving the action back to the era of 1900. O'Neill himself supplied the happy ending."

20. Ward Morehouse, New York *Sun,* Oct. 10, 1946.

21. *Anna Christie* probably comes as near as any important American drama to treating the loneliness of the immigrant, but in reality the fact of the

Christophersons' foreign origin has little to do with the theme. No successful playwright has treated the immigrant's struggle to establish a home in America, as have such novelists as Rolvaag and Willa Cather.

CHAPTER 3

1. *In Search of Theater,* p. 284.

2. *The Burns Mantle Best Plays of 1949-1950,* p. 91.

3. William Hawkins on Jan. 6, 1950.

4. John Wharton, "Our Stylized Dialogue," *Saturday Review,* XXXVII (July 17, 1954), 24-25.   5. New York *Times,* Jan. 6, 1950.

6. In *Generation of Vipers,* pp. 184-204, Wylie flails the American Mom as a son-devouring beast of prey.

7. *The World Within,* ed. Mary Louise Aswell, p. 355.

8. According to Matthew Arnold in "Sweetness and Light," Puritanism had an ill effect upon the state of "life and society" in England. He condemns the Puritan's ideal of perfection as "narrow and inadequate" and claims that either Shakespeare or Virgil would have found the Pilgrim Fathers intolerable company. Puritanism of course existed elsewhere, but O'Neill is particularly aware of its vices in America, where its tenets lasted with peculiar ferocity.

9. In *Theatre Arts,* XXXV (February 1951), 22-23.

10. *The Haunted Heroes of Eugene O'Neill,* p. 126.   11. *Ibid.,* p. 271.

12. *Atlantic,* CXCVII (April 1956), p. 36.

CHAPTER 4

1. *America as a Civilization,* p. 584.   2. *Revolution in American Drama,* p. 172.

3. "Three Introductions" in *Six Plays of Clifford Odets,* p. 432.

4. Gagey, *Revolution in American Drama,* p. 171.

5. *And Keep Your Powder Dry,* p. 143.

6. *The Haunted Heroes of Eugene O'Neill,* pp. 199, 239.

CHAPTER 5

1. "The Peril of City Loneliness," *Literary Digest,* XLIV (February 3, 1912), 215-16.   2. *Revolution in American Drama,* p. 149.

3. *American Magazine,* CX (July 1930), 33.

4. Maxwell Anderson, *Off Broadway,* p. 60.

5. "The Isolation of the Shakespearean Hero," *Sewanee Review,* LII (1944), 315.

6. "Man's Spiritual Situation as Reflected in Modern Drama," in *Spiritual Problems in Contemporary Literature,* ed. Stanley Romaine Hopper, p. 50.

7. "Patterns of Belief in Contemporary Drama," in *Spiritual Problems,* p. 196.

8. Theodore Spencer, "The Isolation of the Shakespearean Hero," *Sewanee Review,* LII (1944), 326.   9. *Eugene O'Neill,* p. 131.

10. *Ibid.,* p. 129.   11. *Ibid.,* p. 127.

12. "The Anatomy of Loneliness," *American Mercury,* LIII (October 1941), 473.

13. George Jean Nathan, Introduction to *The Critics' Prize Plays,* p. 11.

14. *Today in American Drama,* p. 32-33.

15. *Man for Himself,* p. 22. See also page 151.

16. *The Theatre Book of the Year 1948-1949,* p. 120.

17. *The Theatre Book of the Year 1944-1945*, p. 327.

18. *Atlantic*, CXCI (January 1953), 41-45.

19. *Fifty Years of American Drama 1900-1950*, p. 103.

20. "Patterns of Belief in Contemporary Drama," *Spiritual Problems*, p. 206.

21. *Man for Himself*, p. 58.

22. Burns Mantle, *The Best Plays of 1946-1947*, p. 163.   23. *Ibid.*, p. 163.

24. Philip Rahv, "Franz Kafka: The Hero as Lonely Man," *Kenyon Review*, I (1939), 67.   25. *The Best Plays of 1938-1939*, pp. 75-76.

26. *Atlantic Monthly*, CXCII (December 1953), 58.

27. New York *Times*, April 3, 1955.   28. New York *Times*, May 22, 1955.

29. *The American Character*, p. 6.

30. The degeneration in the line of old southern families as seen in men like Uncle Bob Connelly and John Bagtry, "an empty man from an idiot world," is explained by Lillian Smith in *Killers of the Dream*, p. 116. "Because these slaveholders were 'Christian,' they felt compelled to justify the holding of slaves by denying these slaves a soul, and denying them a place in the human family. Because they were puritan, they succeeded in developing a frigidity in their white women that precluded the possibility of mutual satisfaction. Lonely and baffled and frustrated by the state of affairs they had set up in their own homes and hearts, they could not resist the vigor and kindliness and gaiety of these slaves. And succumbing to desire, they mated with these dark women, whom they had dehumanized in their minds, and fathered by them children who, according to their race philosophy, were 'without souls'—a strange new kind of creature, whom they made slaves of and sometimes sold on the auction block. The white man's roles as slaveholder and Christian and puritan were exacting far more than the strength of his mind could sustain. Each time he found the back-yard temptation irresistible, his conscience split more deeply from his acts and his mind from things as they are."

31. P. 140.   32. *The Theatre Book of the Year 1942-1943*, p. 49.

33. Jack Kirkland, *Tobacco Road*, based on the novel by Erskine Caldwell, in *Twenty Best Plays of the Modern American Theatre*, ed. John Gassner, p. 609.

CHAPTER 6

1. P. 349.   2. *Saturday Review*, XXXVII (October 2, 1954), 22-23.

3. *Spiritual Problems*, p. 161.   4. *Man for Himself*, pp. 15, 72.

5. "Saroyan would say that if you discover God through the inner dream, if you discover your kinship with all things through the *aloneness* of the inner dream, then the whole of God's world will be lit up with joy." George R. Kernodle, "Patterns of Belief in Contemporary Drama," in *Spiritual Problems*, p. 200.

6. *The Pulitzer Prize Plays, 1918-1934*, eds. Kathryn Coe Cordell and William H. Cordell, p. 319.   7. *The Theatre Book of the Year 1948-1949*, p. 277.

8. *Eugene O'Neill*, p. 159.   9. *The Haunted Heroes of Eugene O'Neill*, p. 155.

10. Barrett Clark, *Eugene O'Neill*, p. 161.   11. P. 68.

12. Although O'Neill has been criticized for his blatant use of Freudian psychology, he nevertheless shows at least a competent layman's understanding of recent theories in the creation of a character like Dion Anthony. The explanation of the Self advanced by the psychologist, Carl Jung, has significance for the understanding of O'Neill's hero. Individuation is the name Jung gives to the process of attaining wholeness of personality. The process, which may take a lifetime, is accomplished by the individual's understanding more and

more aspects of his unconscious, and by his thereby giving proper values to what were once half-sensed and disturbing urges. See "The Meaning of Individuation" in *The Integration of the Personality,* pp. 3-29.

13. *Man for Himself,* p. 40.

CHAPTER 7

1. "The Decline of Greatness," *The Saturday Evening Post,* CCXXXI (November 1, 1958), 71.

2. *Atlantic,* CXXXII (December 1948), 30-36.　　　3. Dec. 2, 1946, p. 32.

4. "The Anatomy of Loneliness," *American Mercury,* LIII (October 1941), 467-475.　　　5. "The Loneliness of Life," CVIII (October 28, 1914), 45-46.

6. Many books and articles testify to Lincoln's mythical status. See Roy Basler's *The Lincoln Legend,* D. B. Turner's *The Mythifying Theory,* Lloyd Lewis' *Myths after Lincoln.*

7. Marshall W. Fishwick, *American Heroes, Myth and Reality,* p. 15.

8. In a series of essays published under the title, *Off Broadway,* Maxwell Anderson insists that the one fundamental touchstone of every great tragedy is that it have a recognition scene, which, as Sherwood's does, should come at the end of the second act of a three-act play.

9. *American Heroes: Myth and Reality,* p. 8.

10. *The Hero in America,* p. 485.　　　11. *Ibid.,* p. 481.

12. All the heroes of these propagandistic plays display some degree of loneliness in their battle against fascistic forces, but none are in military action during the play: Clare Booth, *Margin for Error* (1939); Robert Sherwood, *There Shall Be No Night* (1940); Elmer Rice, *Flight to the West* (1940); Lillian Hellman, *Watch on the Rhine* (1941); Maxwell Anderson, *Candle in the Wind* (1941); John Steinbeck, *The Moon Is Down* (1942); James Gow and Arnaud d'Usseau, *Tomorrow the World* (1943); Edward Chodorov, *Decision* (1944); Paul Osborn, *A Bell for Adano* (1944).

13. "Tragedy," *Theatre Arts Anthology,* ed. Rosamond Gilder *et al.,* p. 34.

14. P. 203.　　　15. "Loneliness," *Golden Book Magazine,* I (January 1925), 54.

CONCLUSION

1. Besides Thornton Wilder for *Our Town* (1938) and *The Skin of Our Teeth* (1943), Owen Davis won the Pulitzer Prize for *Icebound* (1923), Susan Glaspel for *Alison's House* (1931), Zoe Akins for *The Old Maid* (1935), and Joseph Kramm for *The Shrike* (1952). Two adaptations from books—*The Diary of Anne Frank* (1956), adapted by Frances Goodrich and Albert Hackett, and *Look Homeward, Angel* (1958), adapted by Ketti Trings—have also won the Pulitzer and Critics Circle Awards (through the season 1957-58).

2. *Freud on Broadway,* p. 454.　　　3. P. 105.

4. *The New Yorker,* XXXII (February 25, 1956), 88.

5. Quoted in *The Burns Mantle Best Plays of 1948-49,* p. 53, from the New York *Times,* for which Arthur Miller wrote an article on *Death of a Salesman.*

6. "Tragedy," *Theatre Arts Analogy,* ed. Rosamond Gilder *et al.,* p. 34.

7. *The Art of Loving,* p. 11.　　　8. *The White Goddess,* p. 391.

9. *Off Broadway,* p. 60.　　　10. *The Art of Playwriting,* p. 130.

11. "American Theatre and the Human Spirit," *Saturday Review,* XXXVIII (December 17, 1955), 9.

12. *Freud on Broadway,* p. 455.

13. *Shakespeare and the Rival Traditions,* p. 312.

14. *In Search of Theater,* p. 37.

BIBLIOGRAPHY

BOOKS

ANDERSON, Maxwell. *Off Broadway*. New York: William Sloane Associates, Inc., 1947.

————. *The Wingless Victory*. Washington, D. C.: Anderson House, 1936.

————. *Winterset*. Washington, D. C.: Anderson House, 1935.

ASWELL, Mary Louise, ed. *The World Within*. New York: McGraw-Hill Book Company, Inc., 1947.

BAKER, George Pierce. *Dramatic Technique*. New York: Houghton Mifflin Company, 1947.

BARRY, Philip. *Tomorrow and Tomorrow*. New York: Samuel French, 1931.

BENTLEY, Eric. *The Dramatic Event*. New York: Horizon Press, Inc., 1954.

————. *In Search of Theater*. New York: Alfred A. Knopf, Inc., 1953.

BROGAN, D. W. *The American Character*. New York: Alfred A. Knopf, Inc., 1944.

BROWN, John Mason. *Broadway in Review*. New York: W. W. Norton and Company, 1940.

————. *Two on the Aisle*. New York: W. W. Norton and Company, 1938.

CERF, Bennett A. and Cartmell, Van H., eds. *Sixteen Famous American Plays*. New York: Modern Library, Inc., 1941.

CHANDLER, Frank W. and Cordell, Richard A., eds. *Twentieth Century Plays*. New York: The Ronald Press Company, 1943.

CHAPMAN, John, ed. *The Burns Mantle Best Plays of 1948-49*. New York: Dodd Mead and Company, 1949.

————. *The Burns Mantle Best Plays of 1949-50*. New York: Dodd Mead and Company, 1950.

CHASE, Richard. *Quest for Myth*. Baton Rouge: Louisiana State University Press, 1949.

CLARK, Barrett. *Eugene O'Neill: The Man and His Plays*. New York: The Mc-Bride Company, 1929.

————. *European Theories of the Drama*. New York: Appleton-Century-Crofts, Inc., 1938.

CLARK, Barrett H. and Freedley, George, eds. *A History of Modern Drama*. New York: Appleton-Century-Crofts, Inc., 1947.

COMMAGER, Henry Steele. *The American Mind*. New Haven: Yale University Press, 1950.

CORDELL, Kathryn Coe and William H., eds. *The Pulitzer Prize Plays 1918-1934*. New York: Random House, Inc., 1935.

CORDELL, Richard A., ed., *Twentieth Century Plays*. New York: The Ronald Press Company, 1947.

CRAIG, Hardin, ed. *Essays in Dramatic Literature*. Princeton, N. J.; Princeton University Press, 1935.

The Critics' Prize Plays. Introduction by George Jean Nathan. Cleveland and New York: The World Publishing Company, 1945.

CROTHERS, Rachel. "The Construction of a Play" in *The Art of Playwriting*. Philadelphia: University of Pennsylvania Press, 1928.

DE VOTO, Bernard. *Forays and Rebuttals*. Boston: Little, Brown and Company, 1936.

DOWNER, Alan S., ed., *English Institute Essays 1951*. New York: Columbia University Press, 1952.

219

————. *Fifty Years of American Drama 1900-1950*. Chicago: Henry Regnery Company, 1951.

ELIOT, T. S. *The Cocktail Party*. New York: Harcourt, Brace and Company, 1950.

ENGEL, Edwin A. *The Haunted Heroes of Eugene O'Neill*. Cambridge: Harvard University Press, 1953.

FERGUSSON, Francis. *The Idea of a Theater*. Princeton, N. J.: Princeton University Press, 1949.

FISHWICK, Marshall W. *American Heroes: Myth and Reality*. Washington, D. C.: Public Affairs Press, 1954.

FROMM, Erich. *The Art of Loving*. New York: Harper and Brothers, 1956.

————. *Man for Himself: an Inquiry into the Psychology of Ethics*. New York: Rinehart and Company, Inc., 1947.

GAGEY, Edmond M. *Revolution in American Drama*. New York: Columbia University Press, 1947.

GASSNER, John, ed. *A Treasury of the Theatre*. New York: Simon and Schuster, Inc., 1950.

GILDER, Rosamond, *et al.*, eds. *Theatre Arts Anthology*. New York: Theatre Arts Books, 1950.

GORER, Geoffrey. *The American People*. New York: W. W. Norton and Company, Inc., 1948.

GRAVES, Robert. *The White Goddess*. New York: Creative Age Press, 1948.

GREEN, Paul. *Dramatic Heritage*. New York: Samuel French, 1953.

————. *The House of Connelly and Other Plays*. New York: Samuel French, 1931.

HAINES, William Wister. *Command Decision*. New York: Random House, Inc., 1947.

HAMILTON, Clayton. *The Theory of the Theatre*. New York: Henry Holt and Company, 1939.

HARBAGE, Alfred. *Shakespeare and the Rival Traditions*. New York: The Macmillan Company, 1952.

HELLMAN, Lillian. *Another Part of the Forest*. New York: Viking Press,, Inc., 1947.

————. *The Little Foxes*. New York: Random House, Inc., 1939.

HOPPER, Stanley Romaine. "The Problem of Moral Isolation in Contemporary Literature," in *Spiritual Problems in Contemporary Literature*, ed. Stanley Hopper. New York: Harper and Brothers, 1952.

HOWARD, Sidney. *The Silver Cord*. New York: Samuel French, 1926.

INGE, William. *Come Back, Little Sheba*. New York: Random House, Inc., 1950.

————. *Picnic*. New York: Random House, Inc., 1953.

JUNG, Carl G. *The Integration of the Personality*. trans. Stanley Dell. New York: Farrar & Rinehart, Inc., 1939.

KAHLER, Erich. *The Tower and the Abyss*. New York: George Braziller, Inc., 1957.

KARDINER, Abram, and Associates. *The Psychological Frontiers of Society*. New York: Columbia University Press, 1945.

KELLY, George. *Craig's Wife*. New York: Samuel French, 1926.

KERNODLE, George. "Patterns of Belief in Contemporary Drama," in *Spiritual Problems in Contemporary Literature*, ed. Stanley Hopper. New York: Harper and Brothers, 1952.

KINGSLEY, Sidney. *Men in White*, in *The Pulitzer Prize Plays 1918-1934*, Kathryn Coe Cordell and William H. Cordell. New York: Random House, Inc., 1935.

KIRKLAND, Jack. *Tobacco Road*, based on the novel by Erskine Caldwell, in

Twenty Best Plays of the Modern American Theatre, ed. John Gassner. New York: Crown Publishers, 1939.

KRUTCH, Joseph Wood. *"Modernism" in Modern Drama: a Definition and an Estimate.* Ithaca, N. Y.: Cornell University Press, 1953.

LAWSON, John Howard. *Theory and Technique of Playwriting.* New York: G. P. Putnam's Sons, 1936.

LERNER, Max. *America as a Civilization.* New York: Simon and Schuster, 1957.

MANTLE, Burns. *The Best Plays of 1937-38.* New York: Dodd, Mead and Company, 1938.

MAY, Rollo. *Man's Search for Himself.* New York: W. W. Norton and Company, 1953.

MATTHEWS, Brander. *Playwrights on Playmaking and Other Studies of the Stage.* New York: Charles Scribner's Sons, 1923.

McCULLERS, Carson. *The Member of the Wedding.* New York: New Directions, 1951.

MEAD, Margaret. *And Keep Your Powder Dry.* New York: William Morrow and Company, 1942.

MENNINGER, Karl A. *The Human Mind.* New York: Alfred A. Knopf, Inc., 1930.

MILLER, Arthur. *Death of a Salesman.* New York: Viking Press, Inc., 1949.

MILLETT, Fred B. and Bentley, Gerald Eades. *The Art of the Drama.* New York: Appleton-Century-Crofts, Inc., 1935.

MILLET, Fred B. *Reading Drama.* New York: Harper and Brothers, 1950.

MODERWELL, Hiram Kelly. *The Theatre of To-Day.* New York: Dodd, Mead and Company, 1927.

NATHAN, George Jean. *The Theatre Book of the Year.* 8 volumes (1942-1943 through 1949-1950). New York: Alfred A. Knopf, Inc., 1943-1950.

ODETS, Clifford. *Golden Boy,* in *Six Plays.* New York: Modern Library, Inc. 1939.

————. *Night Music.* New York: Random House, Inc., 1940.

————. *Paradise Lost,* in *Six Plays.* New York: Modern Library, Inc., 1939.

————. *Rocket to the Moon,* in *Six Plays.* New York: Modern Library, Inc., 1939.

O'HARA, Frank Hurburt. *Today in American Drama.* Chicago: University of Chicago Press, 1939.

O'NEILL, Eugene. *Anna Christie.* New York: Boni and Liveright, 1925. Same volume includes *All God's Chillun Got Wings* and *Diff'rent.*

————. *Desire Under the Elms,* in *Nine Plays.* New York: Liveright, Inc., 1932.

————. *The Great God Brown,* in *Nine Plays.* New York: Liveright, Inc., 1932.

————. *The Hairy Ape,* in *Nine Plays.* New York: Liveright, Inc., 1932.

————. *The Iceman Cometh.* New York: Random House, Inc., 1946.

————. *Long Day's Journey into Night.* New Haven: Yale University Press, 1956.

————. *Mourning Becomes Electra,* in *Nine Plays.* New York: Liveright, Inc., 1932.

————. *Strange Interlude,* in *Nine Plays.* New York: Liveright, Inc., 1932.

PEACOCK, Ronald. *The Poet in the Theatre.* New York: Harcourt, Brace and Company, 1946.

RICE, Elmer. *Street Scene.* New York: Samuel French, 1929.

RIESMAN, David, with Denney, Reuel, and Glazer, Nathan. *The Lonely Crowd.* New York: Doubleday and Company, Inc., 1953.

SANDBURG, Carl. *The Sandburg Range.* New York: Harcourt, Brace, 1958.

221

SAROYAN, William. *The Time of Your Life.* New York: Samuel French, 1941.

SELDES, Gilbert. *The Great Audience.* New York: Viking Press, Inc., 1950.

SHERWOOD, Robert. *Abe Lincoln in Illinois.* New York: Charles Scribner's Sons, 1939.

————. *Idiot's Delight.* New York: Charles Scribner's Sons, 1936.

————. *The Petrified Forest.* New York: Charles Scribner's Sons, 1935.

SIEVERS, W. David. *Freud on Broadway.* New York: Hermitage House, 1955.

SMITH, Lillian. *Killers of the Dream.* New York: W. W. Norton and Company, 1949.

SPENCER, Theodore. "Man's Spiritual Situation as Reflected in Modern Drama," in *Spiritual Problems in Contemporary Literature,* ed. Stanley Romaine Hopper, New York: Harper and Brothers, 1952.

STEIN, Gertrude. *Narration.* Chicago: University of Chicago Press, 1935.

STEINBECK, John. *Of Mice and Men.* New York: Modern Library, Inc., 1937.

THOMPSON, Alan Reynolds. *The Anatomy of Drama.* Berkeley and Los Angeles: University of California Press, 1946.

TYLER, Parker. *Magic and Myth of the Movies.* New York: Henry Holt and Company, 1947.

WEBB, Walter Prescott. *The Great Frontier.* Boston: Houghton Mifflin Company, 1952.

————. *The Great Plains.* Boston: Ginn and Company, 1931.

WECTER, Dixon. *The Hero in America: A Chronicle of Hero-Worship.* New York: Charles Scribner's Sons, 1941.

WHIPPLE, T. K. "Eugene O'Neill," in *Spokesman.* New York: Appleton-Century-Crofts, Inc., 1928.

WILLIAMS, Tennessee. *Cat on a Hot Tin Roof.* New York: New Directions, 1955.

————. *The Glass Menagerie.* New York: Random House, Inc., 1945.

————. *Orpheus Descending.* New York: New Directions, 1958.

————. *A Streetcar Named Desire.* New York: New Directions, 1947.

WILSON, Colin. *The Outsider.* Boston: Houghton Mifflin Company, 1956.

WOLFENSTEIN, Martha and Leites, Nathan. *Movies: A Psychological Study.* Glencoe, Illinois: The Free Press, 1950.

WYLIE, Philip. *Generation of Vipers.* New York: Rinehart and Company, Inc., 1942.

PERIODICALS

ALEXANDER, Doris. "Psychological Fate in *Mourning Becomes Electra,*" *PMLA,* LXVIII (December 1953), 923-934.

ATKINSON, Brooks. "Tragedy Behind a Tragic Masque," New York *Times* (February 19, 1956), Sec. 7, p. 1.

————. "Two by Rattigan," New York *Times* (May 22, 1955), Sec. 2, p. 1.

BENSON, Arthur C. "The Loneliness of Success," *North American Review,* CXXCVI (November 1907), 394-399.

DIMNET, Ernest. "The Case for and against Loneliness," *American Magazine,* CX (July 1930), 33.

DOWNER, Alan S. "Eugene O'Neill as Poet of the Theatre," *Theatre Arts,* XXXV (February 1951), 22-23.

GARRETT, H. T. "The Imitation of the Ideal," *PMLA,* LXII (1947), 735-744.

HANDLIN, Oscar, "Second Chance for the South," *Atlantic,* CXCII (December 1953), 54-58.

HOPKINS, Arthur. "The Theatre Seeks the Rhythm of the Times," *Literary Digest,* CXVII (June 30, 1934), 21, 35.

KERR, Walter, "Killing Off the Theater," *Harper's Magazine,* CCX (April 1955), 55-62.

"The Loneliness of the Modern Man," *Current Opinion*, LXXII (May 1922), 670-672.

MANN, Thomas, "The Making of 'The Magic Mountain,'" *Atlantic*, CXCI (January 1953), 41-45.

MARQUIS, Don. "Loneliness," *Golden Book Magazine*, I (January 1925), 54.

MILLER, Arthur. "The Family in Modern Drama," *Atlantic*, CXCVII (April 1956), 35-41.

————. "Tragedy and the Common Man," *Theatre Arts*, XXXV (1951), 48-50.

MONTAGU, Ashley. "The Annihilation of Privacy," *Saturday Review*, XXXIX (March 31, 1956), 9-11, 32.

"Nineteen American Playwrights Look at Themselves," *Saturday Review*, XXXVIII (September 3, 1955), 18-19.

"The Peril of City Loneliness," *Literary Digest*, XLIV (February 3, 1912), 215-216.

PITKIN, Walter B. "Get Acquainted!" *The Rotarian*, LVI (February 1940), 20-22.

RAHV, Philip. "Franz Kafka: the Hero as Lonely Man," *Kenyon Review*, I (1939), 60-74.

RICE, Elmer. "American Theatre and the Human Spirit," *Saturday Review*, XXXVIII (December 17, 1955), 9, 39-41.

SCHLESINGER, Arthur, Jr. "The Decline of Greatness," *The Saturday Evening Post*, CCXXXI (November 1, 1958), 25, 68-71.

SPENCER, Theodore, "The Isolation of the Shakespearean Hero," *Sewanee Review*, LII (1944), 313-331.

TAYLOR, Francis Henry. "Modern Art and the Dignity of Man," *Atlantic*, CXXCII (December 1948), 30-36.

THOMPSON, Clara Belle and Will. "There's No Need to Be Lonely," *Coronet*, XXXIII (January 1953), 65-67.

"Untragic America," *Life*, XXI, Part 3 (December 2, 1946), 32.

WHARTON, John. "Our Stylized Dialogue," *Saturday Review*, XXXVII (July 17, 1954), 24-25.

WILDER, Thornton. "The American Loneliness," *Atlantic*, CXC (August 1952), 65-69.

————. "Emily Dickinson," *Atlantic*, CXC (November 1952), 43-48.

————. "Toward an American Language," *Atlantic*, CXC (July 1952), 29-37.

WOLFE, Thomas. "The Anatomy of Loneliness," *American Mercury*, LIII (October 1941), 467-475.

YARROW, Victor S. "Isolation and Social Conflicts," *American Journal of Sociology*, XXVII (September 1921), 211-221.

ZILBOORG, Gregory. "Loneliness: its Relation to Narcissism," *Atlantic*, CLXI (January 1938), 45-54.

INDEX